COMMERCE 3MC3

MW00964320

TABLE OF CONTENTS
& ACKNOWLEDGEMENTS

PAGE

MARKETING - STRATEGY AND TACTICS

Every textbook defines marketing differently. For our purposes, marketing is the art of finding out what people want and giving it to them in a way better than the competition, while generating revenue over the long term. There are, of course, some limitations to this definition. "Revenue" connotes "dollars and cents" yet non-profit organizations do engage in marketing. Revenue should, therefore, be more broadly considered as a response – it may be the number of pints of blood donated, attendance figures at a little-league game, or even the amount of money a foundation donates to others. The timing of revenues is also important. Successful marketers look for revenue over the long term. It may be necessary, for a year or two, to have lower revenues to fully satisfy consumers. When Johnson & Johnson was faced with the discovery of poisoned capsules in some bottles of its best-selling pain reliever, Tylenol, it ordered a worldwide recall of the product costing hundreds of millions of dollars. While it did not generate revenue for the company in the short term, this action helped ensure revenues for Johnson & Johnson over the long term by inspiring trust in the consumer.

Another limit to the definition is that some things that people want they should not have. There are members of society who want access to prostitution, drugs and child pornography. The rest of society imposes stiff penalties on the promotion and selling of these commodities. The inverse is also true: some things people do not want they should have. Many people don't want to wear seat belts in automobiles or safety helmets while riding motorcycles, but the rest of society has demanded that these precautions be promoted. Only serving consumer wants can lead to tunnel vision. Consumers are not well versed in technological capabilities – they cannot see large technological leaps. Relying strictly on consumers, companies might not have envisioned compact-disc players, personal computers, or the Internet.

Though elements of marketing can be traced to ancient Rome, the first marketing course did not appear until the early 1900's. Why? For marketing to exist, consumers must face a surplus of goods. In Somalia, Ethiopia, and parts of the former Soviet Union, there is a shortage of goods. We call that a seller's market. Finding out what consumers want is a mostly pointless exercise if a constant flow of product cannot be guaranteed. So it was in North America until the end of the Second World War. The assembly line and corresponding mass-production technology were not invented until the twentieth century, and were not perfected until the 1940's. As the soldiers returned home, there was, for the first time, a surplus of goods, or a buyer's market. When we move from a seller's market to a buyer's market, power is transferred from the producer to the consumer. A company that pays close attention to the needs of consumers can obtain a competitive advantage.

Ask the general population about marketing and the words you are most likely to hear in response are "sales" and "advertising." For many people, selling is a negative activity, which implies that consumers are forced or tricked into buying something that they do not want. Others view advertising more positively, but place a remote-control unit in the hands of someone watching a television program and you will soon see how much people dislike advertising. Marketing is, therefore, not viewed very favourably by the public. Perhaps if the marketing concept was understood in a broader context, marketing would gain a better reputation.

◊◊ The Four P's of Marketing

In battle, one force fights for territory using the weapons of its army, navy, air force and marines. In business, one company fights for consumer purchases using the four P's of marketing: product, promotion, price and place (or distribution) (see fig. 1). The concept of product goes far beyond the physical product itself, and includes package design, brand names, trademarks, warranties, guarantees, product life cycles, and new- product development. The product concept also includes the increasingly important service sector. Pricing begins with a consideration of economic principles

Figure 1.   THE FOUR P'S OF MARKETING

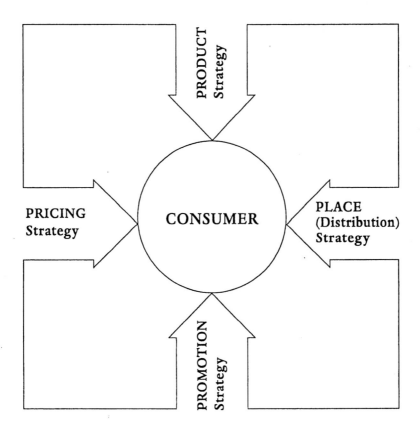

SOURCE: Dale Beckman, David Kurtz, and Louis Boone, *Foundations of Marketing*, 4th ed. (Toronto: Holt, Rinehart and Winston of Canada, 1988), 14.

and then takes into account consumer expectations, manufacturing costs, mark-ups, discounts, and transportation costs. Promotion represents all forms of communication to consumers including advertising, social media, personal selling, public relations, and sales- promotion techniques (that is, coupons, samples, point-of-purchase displays). Place includes the activities of wholesalers and retailers, as well as choices involving the physical distribution of the product, and storage and inventory handling.

◊◊   The Environment for Marketing Decisions

Even with good weapons, superior forces have been beaten in battle by inferior forces. Why? No doubt the superior forces did not do a full reconnaissance and failed to consider the uncontrollable forces during battle. Many battles have been won or lost because of the weather or the unforeseen existence of a swamp. Marketers must realize that their deci-

Figure 2.   THE ENVIRONMENT FOR MARKETING DECISIONS

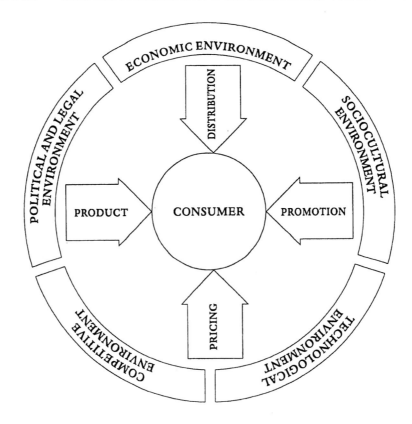

SOURCE: Dale Beckman, David Kurtz, and Louis Boone, *Foundations of Marketing*, 4th ed.
(Toronto: Holt, Rinehart and Winston of Canada, 1988), 22.

4

sions involving the four P's are made in a context where the environment is uncontrollable. While marketers may influence some of these environmental factors, control eludes them (see fig. 2).

The competitive environment has become increasingly important as trade becomes more globalized. A company must be concerned with other firms in the industry, other firms that compete for the same customers, and it must contend with potential new competitors, both national and international. McDonald's Restaurants closely watches Burger King, Wendy's, and Harvey's, its competition in the hamburger industry. It also watches Pizza Hut, Tim Horton's, and Swiss Chalet, which compete for the same quick-service customers. McDonald's is also watching those quick-service companies from other parts of the world that would like to enter the affluent North American market.

The economy operates in a cyclical manner. Over a ten-year period, a marketer will see periods of recession, depression, recovery, and prosperity. Unemployment, inflation, and the economy in general influence many consumer decisions, including those concerning marriage, having children, buying a home, buying a car, and retirement. Closely connected is the political/legal environment. Government rules and regulations at the municipal, provincial, and federal level affect pricing (for example, the harmonized sales tax – HST), promotion (advertising to children, misleading advertising), distribution (where and how liquor, wine, and beer can be sold) and product (listing of ingredients, defining product terms). Society expects governments to control business and maintain a free-enterprise system. The rules of the Competition Act come into play here as they seek to prevent actions which greatly lessen competition (including mergers and acquisitions) and to prevent deceptive trade practices. Of course, a nation's laws are not static and can change as governments are replaced. As well, with increased emphasis on international trade, the political/legal environments of other nations become much more important.

Technology refers to knowledge gained from scientific investigation, discovery, and invention. It affects marketing in many ways. Technological advancement is the source of new products and product refinements. Through improved production efficiency, costs can be lowered and the savings shared with consumers. Technological advances in animation and sound recording have changed the production of television commercials. The universal product code and scanner technology have improved inventory handling and reduced the time consumers spend at retail checkouts.

The final environment looks at the interpersonal relationships of humans through their societies and cultures. As cultures and sub-cultures evolve, demand for products change and new products are needed. As Canada has welcomed immigrants from around the world, the food options at restaurants have evolved from meat with potatoes to quesadillas, pad Thai, and kimchee. More importantly, as we engage in global trade, the cultures of different countries need to be explored and respected. Similarly, understanding how consumers behave and how they choose products to purchase can improve the chances of success for a marketer.

◊◊ Developing a Marketing Strategy

A CFL football player and his wife asked for my opinion on a new business venture. He was an offensive lineman: three hundred pounds of muscle standing six feet six inches with a twenty-inch neck, looking for all the world like a brick wall. He liked fashionable clothing, but had a problem finding things that would fit. "So what do you think about us opening a fashionable big and tall man's clothing store?" he asked. "I would be personally involved in the off-season, and it would give me some security for when I retire in a few years."

"I think it could work," I replied. "But I need a few details."

"We see the store operating in about six hundred square feet in a major downtown shopping mall. We would carry some casual pants and shirts, belts, some sports jackets and suits. And great labels like Polo, Gant, Hugo Boss, and Armani."

"Sounds good to me," I said, "and I assume you will be using your celebrity status to draw customers."

"Don't forget his teammates," his wife added. She, too, was striking. She stood five feet eleven inches and had dabbled in bodybuilding. "I thought that we would probably have enough room in the store to include some clothes for the large and tall woman."

"Oh?" I was starting to get worried.

"Yes, and don't forget the shoes. I have a size fourteen foot, and I can't find good-quality shoes in my size," the football player chimed in.

"Men's and *women's* shoes," she added. "And, of course, we would need some accessories. Handbags, hats, some jewellery. I was even thinking of watches."

"Of course," was all I could say.

"And we would need to have coats for the fall and winter. Maybe some ties, and then there would be men's jewellery," he said.

I was flabbergasted. In thirty seconds, this couple had described a big-and-tall, high-class department store crammed into six hundred square feet. I knew this strategy wouldn't work. They were trying to satisfy too many consumers and too many needs at once. As the saying goes, a jack-of-all-trades is a master of none. Translation? A company that tries to do too many things at one time is likely to do none of them well.

As far as I could tell, I only had one problem.   How would I tell a three-hundred-pound CFL lineman that his strategy was doomed to fail?

◊◊   Strategy and Tactics

Strategy is difficult to define. In an academic context, it can be described as the plan used to determine the direction of an organization and to achieve its long-term goals. When a company enacts its marketing strategy, it blends product, pricing, distribution, and promotion decisions to satisfy its chosen target market over the long term. As its reward for satisfying its customers, the company receives sales revenue and, ideally, sees profits. Strategic plans are often quite broad, they use a three-to-five-year time frame, and they encompass major overall objectives. Strategy has always been important in a military context. For instance, in the Gulf War of the early 1990's, the long-term military goal of the United Nations forces was the liberation of Kuwait.   On the market battleground, the goal of a company might be to introduce its product to ten new countries or to create awareness of a new product in 50-percent of the population in a three-year period.

Tactics are narrower in scope than strategies. They focus on the implementation of those activities specified in the strategic plan. In fact, two different companies might use completely different tactics to accomplish the same strategic goals. Suppose the strategic goal is to introduce a product to ten new countries in three years. One company might choose to employ an export strategy that includes manufacturing the product in Canada and signing agreements with distributors in the new countries. Another company might purchase a factory in each of the ten countries to save on shipping costs and to exploit cheaper local raw materials. Generally, tactics are reviewed every six months, focus on short-term accomplishments, and involve actual resource allocation.

Everyone in an organization does some strategic and tactical planning, though the percentage of time an employee spends on these activities increases as that person moves to higher echelons of management. There is a long-standing debate about whether strategy formulation is an art or science. Those who think it is a science have spent considerable time developing rigorous techniques with which to turn specified inputs into generic strategies. Let's examine a couple of these techniques or strategy models.

◊◊ Generic Approaches to Strategy

One of the first generic approaches to strategy was championed by General Electric (GE) in 1971. With sales revenue measured in the billions and plants situated around the world, GE needed to focus its strategic planning. The first step in this process was to form strategic business units – groupings of companies that serve the same consumers with products requiring much the same resources to produce. The most important innovation from a strategic-planning perspective was the development of the GE business screen (see fig. 3).

There are two dimensions to this screen. One dimension is an internal measure called business strengths, and includes an assessment of the strength of the strategic business unit in the areas of production, human resources, information systems, finance, marketing, and research and development. If a unit shows outstanding strengths, it is rated high on the business-strengths dimension. The other dimension is an external measure called industry attractiveness, and includes an assessment of the competition, the sales growth rate, consumer behaviour, technological developments, government intervention, and economic conditions. If the environment facing a strategic business unit is quite threatening, industry attractiveness is rated as low.

Once these dimensions are plotted on the screen, one of three generic strategies is suggested. Where both dimensions received a high rating, the company should invest money in making the business unit grow. The future-earnings potential of the company lies in such a unit. Where both dimensions received a medium rating, the strategy should be more cautious. Management is told to be more selective about investing money in these units, and to do so only if the investment is made to support the current-earnings potential of the unit. Where both dimensions received a low rating, management is advised to cease investing and to work at squeezing every last ounce of profits from the unit. If the unit is not profitable or cannot be made profitable in short order, management is told to sell off or close the unit.

Figure 3.   *THE GE BUSINESS SCREEN*

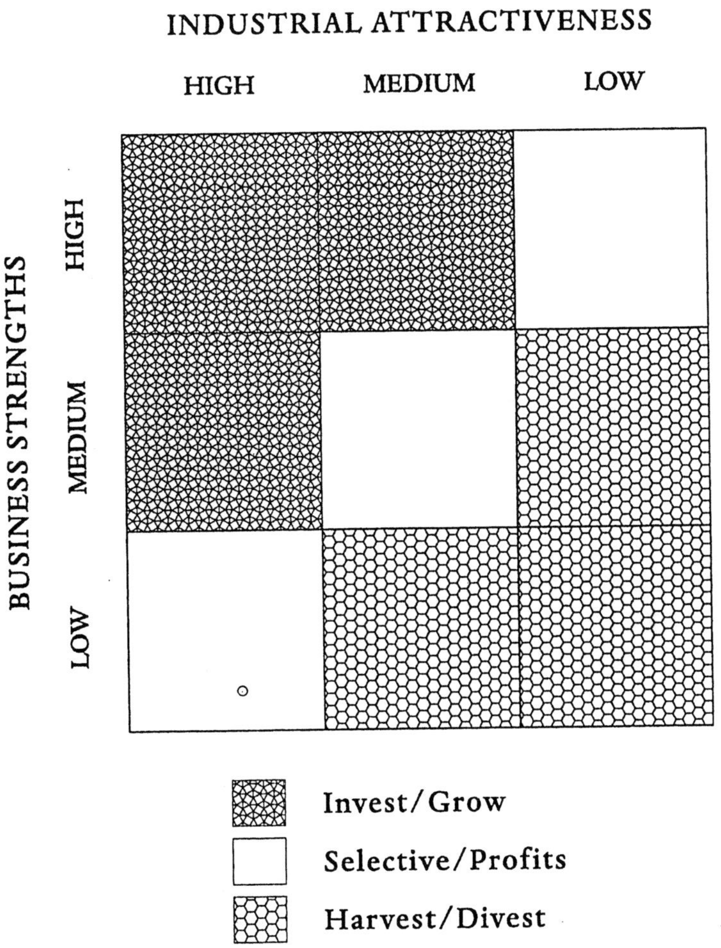

INDUSTRIAL ATTRACTIVENESS

SOURCE: Dale Beckman, David Kurtz, and Louis Boone, *Foundations of Marketing,* 2d ed. (Toronto: Holt, Rinehart and Winston of Canada, 1982), 131.

One problem with this screen is that it is supposed to be applied to strategic business units only. Not every company is large enough to be organized around to the business-unit concept. However, companies have successfully used the screen for individual products or target markets. Another set of problems involved the differences between high and medium, and between medium and low. Companies found that managers can interpret them quite differently

In the late 1970's, it was determined that a simpler screen was needed. A group of Harvard business professors, working through their independent consulting company, proposed a new model. Known today as the Boston Consulting Group (BCG) Matrix, it, too, has both an external and internal dimension (see fig. 4).

The external dimension is market growth. The assumption is that for high market growth to occur, technology, competition, economic conditions, the government, the laws, and the customers must all be favourable. As well, only one decision need be made, and that is whether market growth is high or low.

Figure 4. THE BOSTON CONSULTING GROUP MATRIX

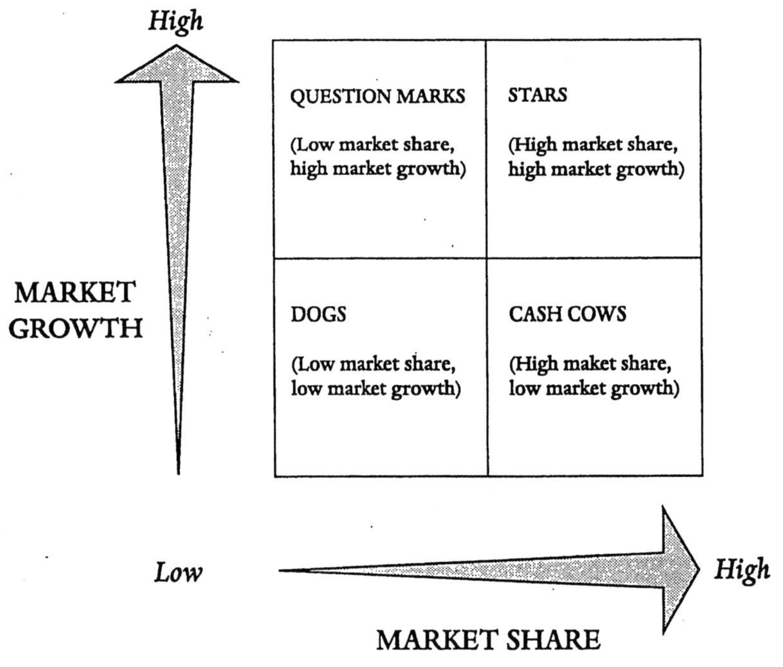

	QUESTION MARKS (Low market share, high market growth)	STARS (High market share, high market growth)
	DOGS (Low market share, low market growth)	CASH COWS (High maket share, low market growth)

MARKET GROWTH

Low — High

MARKET SHARE

SOURCE: Barry Hedley, "Strategy and the Business Portfolio," *Long Range Planning*, February 1977: 12.

The internal dimension is market share. The assumption, in this case, is that for a business unit to have high market share, the production, finance, information systems, marketing, human resources, and research and development capabilities of that business unit must be above average. Again, only one decision has to be made. It must be decided whether the market share is high or low.

The resulting four matrix positions have each been given a name and a generic strategy. High-market-share, low-market-growth units or products are called cash cows. These are the most profitable ventures for a company, and help to generate strong cash flows. Investments should be made to sustain their cash-generating ability. High-market-share, high-market-growth units or products are called stars. They will become cash cows as market growth inevitably slows. While these ventures are profitable and generate cash, they also require investment to maintain their high market share as the market grows. Investments may be made in promotion, getting and keeping shelf facings, aggressive pricing (especially in the face of price wars) and product improvements through continued research and development.

Low-market-share, high-market-growth units or products are called question marks, and are, typically, new ventures for a company. It is always best to launch new ventures when the market is growing. As they are launched, they will, of course, have low market shares and will require substantial investment from the company so that awareness may be built through promotion, and wholesalers and distributors may be encouraged to carry the product. These new ventures will have already sustained heavy research-and-development and market launch costs, which will need to be recouped. Low-market-share, low-market-growth units or products are called dogs. If these are question marks that do not gain consumer acceptance before the market slows, it is probably best to sell off or close these ventures. If they are former cash cows which have lost their popularity due to changes in consumer needs or desires, or in technology, it is probably best to manage the ventures carefully until they are no longer contributing profits to the company.

The key problem with these two strategic approaches is that both a company and its competitors can perform the same analysis. It is hard to win a battle when your opponent knows exactly what moves you will be taking. Some of the most innovative marketing has been done by companies that did not follow the proposed strategy models. Carling Black Label beer was a dog, but some significant re-investment in the brand saw it resume cash-cow status for a few years. Most marketers favour more artistic models of strategy.

◊◊ Other Strategy Models

Harvard University's Michael Porter suggests there are five factors that need to be fully analysed before a strategy is developed (see fig. 5). One factor is the power of suppliers. If only one or two can supply the raw materials a producer needs, power rests with those suppliers, and the producer is made weaker. One also needs to assess the power of buyers or consumers. If hundreds or thousands of consumers purchase a company's products, power rests with that company. Will new companies be able to enter the marketplace? If there are many barriers to market entry, the opportunities for new competition are decreased, and power is gained by the established company. Are there products that can be easily substituted for those of the established company? The more substitute products that exist, the less power the company with the original product has. Finally,

Figure 5.   *MICHAEL PORTER'S FIVE-FACTOR MODEL*

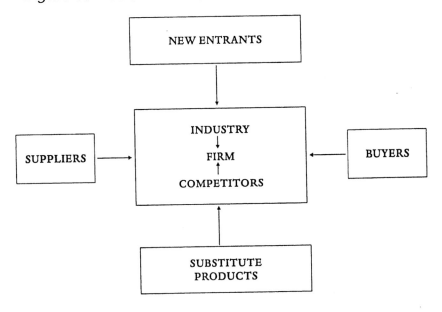

SOURCE: Michael E. Porter, *Competitive Strategy: Techniques for Analyzing Industries and Competitors* (The Free Press, 1980), 4.

one needs to assess the power of competitors. The more the dynamics of the marketplace are dictated by competitors, the less power a company has.

When a company develops a competitive strategy, it increases its power. Such a strategy works to raise barriers that prevent competitors from entering the market, to secure supply, to increase the number of potential consumers, to improve the company's position among competitors, or to make substitute products obsolete – but these actions cannot all be predicted from the strategy model alone. The additional insight of a manager is required, and that makes each strategy unique.

A different strategy model involves an analysis of the product/market focus of the company, both in the present and in the future. It is a useful brainstorming tool that can be used to generate and scrutinize the risks and rewards of future strategies (see fig. 6). Strategies can be designed for the existing target market to better serve its needs (a product may be relabelled or put in a new container) or for a new target market (a product may be launched in a different country, or its benefits may be adjusted to suit new demands). Strategies can also be designed to exploit existing products (a new scent to a laundry detergent or the product may be concentrated so less packaging is needed) or to develop new products (for example, Coca-Cola popsicles or Tide toothpaste).

Figure 6.   THE PRODUCT/MARKET FOCUS MODEL

	Old Product	**New Product**
Old Market	Product Improvement	Market Improvement
New Market	Product Diversification	Product Development

SOURCE: Dale Beckman, David Kurtz, and Louis Boone, *Foundations of Marketing*, 5th ed. (Toronto: Dryden, Holt, Rinehart and Winston of Canada, 1992), 276.

The easiest strategies to implement, and those that pose the least risk, are in the upper left hand corner of figure 6. But serving existing markets with existing products will also result in the lowest additional rewards. Risk increases diagonally. The riskiest strategies are those that involve serving new markets with new products, but the rewards of such an approach can also be much greater.

A final strategy model, used extensively in introductory marketing courses, is shown in figure 7. The first step in S/W/O/T Analysis is to identify in detail the current strategy (the product, price, distribution, promotion, and target-market elements) for a company. Then the activities taking place beyond the control of the company, environmental factors, must be assessed. The concept of control is important here. Whatever a company can control becomes part of its resources as either a strength or a weakness. If a company can merely influence a factor, it is considered either an opportunity or threat in the environment. It is also important to evaluate the ethical standards of doing business; this has become an increasingly important concern.

Figure 7.   S/W/O/T ANALYSIS

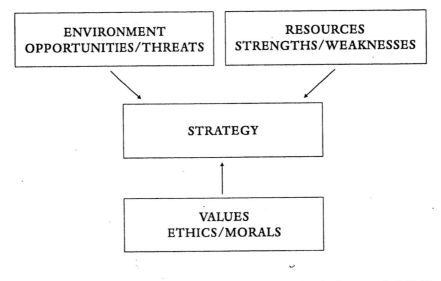

SOURCE: Renato Mazzolini, "European Corporate Strategies," *Columbia Journal of World Business*, Spring 1975: 99.

The next step is deciding whether the current strategy can work in conjunction with the environmental and resource analysis just undertaken. If changes are necessary, they must fall within the ethical ground rules identified. For instance, the Sierra Leone government might decide to privatize a diamond mine. A certain company may have expertise in diamond mining, but, clearly, before company management moves to acquire the mine, it must consider the ethical and moral consequences of its decision.

In this model, strategies always start from a position of strength and are designed to: block environmental threats, take advantage of environmental opportunities, or correct resource weaknesses.

◊◊   A Word About Tactics

All of these strategy models might seem confusing, and no one model is right for every situation. Tactics are even more closely tailored to the situation at hand, and models are harder to find. Generally, a set of tactics is the implementation plan for the long-term strategy undertaken by a company. As a result, tactics involve the specification of a time frame, a set of prioritized actions, and control or check points, which are put in place to ensure that a given set of tactics is working. When formulating a tactical plan, one would never simply say to a company, "Do some advertising." One would specify the media to be used; the hours, weeks, or months of the campaign; and the type of message. In that tactical plan, one would list the most critical actions first, and the less important, optional actions second. A person would be unlikely to undertake a journey by car without specifying a goal, such as "I want to be in Moose Jaw by five o'clock tomorrow." In making a tactical plan, one must set or predict goals, and if these are not realized, some corrective action may be necessary.

When you work with case studies, you are developing your skills in specifying both strategic and tactical plans. Like all skills, these improve with practice. Case-study work will also teach you what famous strategists discovered years ago: drawing on the experience, perceptions, and viewpoints of your peers will improve your own strategic perspective.

MARKET
SEGMENTATION

Many children are familiar with Saturday-morning television commercials for breakfast cereals such as Lucky Charms and Count Chocula. The brightly coloured animated characters that populate these commercials capture children's imagination, and the promise of special prizes inside the boxes of these sugary cereals makes their appeal almost irresistible. But did the manufacturers of those cereals make a mistake?

While children are more than willing to purchase their products, most do not buy them. The actual cereal purchasers are parents. There is no doubt children have an influence, but their parents make the actual purchase decisions. And their decisions aren't always correct. After buying a box of strawberry-flavoured cereal, a parent, rather than his or her children, may have to finish the remainder of the box.

Today, manufacturers understand that a cereal has to appeal both to the child and to the parent. Those who sell cereals must provide lists of ingredients, notations about added vitamins and minerals, labels highlighting all natural ingredients, and mentions of reduced sugar and salt. There are still special toy surprises and animated characters to encourage children to influence their parents, but the role of children in the purchase process is much better understood.

◇◇ The Marketplace

While we think of a marketplace as being a location, it is more correctly defined as people. Manufacturers do not sell goods to places; they sell them to individuals. This is true of both consumer goods, which are sold to individuals for their own personal use, and industrial goods, which are products used directly or indirectly in the production of other goods or for resale. It is people making decisions for themselves or for their company who buy products.

But the marketplace is not just people. If it were, companies would be focusing on the most highly populated places in the world – China and India. But they don't. A market also requires a willingness to buy. The introductory example of breakfast cereals shows that willingness to buy is a necessary, but not in itself sufficient, criterion for a market to exist. Children are willing to buy many things, yet they do not make many purchases. To have a true marketplace, we need people who also have purchasing power and authority. While China and India have, together, nearly three billion people, the per-capita income or purchasing power for these people is so low that they cannot afford to purchase many of the standard household goods we take for granted in North America. Authority to buy becomes a significant issue in industrial markets. A company trying to sell a new line of personal computers to a university can waste much time talking to individual faculty and staff members who do not have any authority to sign a purchase requisition or place an order.

Remember our definition of marketing: the art of finding out what people want and giving it to them in a way better than the competition while generating revenue over the long term. Even when a market can be identified, it probably contains so many people that determining and satisfying all their needs is impossible. For instance, ask the people in your class what they want in an automobile and you will receive a gamut of responses. Trying to build the one automobile that will satisfy those heterogeneous desires is impossible. One would be wiser to find groups of people within the market who have similar desires and build an automobile to satisfy them. It is nearly impossible to satisfy all of the people, all of the time with one product, so marketers try to satisfy some of the people, all of the time. Even manufacturers of food staples such as sugar and flour have recognized that their products are consumed by several different groups in the marketplace and have developed product variations to increase customer satisfaction.

This process of dividing the heterogeneous marketplace into smaller, more homogeneous chunks is called market segmentation. Once the market is segmented, a marketer can develop products and a marketing plan that will better meet the needs of the people who make up each segment and improve the chances of making a sale. The ways in which the marketplace can be segmented vary for consumer and industrial products.

◊◊ Bases of Consumer Market Segmentation

There are four bases for segmenting the market for consumer products (see fig. 1). The oldest basis is segmentation by geography. In Canada, a little over sixty-one percent of the population live in Ontario and Quebec. Cities account for eighty percent of Canada's population. The country's three largest cities – Toronto (6.1 million), Montreal (4.1 million) and Vancouver (2.5 million) – account for thirty-five percent of its population. Climate is also a basis for geographic segmentation. People in Vancouver rarely see snow, and people in Regina have more sunny days than those in any other provincial capital. If one is looking for a suitable location for a professional-sports franchise, it is important to consider gross city size. Many believe that Saskatoon and Hamilton are too small to support an NHL hockey team. If one is considering selling products on a door-to-door basis, population density is an important factor. Rural areas, with low population densities, make selling door-to-door very impractical.

As the mass media grew in importance during the late 1800's and early 1900's, a second basis of segmentation was born: demographics. Age, gender, income, occupation, education, whether a person's home is owned or rented, number of children, and ethnicity are some demographic variables. As an aid to advertisers in deciding which medium to use, companies began to gather and share this type of information. Demographics are easy to gather and common sense dictates that they are associated with the purchase of many products. Diapers are consumed mostly by people with children under the age of two. High-heeled shoes are consumed mostly by women. University textbooks are consumed mostly by people aged eighteen to twenty-two. Pasta is consumed twice as often by people of Italian heritage.

Figure 1. FOUR BASES OF CONSUMER MARKET SEGMENTATION

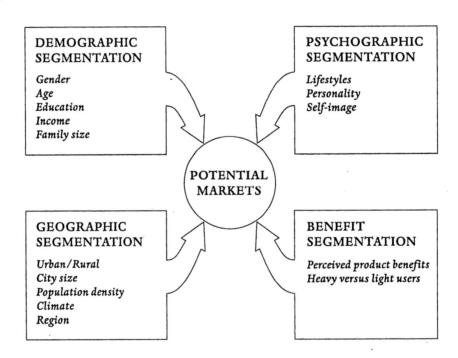

SOURCE: Adapted from Jack Z. Sissors, "What Is a Market?" *Journal of Marketing*, July 1966: 21.

You should know a few current demographic trends. Baby boomers, those born between 1946 and 1964, are getting older (see fig. 2). In North America, the segment of people over the age of fifty is expected to show double-digit growth over the next decade – a much higher rate of growth than that of any other segment. Compared to twenty years ago, people are marrying at a later age and they are having fewer children. More than one in two marriages will end in divorce. People are saving money for their retirement, especially those with higher incomes. In fact most of the disposable wealth in Canada is controlled by those over the age of fifty. Compared to twenty years ago, people are also more educated and more are employed in white-collar jobs.

Figure 2. ANNUAL NUMBER OF BIRTHS IN THE UNITED STATES

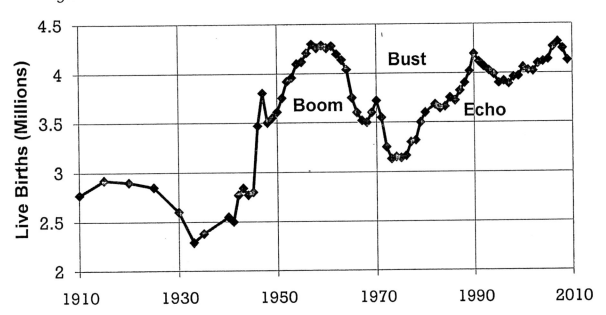

Demographics, however, are not as good a predictor as they were a generation ago. Television, the other mass media, and social media are partly to blame for this. Today, there are people over the age of sixty running triathlons, while many people under the age of thirty are out of shape. Some people with low incomes drive expensive luxury cars while some people with high incomes drive economy cars. As marketers have discovered, an increasingly important basis of segmenting the market is psychology. Psychographics attempts to blend demographic data with psychological factors, such as attitude and lifestyle, to develop a behavioural profile of consumers. As a result, we find that some consumers are old-fashioned while others are adventurous, and that some groups are family-centred and others live for the moment. Each of these groups will buy different products to satisfy their emotional needs.

A final basis of segmentation is by expected product benefits. While you and I may each purchase a box of baking soda, you may be buying it to deodorize your refrigerator while I plan to do some baking. Take this test. What brand of toothpaste did you use this morning? Chances are that if you used Crest or Colgate, you wanted cavity prevention and plaque protection. If you bought Close-up or Pearl Drops Tooth Polish, you wanted a sexy, white smile. If you bought Aquafresh, you wanted triple protection using its three stripes: fresh breath, cavity prevention, and white teeth. People buying Macleans or Pepsodent wanted to save some money. One might also segment the market by the volume consumed. An old rule of thumb is that 20-percent of a company's customers account for 80-percent of the volume sold. There are people who consume five cups of coffee per day. Companies do not want to offend these people with any new marketing activity. Furthermore, companies like to identify these consumers to determine how lighter users can be turned on to the product and be made heavy users.

◇◇ Bases of Industrial Market Segmentation

There are three ways to segment the industrial market (see fig. 3). As it can in the consumer market, geography can be used. In Canada, nearly three-quarters of the industrial market is located in a narrow band running from Windsor, Ontario through Toronto and Montreal and ending in Quebec City. While there are over thirty-five million consumers, there are only several hundred thousand industrial customers. Often industrial customers cluster around geographic features. For instance, deep-sea fishing firms are concentrated along the east and west coasts, while mining concerns are concentrated in the Canadian Shield regions of Ontario and Quebec.

A consideration of the end use of a product can help marketers to segment the industrial market. Consider the industrial market for personal computers. Firms may purchase personal computers to act as print servers, stand-alone workstations, monitoring workstations for industrial processes, database servers, desktop-publishing centres, or as hubs of e-mail networks. While the computer required to work with each of these applications is essentially the same, the marketing plan developed by a computer company to reach each industrial customer is different.

Finally, the need for special products can be used to segment the industrial market. A valve that can be opened and closed to permit or cut off the flow of liquid might, at first, seem to be a standard product. However, different industries have needs for valves with different properties. The transport of pressurized gases requires a valve that can operate at subzero temperatures. In the transportation of drinking water, valves need to be quite large to accommodate the volume of water moved in a city. In a chemical plant, valves will need to be designed to withstand chemical reaction. For an industrial marketer, it might be convenient to segment companies on the basis of their unique product needs.

Figure 3. THREE BASES OF INDUSTRIAL MARKET SEGMENTATION

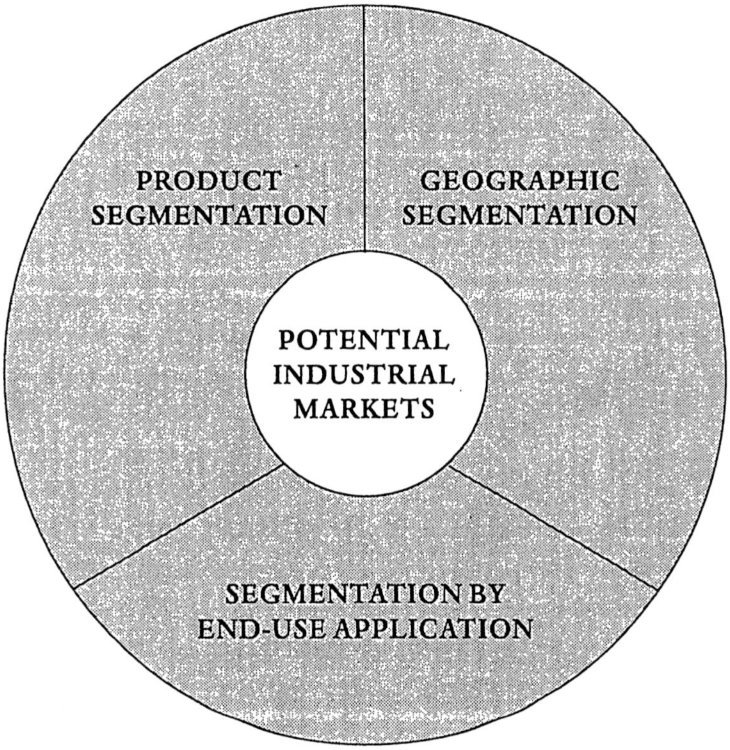

SOURCE: Dale Beckman, David Kurtz, and Louis Boone, *Foundations of Marketing*, 5th ed. (Toronto: Dryden, Holt, Rinehart and Winston of Canada, 1992), 75.

◊◊ Market-Segmentation Strategies

How should a company use this knowledge of market segmentation? There are three potential strategies that can be used. The first is to treat the entire market as an undifferentiated whole and offer it a single product.

Companies taking this approach admit that they cannot satisfy all of the people all of the time, yet they try to satisfy most of the people, most of the time. Coca-Cola was invented just over 125 years ago. For the first eighty years of its life, it produced only one kind of Coke - with sugar and caffeine. Such a single-offer strategy allows for economies of production and savings on promotion and inventory costs, yet reduces satisfaction among consumers.

A second strategy is to recognize that there are many different consumer segments and to develop a product for each segment's special needs. The history of marketing has shown us that after two brands have competed head to head using an undifferentiated strategy, it is most often the number two brand which sees the differentiated strategy as an opportunity to wrest the lead from its competitor. In the cola battles, it was Pepsi-Cola which first introduced artificially sweetened Diet Pepsi, caffeine-reduced Pepsi Free, and eliminated artificial colours in Crystal Pepsi. While production efficiencies declined and promotion and inventory costs climbed, Pepsi was rewarded with increased sales, increased consumer satisfaction, and increased profits. Not surprisingly, Coca-Cola quickly abandoned its old, undifferentiated strategy and followed suit.

A final strategy is, again, to recognize that there are many different consumer segments, and to simultaneously recognize that a company may not have the financial, production, or marketing resources to pursue a multi-offer strategy. Instead, it may choose one market segment and develop a product especially for it. In the soft-drink market, Orange Crush, Dr. Pepper, Canada Dry, Schweppes, Red Bull, and Hires Root Beer are all examples of brands that have followed a concentrated or niching strategy. The only trick to choosing a market niche is to make sure the niche is large enough to justify pursuing it, and that it is stable enough to endure. For a brief time in the 1970's and 1990's, platform shoes made a fashion statement. However, by the time some companies had developed their line of platform shoes, the fashion trend had passed on.

PRODUCT
STRATEGY

In 1993, Lee Iacocca retired as Chairman of the Chrysler Corporation. By the time Iacocca had become President in the early 1980's, Chrysler had suffered major losses and was rapidly losing market share. Though Chrysler was the third largest car company in America, most analysts predicted that Iacocca's appointment was too little too late to save the company. Stock prices had fallen and commercial debt had been so devalued that someone buying a bond could expect a 40-percent return, assuming the company survived.

By 1993, Chrysler's market share had recovered, though the company remained in third place, and its quarterly profits exceeded those of both its competitors. Iacocca has written several books on his successful turnaround of Chrysler Corporation. In these, he attributes his success to several factors, but much of it can, in fact, be attributed to his product strategy.

Chrysler was the first American car company to offer an extended warranty plan. Its seven-year, seventy-thousand mile warranty on the automobile powertrain nearly doubled the best American car warranty at the time, and set a new standard that its competitors had not managed to emulate fully by 1993. Chrysler was the first American company to introduce front wheel drive vehicles. It was the first to develop an automobile resembling a crossbred van and station wagon: the mini-van. Chrysler successfully reintroduced the convertible, which had disappeared in the early 1970's. Through its acquisition of Jeep, Chrysler became the first company to introduce "shift-on-the-fly" two-wheel-drive-to-four-wheel-drive vehicles. Chrysler was the first American company to make air bags a standard feature of its cars. As a parting salvo, Iacocca introduced cab-forward design. By moving the wheels of the automobile closer to the front and back corners, and by extending the passenger compartment, the company created a car that was both more spacious and more stable on the highway.

Lee Iacocca recognized that a company's product strategy goes beyond the physical properties of the products it sells. The total product strategy incorporates brand names, trademarks, labelling, packaging, consumer credit plans, warranties or guarantees, and brand image. It also includes service – the intangible aspects of a purchase.

◊◊ Products and Services

In 1945, half of all people who worked did so in the manufacturing sector. Today, people who make products account for only 15% of the workforce. Half of all people who work are now employed in the services sector. Services are different from products in several important ways. First, services are intangible. You cannot see, feel, or sample a service before it is performed. Services are difficult to standardize. Even if the same person was to cut your hair, no two visits to the hairstylist would yield exactly the same result. Services cannot be produced in advance and inventoried; idle capacity is, therefore, an important concern. We design ambulance services to have plenty of idle capacity, but dentists would go out of business without a full schedule of appointments. Finally, most services are produced and consumed simultaneously. When you travel by plane, the type of flight you experience depends as much on the other passengers aboard and the weather you encounter as it does on the flight attendants and cockpit crew.

Both products and services can be classified by the amount of effort they require of consumers. Convenience products and services are purchased frequently, as soon as they are needed, and with a minimum of effort. These might include bread, milk, potato chips, gasoline, dry cleaning, and fast-food meals. Shopping products and services are purchased only after the consumer has made comparisons between brands or stores. Consumers expect the monetary savings or greater satisfaction to outweigh the costs of shopping. Shopping products and services might include clothing, furniture, appliances, auto repairs and insurance. Specialty products and services possess some unique characteristics that cause consumers to prize them, and go out of their way to buy them. These might include services of specialized surgeons and divorce attorneys, or imported crystal, handmade sweaters, and classic automobiles.

◊◊ The Product Life Cycle

A key concept is the product life cycle. This represents the typical path a product or service follows from introduction to deletion (see fig. 1).

In the introduction phase, a company builds awareness of, and stimulates demand for, the new product. Promotional campaigns stress information about the product to educate the general public. Wholesalers and retailers are convinced to carry the new product and to give it shelf space. Continuous research and development is undertaken to refine the product to match consumer expectations. Though pricing policies can be adopted that increase returns, losses are expected during this phase because of significant promotion and research costs.

In the growth phase, sales rise dramatically as consumers first try, and then accept, the product. As profits grow, so does the number of competitors, as introducing a new brand of a product is easiest when the market is growing. Promotional campaigns begin to stress corporate brand names and consumers are induced to make trial purchases.

Mass-media advertising is used to reach consumers and to stimulate publicity. It becomes easier for a company to add more wholesalers and retailers to its lists as its product develops a sales track record. In the late growth phase, prices begin to decline as competition increases. Research and development remains intensive as producers search for the consumer ideal.

Figure 1. *PHASES IN THE PRODUCT LIFE CYCLE*

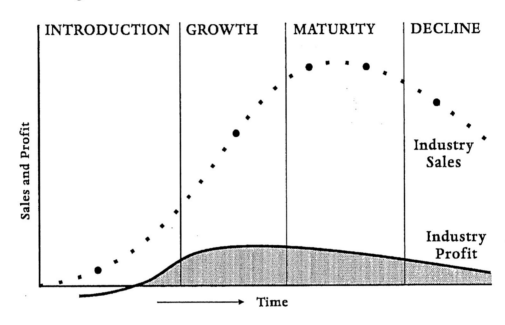

SOURCE: Dale Beckman, David Kurtz, and Louis Boone, *Foundations of Marketing*, 5th ed. (Toronto: Dryden, Holt, Rinehart and Winston of Canada, 1992), 243.

In the maturity phase, sales reach a plateau and competition is at a maximum. This inevitably leads a company to a state of overcapacity and to make cutthroat competitive moves in order to hold market share and force weaker companies out of the market. Prices continue to decline, and price wars often occur. Profitability of the entire industry suffers. Those who have done the research-and-development work have identified customer ideals so well that products are virtually indistinguishable. Promotion emphasis shifts to retaining customers and building repeat purchases. Brand names and subtle product differences are stressed in expensive mass media campaigns. The number of wholesalers and retailers carrying the product reaches a maximum during this phase. As competitors are forced out of the market, some wholesalers and retailers begin to drop the line from their product mix.

The decline phase is characterized by a permanent drop in industry sales caused either by new technological innovations or by changes in basic consumer preferences. Competition for fewer sales means more overcapacity and more companies leaving the market. Industry profits continue to fall, and may become losses. No money is spent on research and development – products are not improved. Because there are fewer competitors, prices begin to stabilize and may increase slightly. The number of distributors continues to fall. Promotion is cut back to minimal levels and messages are more reminder-oriented.

The time it takes for a product to move through its life cycle can vary dramatically. The incandescent light bulb was invented more than 140 years ago by Thomas Edison, and is just entering the early decline phase of its life cycle. The black and white television set was invented in the early 1940's and today it is in the late decline phase – about to disappear. Laser disc players had a complete life span of less than a decade in the late 1990's and early 2000's.

◊◊ Exploiting the Product Life Cycle

A single-product company lives and dies by the product life cycle. Most company managers have a portfolio of products at different stages of their life cycles. One should also realize that, if they are properly managed, products in the decline phase of the product life cycle can still be profitable.

The decline phase does not have to follow the maturity phase if sales of the product can be kick-started (see fig. 2). There are three ways to extend the product life cycle: by finding new uses, by finding new users, or by increasing usage among current users. Baking soda faced a decline, as people did not have the time or inclination to continue home baking. To keep the product alive, many new uses for baking soda were devised; it could serve as a freezer or refrigerator deodorant, cat-box freshener, bathwater additive, toothpaste whitening ingredient, rug cleaner, breath freshener, or household cleanser.

Soft drinks are mostly consumed in much greater quantities in the summer, when a cold beverage is most welcome. In the winter months, people turn to coffee, tea, and hot chocolate. In an effort to rejuvenate soft-drink sales, many companies are experimenting with hot versions of their product to appeal to a new group of consumers. Just imagine a steaming cup of cola on a cold winter's day.

Figure 2.   EXTENDING THE PRODUCT LIFE CYCLE

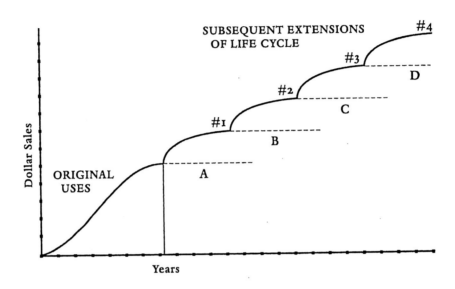

SOURCE: Theodore Levitt, "Exploit the Product Life Cycle," *Harvard Business Review,* November–December, 1965: 88.

As a rule of thumb, 20-percent of customers account for 80-percent of a product's sales. If a company could transform more light users into heavy users, it could extend the product life cycle. Some companies have added a second target market to add new users. A Canadian company could start selling in China or India. A company targeting men could target women as well.

To increase usage, one could change the package size. In Canada, twenty years ago, soft drink companies changed their can size from 280 to 355 millilitres, thus triggering a 25-percent increase in sales volume. Another ploy would be to have consumers save many box-tops for a limited time or they could collect punches on a card each time they purchased a cup of coffee. Consumers would thereby be encouraged to increase their product usage if they wanted the bonus prize.

Some texts suggest a fourth way to rejuvenate a product's life cycle: by reformulating the product, changing its quality, using a new package, or changing the label. However, these are simply tactics to increase usage, attract new users or find new uses.

◊◊ Developing New Products

To fully exploit the product life cycle, companies must always be seeking new products. A company might use internal research-and-development projects, or it could find externally generated technologies that lead to new products. A product is considered new when it involves an area of activity or a production process new to the company. Historically, developing successful new products has not been easy. Studies conducted in the 1960's, showed that two in three new products were a commercial failure. Academic researchers and private corporations have tried to determine why new-product development is not more successful.

As we see in figure 3, all new-product projects must move through six phases of development. At any phase, a project idea might be dropped. The first phase is idea generation. This is the least costly of the six phases, yet it can be the most difficult. People who are asked to brainstorm new-product ideas need to set aside their critical judgement and be free to create. Often the first idea generated is not practical, but that idea may lead to another idea, and yet another, which then can be commercially developed. The key is not to dismiss any idea as being too crazy. As an exercise, examine a belt. Focusing on the belt itself or on the process by which it was produced, try to think of other products that could be developed. Those people who can "ideate" freely are able to generate more than thirty new product ideas in fifteen minutes or less.

The following phases require an increasing commitment of company resources to the new-product project. A company must carefully screen this creative list of new-product ideas. Inferior ideas must be filtered out in such a way that potential winners are not inadvertently dropped. Screening involves a quick assessment of the five environments (technology, competition, political/legal, economic, and socio-cultural) as well as the company's strengths and weaknesses. Ideas that pass this initial screen are developed into full business plans. Detailed assessments of competitors, spreadsheets showing estimated capital expenditures and operating income, and market research into consumer attitudes are assembled. Rigorous quantitative hurdles are set for these business plans so that company resources are invested in projects that will increase shareholder wealth.

Figure 3. DECAY CURVE OF NEW-PRODUCT IDEAS

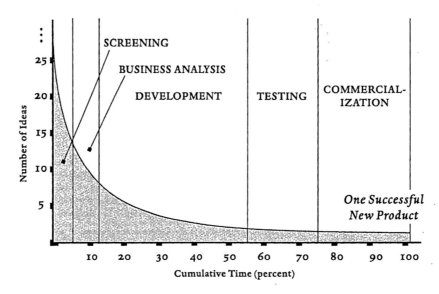

SOURCE: Adapted from *Management of New Products* (New York: Booz, Allen & Hamilton, 1968), 9.

Those plans that are approved lead to product development. At this stage, product prototypes are developed and tested with actual consumers. In the industrial market, new process technologies are tried in pilot plants to ascertain optimal operating conditions and guarantee quality of output. Forty years ago, the Carnation Milk Company discovered a market opportunity for chocolate skim milk powder. The new-product project died in the product development stage, as no formulation could be developed to meet the government standards for fat and calorie content in skim milk.

If a company is certain about the viability of a product and its marketing plans, it might move straight to commercialization – making the product available in the national marketplace. Sometimes, companies have some details to fine tune. A test market – an optional stage – could be undertaken at this point. To conduct this test, marketers choose a small city that is representative of the target population. The product is introduced here, and a small-scale replica of the marketing plan is reproduced – down to the level of couponing, advertising and store displays. The results are closely monitored and activities adjusted to find the optimal marketing plan.

While test markets can cost a half million dollars each, they can be cheap insurance to prevent problems that can arise in a multi-million-dollar national product launch. McDonald's Restaurants has used test marketing successfully to gauge reaction to salads, pizza, chicken nuggets, wraps, and a ground-pork sandwich. However, a test market can reveal a company's plans to its competitors. Colgate has been fighting for nearly five decades to regain, from Crest, its position as the number-one-selling toothpaste. For adults, the number-one dental problem is not cavities but gum disease. Colgate developed an adult toothpaste formulation and used test marketing to gauge reactions. While the new formulation was a success in test market, a short time after Colgate introduced it nationally, Crest introduced its own version of the toothpaste. Crest had learned of the innovation during the test market. Colgate was unable to gain a sustained competitive advantage.

Some companies try to foil a competitor's test market by changing their own marketing activities. For instance, they may distribute extra-value coupons or free samples, temporarily lower prices, or increase their volume of advertising to make the competitor's test market seem unsuccessful. The blockage of potentially successful new products is part of the free-enterprise system.

To increase the success rate of new product commercialization, Dr. Robert Cooper and Dr. Elko Kleinschmidt of McMaster University studied successful and failed product launches. They revised the old model slightly (see fig. 4). They proposed that an effective new-product process was a series of stages and gates. The gates represent hurdles to be overcome. Their research indicates that new products fail because companies don't do all the groundwork required in a given stage, and that hurdles or gates, at which go/no-go decisions are made, are sometimes skipped or hurdles lowered. They advocate for a rigorous approach to new-product development in which full research is conducted with the consumer at every stage. After four decades, their research is paying dividends. Their approach has been adopted by most of the Fortune 500 with those companies seeing two in three commercially launched new products succeeding.

Figure 4.   *A STAGE-GATE APPROACH TO NEW-PRODUCT DEVELOPMENT*

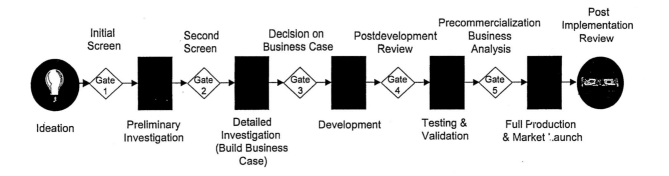

SOURCE: *Winning at New Products* (Toronto: Addison Wesley, 1991), 73.

◊◊ Product Identification

Many products are in the maturity phase of their life cycles, and it is their brand images that affect a consumer's willingness to purchase them. Brand image can be conveyed through the use of logos or symbols, brand names, and packaging. As trade becomes more globalized, the use of logos or symbols will increase, because these devices do not need to be translated from one language to another. Witness the success of McDonald's golden arches or Disney's Mickey Mouse.

The average university graduate has a speaking vocabulary of eight thousand words, yet the average supermarket has over ten thousand individually branded products. Certainly, not all brand names will be equally effective. What makes a brand name good? First, it should be easy to pronounce, recognize and remember. Most effective brand names have one or two syllables and just a few letters: Tide, Bold, Cheer, Dial, Joy, Dove, Kraft, Coke, Pepsi, Jell-o, Blue and Canadian. A study of trademark files indicates that almost all four- and five-letter words have been used in North America as brand names. Some companies are legally protecting six- and seven-letter words for that future time when they will need to introduce new products.

Second, the name should give the right connotation to the buyer. *Connotation* refers to a suggested or implied meaning. *Denotation*, however, refers to the exact meaning of a word – its dictionary definition. *Tubular* means "pertaining to, shaped like, or consisting of, one or more hollow cylinders, or tubes." When a Teenage Mutant Ninja Turtle says, "It's like tubular, dude," the word has a connotative, not a denotative, meaning: it connotes "special," "excellent," "radical." The name given to a product should always have the correct connotation. "Slender" is a great name for a diet drink; "Gaunt" is not.

Finally, the name should be capable of being legally protectable. In this day of designer waters with foreign names, expect to see Perrier, Evian, and Montclair facing competition from L'Eau. But the latter is not a brand name that can be protected. You cannot force French-speaking people to stop using the word *eau* ("water") in their advertising. This inability to legally protect generic terms has come to haunt some companies. Twenty years ago, a court ruling prevented Labatt Breweries from protecting the name Blue, and, by the same token, Molson Breweries cannot protect the name Canadian. Some companies fight to remind consumers that their brand name is not the same as the products they represent. Scotch Tape is an adhesive tape. Aspirin is an acetyl-salicylic-acid pain reliever. Kleenex is a facial tissue and Jell-o is a gelatin dessert. If the fight is lost, these names may be declared unprotected, just like escalator and zipper, former brand names that are now free to be used by any company.

Firms can choose either a family-brand or an individual-brand approach. Kraft is a brand name for a family of food products: cheese slices, peanut butter, cream cheese, salad dressings, mayonnaise, and margarine. Family brands allow for an economy of promotion. Money spent to advertise any one product benefits, to some degree, all the other products in the line. Also, consumers who have a positive experience with one item in the product line often make trial purchases of other items in that line.

In the case of individual branding, each item in a product line receives a unique brand name. You might be hard pressed to name all the products manufactured by Procter and Gamble because the Procter and Gamble name is not made prominent on most of the company's packaging. Individual brands allow for better targeting of products to specific (and probably different) markets. A company that employs individual brands can also have more than one brand competing in the same product class. Procter and Gamble manufactures three different laundry detergents, and they compete against each other. While individual brands are more expensive, companies hope that improved customer satisfaction will increase revenues.

Packaging and labels also define a brand image while serving many other functions. Clearly, packaging protects the contents from damage and spoilage. It helps reduce shoplifting. Small items are placed in larger boxes to prevent the item from being slipped up a shoplifter's sleeve or down his or her boot. Packaging allows consumers to re-use a product. Cereal boxes are designed to store the product between servings, and to keep it fresh over time. In a retail store, package fronts act as small billboards. Consumers may have no idea which brand they will purchase until confronted by the packages in the store.

Labels contain information in both of Canada's official languages. Examine a package of cigarettes, a can of soda or a bag of potato chips, and you will discover more than the brand name or company logo. You should find the name and address of the manufacturer and/or distributor, information about the product composition and the package size, the weight of the contents, recommended uses of the product, promotional information, and the universal product code. The latter has been designed to speed consumers through checkouts, to reduce salesclerk errors and to improve inventory control.

PRICING
STRATEGY

A child opens a package of hockey cards. "Look Mom," the child exclaims, "it's a Sidney Crosby rookie card. I bet it's worth five hundred dollars." Mom doesn't look nearly as excited as the child. Perhaps it's because Mom knows that she couldn't take the hockey card to her bank and use it to reduce her mortgage payment by five hundred dollars.

In the classic sense, price has often been defined as the exchange value of a product or service. The definition implies that something is only worth what someone else is willing to trade for it. Perhaps someone might have been willing to trade five hundred dollars for the hockey card, but it is doubtful that a plumber would take the card in exchange for services rendered.

From time to time, especially when the economy is in a recession, the practice of bartering generates renewed interest. In those unique times, a few individuals revive the concept of exchanging one product or service for another. However, most companies deal in cash dollars, so price represents the cash amount a person or a company is willing to exchange for a product or service.

Producers of products or services must make three classic business decisions: what price level will be set; what discounts will be allowed to purchasers; and what impact the first two decisions will have on the profitability of the business. Let's examine each of these questions in a little more detail.

◇◇ Setting a Price

Classic microeconomic theory suggests that a company needs to determine two curves. One represents the quantity that consumers will demand at various price points. Its shape depends very much on the competitive circumstances in the market (that is, whether a company has a monopoly or whether it faces some degree of competition). The second curve represents the cost a company faces in producing various quantities of a product. Using calculus, one can take the first derivative of each curve to give both a marginal-cost and marginal-demand curve. By finding the intersection of the marginal curves, one has found the point at which the last dollar of cost has been balanced by the last dollar of revenue. Having made this determination, a company would then price the product at that point.

There are two major problems with that approach. The first concerns the construction of the curves. Estimating a reliable cost curve for a company is a fairly easy task. The same is not true of a demand curve. Even if one could reliably determine a demand curve at 9:00 a.m., because consumer tastes and wants are constantly in flux, that demand curve would be out of date by 10:00 a.m. Conceivably, if one used microeconomic theory, the price of a good could change in the time it took for a consumer to pick it from the shelf and pay for it at the checkout counter. As we need an easier and more stable method of pricing, microeconomic theory is generally rejected.

The typical approach to pricing is a cost-plus approach. With the help of its accounting department, a company can determine all the costs of producing a product. There are two types of cost: fixed costs, which do not vary much with the quantity produced; and variable costs, which vary directly with each unit produced. Typical fixed costs include administrative salaries, heating and electricity, property taxes, rent, and promotion budget. Variable costs include raw materials, component parts, and assembly labour. At a minimum, the price paid by consumers must cover all variable costs and should include an extra amount to cover the fixed costs and a contribution to profits.

This extra amount is called the mark-up. While many marketing texts like to define mark-up based on price, it is easier to think of it as based on cost. For instance, if the variable costs of a product are three dollars and a company chooses to sell the product for four dollars, the mark-up of one dollar could also be expressed as a 33.3 percent mark-up based on cost.

The classic business dilemma here is just how big a mark-up to take. Clearly a mark-up which is too big will not be well-received by consumers, and the product won't sell. A mark-up that is too small will be well-received by consumers, but the sales won't generate enough money to cover the fixed costs of doing business. This dilemma is further complicated when a producer realizes that marketing intermediaries, such as wholesalers and retailers, will also mark-up a product to cover their costs. Determining the price at which to sell a product to wholesalers while also calculating a suggested retail selling price is something of an art (see fig. 1).

The size of a mark-up is generally related to stock turnover. The more frequently an item is sold, the less money has to be made on each sale to cover costs. Milk is a product that is sold frequently. Typically, a grocery store's inventory of milk is completely sold in forty-eight to seventy-two hours. Given this high turnover rate, the mark-up on milk is typically 1 or 2 percent. In that same grocery store, one may find dishware or glassware. This inventory will be completely sold in four to six months. Given this low turnover rate, the mark-up on these products could be as much as 100 percent. The average grocery store mark-up is probably 5 to 8 percent. In another industry – for example, retail sporting goods – the average is probably 100 percent, with some items marked up as high as 300 percent.

Figure 1. *THE MARK-UP CHAIN*

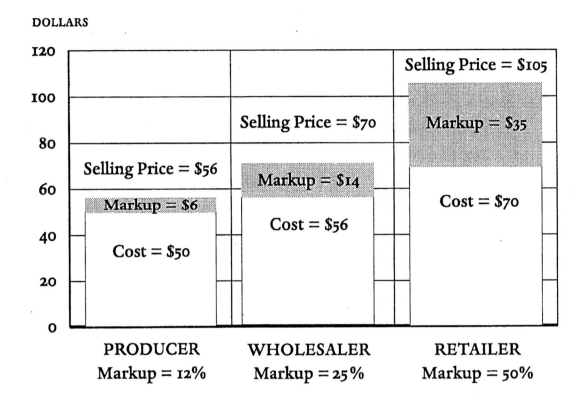

DOLLARS

PRODUCER
Markup = 12%

WHOLESALER
Markup = 25%

RETAILER
Markup = 50%

◊◊ A Look at Discounts, Allowances and Rebates

Although a product is assigned a suggested selling price, the price a company or consumer actually pays for it can be quite different. This market price might reflect various discounts or additional charges.

Discounts are reductions in the price one pays. The need to move inventory is one reason that companies apply discounts to their products. For example, a tomato-juice manufacturer could still have inventory on hand when the new harvest of tomatoes begins. The company needs to clear the warehouse before the new production run, and so it might consider a quantity discount. If a typical case price to the wholesaler is twelve dollars, it could be reduced to ten dollars, but only if the wholesaler agrees to purchase a minimum of one thousand cases.

Another reason a company might offer a discount is to encourage consumers to pay their bills quickly. The company can thus generate a larger or more liquid cash flow. In recessionary times, making a sale may not be enough. Prompt settling of accounts receivable helps to generate the cash lifeblood of a company. In purchasing five thousand dollars worth of lumber from a building-supply store, a contractor might be offered a 2 percent discount if he or she is willing to pay in cash rather than being issued a bill payable in thirty days.

Finally, a discount may be given in exchange for marketing functions that might normally be performed by the manufacturer. Sometimes wholesalers or retailers perform special marketing services for a manufacturer. For instance, a retailer might allow a manufacturer to display its product in an end-of-aisle display, or to set up an in-store tasting. Likewise, a wholesaler may agree with the manufacturer to implement a new shipping and storing arrangement using a new pallet size. In these cases, manufacturers offer discounts to thank and reward intermediaries for their efforts.

The three discounts discussed may be pass passed along to consumers in their entirety, or in part, or not at all.

Allowances should be considered separately. These do not change the price paid for an item, but represent credits that can be applied to a purchase. Consumers are well aware of trade-in allowances. When purchasing a new car, a consumer will negotiate with the car retailer to obtain the best price possible. With that deal completed, the consumer might offer to sell the car he or she is currently using to the dealer. A new negotiating process ensues, and a final trade-in allowance is determined. The allowance does not change the negotiated price for the new car, but represents a credit that can be applied to the purchase price. When purchasing a new car, you may not like the trade-in allowance offered by the dealer. So, instead, you may try to sell your used car privately hoping to get more than the trade-in allowance.

Another type of allowance is for promotion of the manufacturer along with the retailer. Every fall, car manufacturers must unveil all their new-car models for the coming year. Car retailers are often given promotional allowances to organize unveiling events that promote both the dealership and the new cars. You might know dealerships that have hosted barbecues, installed special lighting, or temporarily erected tents to announce their new models. These were all financed by allowances.

When the economy slips into a recession or depression, it is not uncommon to see the rebirth of the rebate. A rebate is a refund by the seller of a portion of the purchase price. A sure sign of a slipping economy is the renaissance of rebates on new-car purchases; automobile manufacturers have used this technique extensively. It is also possible to have smaller rebates on the purchase price of household appliances.

◊◊ Shipping Charges

A final adjustment to the market price involves freight or shipping charges. One can imagine two extremes here. The first would be that the purchaser pays all shipping charges. This is often quoted as free-on-board (or FOB) plant pricing, and suggests that the price quoted is applicable at the plant gates. Should the purchaser want the product delivered anywhere else, it is responsible for all shipping charges.

The other extreme would be a delivered price. This is called freight-absorption, and refers to the price of goods when they have been delivered to wherever the purchaser specifies. A smart purchaser will ask for quotations of both the FOB plant price and the freight-absorption price. The difference represents the cost of freight for the seller. If the purchaser can arrange delivery more cheaply, it will accept the FOB plant price. If it cannot, it will accept the freight-absorption quotation.

Calculating the actual freight charge for each and every order would be a time-consuming task. Instead, a company can calculate an average delivery charge by adding all delivery charges over the previous twelve months and dividing that total by the total number of products shipped. The result is called a uniform-delivered price. Unfortunately, employing this pricing strategy penalizes those who are located close by; they must subsidize the freight costs for those who are situated farther away. The Canadian post office, for example, charges the same price to deliver a letter across the street as it does to deliver a letter to an address several provinces away.

To modify the uniform-delivered pricing plan, one could create concentric zones around the seller's location. Within a zone, there is a uniform-delivered price, but that price increases when one moves from a zone closer to the seller to a farther one. This is called zone-delivered pricing (see fig. 2).

Figure 2.   ZONE-DELIVERED PRICING

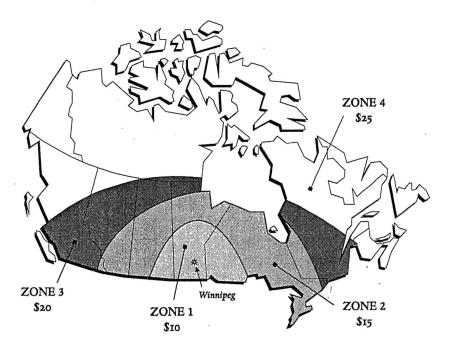

SOURCE: Dale Beckman, David Kurtz, and Louis Boone, *Foundations of Marketing*, 5th ed. (Toronto: Dryden, Holt, Rinehart and Winston of Canada, 1992), 372.

◊◊ How the Market Price Affects the Firm

What size mark-up should a producer take? What size mark-up should be allowed for wholesalers and retailers? What kinds of discounts, allowances, and rebates should be granted? How will freight be handled? While each of these questions require some type of policy decision, it is always important to realize that every policy decision will have an effect on the financial health of the firm. A price set too high will not be accepted by consumers. A price set too low will not allow the firm to be profitable.

In classic microeconomics, the consumer is represented by a demand curve. While these are very difficult to estimate, one does need to think about the consumer as one makes each of the policy decisions listed in the previous paragraph.   One technique that takes the consumer into consideration is break-even analysis.

Calculating a break-even point is fairly easy.   It is the intersection of two lines – the total-revenue line and the total-cost line.   The total-revenue line has a slope equal to the market price per item and no intercept (as there is no guaranteed revenue if no units are sold). The total-cost line has a slope equal to the average variable cost per item and an intercept equal to the total fixed costs (see fig. 3).

If we have a market price, it is fairly easy to calculate the break-even point. Any units that can be sold in excess of the break-even point will be profit for the firm. Any shortfall in sales will result in losses. As the total-cost line is unaffected by the market price, the only detail that can change the break-even point is price differences. Higher prices represent more steeply sloped total-revenue lines and a lower break-even point in units to be sold. Lower prices have the opposite effect. Now with different break-even points calculated for different market prices, the marketer's understanding of the consumer comes into play. Will consumers buy enough units at the higher price or the lower price for the company to break-even?

Break-even analysis is deceptively simple. It is, in fact, one of the most powerful techniques in a marketer's arsenal of analytical weapons.

Figure 3.   BREAK-EVEN ANALYSIS

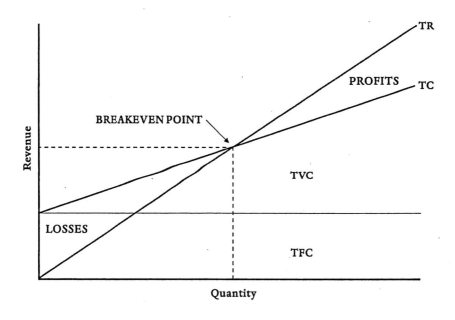

Break-even point in units = $\dfrac{\text{Total Fixed Costs (TFC)}}{\text{Price (P) – Average Variable Cost (AVC)}}$

PROMOTION STRATEGY

If a tree falls in the wilderness and no one is present, does it make a noise? While this old philosophical question has been debated for centuries, it is easy to answer when it is adapted to a modern marketing context. If a company advertises in a magazine that nobody reads, has it communicated with anyone? The answer is no.

Promotion is all about communications. Any messages that a company sends to inform, persuade, or remind customers as they make a purchase decision perform a promotional function. This communication task can be performed on a one-to-one basis (a salesperson talking to a potential client) or on a one-to-many basis (an impersonal television advertisement broadcast to millions of viewers).

A promotional mix is ultimately a blend of personal and nonpersonal selling choices. Along with advertising, nonpersonal selling involves public relations and the field of sales promotion, some of the tools of which are coupons, free samples, contests, and in-store displays. Unlike the stereotypical vacuum-cleaner salesperson of an earlier era, the modern salesperson must understand consumers and help them to satisfy their needs.

Producers of goods or services must investigate four areas: the communications process; the choice of advertising medium; the field of sales promotion; and the personal-selling process. Let's examine each of these in more detail.

◊◊ The Communications Process

Communications begins with a sender, generally a company with a message it wishes to relay. The message can be either a piece of information, a question or request, or an opinion or piece of advice. Good messages must: gain the attention of a receiver; be understood by both the receiver and sender; and stimulate the needs, change the attitudes, or reinforce the learning of a receiver, and suggest an appropriate action or reaction.

For communications to be effective, there must also be a receiver. This could be a single individual or millions of people. In deciding how to reach the receiver, the firm must choose a transfer medium with which to deliver the message. This medium can be a salesperson or a television commercial or a flyer or a Facebook page or a free sample brought to someone's door. Generally, the more receivers that can be reached with a transfer medium, the lower the per-capita cost for its use. During the Super Bowl, television-commercial time may cost four million dollars but reach hundreds of millions of people for a per-capita cost of pennies per person. A flyer delivered by Canada Post will reach far fewer people and its cost, as third class mail, can be measured in tens of cents per person.

Messages must be encoded or translated into understandable terms. A company with a new brand may want to build awareness. Its message may be nothing more than, "Hello Canada. I want you to meet my new brand." The translation of that message is done once a transfer medium is chosen. If a company chooses a television commercial to promote its product, it might use a recognizable celebrity, humour, and rock-and-roll music. If it decides on personal selling, then it might use a four-colour flyer, a gift pencil, and an attention-getting demonstration. The message must be decoded by the receiver. While watching a television commercial for Obsession cologne, you may wonder what message you are supposed to extract. A recent public-service message on the dangers of steroid abuse was tested on a group of teenagers. When asked what message they had received, most identified it as "Taking steroids makes you more muscular." The message about the dangers of steroids had been either encoded or decoded incorrectly.

An enemy of good communications is noise, which can be defined as anything that interferes with the transmission of a message or reduces its effectiveness. Noise can be something as simple as the static you hear while listening to a radio station or the sound of children playing in the room where you are watching television. It can also refer to the thousands of marketing messages we receive every day. As we cannot possibly comprehend them all, we build up perceptual screens. These are an impediment to marketing communications. We also use our television remote-control to filter communications.

Marketing communication is not one-way, or simplex, from the manufacturer to the consumer. If one truly embraces the marketing concept, one knows that consumers also need to be heard. They provide much-needed feedback on a producer's message. Perhaps consumers buy a product, perhaps they don't. After buying the product, they may have problems or suggestions about how to improve the product that need to be communicated to producers. WATS lines (1-800 numbers), social media posts, and marketing research studies are just a few vehicles that allow consumers to be heard.

Of course, marketing communication is not a one-time process. It is a never ending loop of sending and receiving (see fig. 1).

◊◊   Choosing Between Advertising Media

Given the cost of developing an advertising campaign, the correct choice of a medium is critical. The key is to determine, through research, a specific description of the target market, including a determination of its size, key characteristics, attitudes, opinions, and preferred activities. One must balance the cost of an advertising medium with the reach or coverage of the target market. Overcoverage (spilling into unwanted target markets) can be as bad as undercoverage.

Figure 1. THE COMMUNICATIONS PROCESS

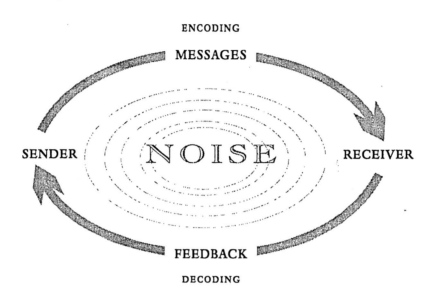

The largest fraction of advertising dollars, about 38-percent, goes to television – network and cable combined. Television's share of advertising dollars changes little annually, in part, because the quantity of its advertising is fixed. Typically, no more than eight minutes of advertising are allowed during a thirty-minute television broadcast. With the supply fixed and demand growing, it comes as no surprise that the cost of television advertising time is growing faster than the rate of inflation. Television is popular because of its impact on a range of senses. A television advertiser can combine sound, motion, and colour to create advertising with impact – impact that might break through our perceptual screens. Also, one national television advertisement reaches many millions of people and, through repetition, has the potential to reach many millions more. Of course, the costs of producing a television advertisement (sometimes as much as five million dollars) can be prohibitive for many companies. Television commercials rarely run longer than thirty seconds, and some only last fifteen seconds. A company may have to pack its commercial with information, but because that information is so dense, the viewer could have trouble retaining it. Finally, the effectiveness of television commercials decays quickly. Most have a life span of thirteen weeks; they must then be retired. Some lose their effectiveness because the public do not trust the actors or the information presented.

Internet advertising receives 30-percent of advertising dollars annually. This has been the fastest growing medium starting with virtually no spending in this area fifteen years ago. Like a magazine, some websites have banner ads at the bottom, top, or sides of a page. When you search for information, engines like Google, Yahoo, or Bing suggest some sites because they are paid to do so. Advertisers can spend a fixed amount for an advertisement to appear or they can pay-per-click only paying when a viewer clicks on its ad. The effectiveness of Internet advertising is still uncertain. Some automobile companies have discontinued banner advertising as they found many people simply clicked accidentally on their banner ads. For some free Internet services, like Facebook or LinkedIn, Internet advertising is the revenue stream which allows it to survive. In the first quarter of 2016, Facebook generated a little over $5.00 per user per quarter in advertising revenues.

About one-eighth of advertising dollars goes to newspapers. They suffer from a short lifespan (often less than a day), the fact that most readers skim them quickly (usually less than twenty minutes), and the smudgy quality of their images and text. Though inks have been improved in recent years, and full and partial colour are more easily used, newspaper images cannot compare with those of magazines and other periodicals. On the plus side, newspapers reach nearly 90-percent of households; readers can refer back to previously read sections, or can keep advertising handy until it is needed (say for shopping); and newspaper advertising can be easily moved from one day to another, or from one page or section to another, or from one city to another.

Magazines and periodicals are the fourth most popular medium, garnering 7.5-percent of advertising expenditures. Because magazines are designed for very specific target markets, advertisers are given an excellent range of consumers to target. Just imagine the diversity of readers for *Architectural Digest, National Geographic, Seventeen, Soldier of Fortune*, GQ, and *Out*. Magazines have longer life spans (typically thirty days), and a better quality of image reproduction than newspapers. Magazines lack the flexibility of placing advertising in certain geographic markets and not in others. Magazines need a certain minimum subscription base to remain in business. A magazine designed for the north end of Saskatoon just wouldn't have enough readers to justify its existence.

Radio has seen its share of advertising dollars decline since its heyday in the 1930's and 1940's. With the advent of television, radio became a medium of music and talk shows. Today radio attracts only 7-percent of advertising dollars spent. Like television, radio suffers from an over-abundance of stations, and this in turn, fragments the market. In Windsor, one can listen to more than thirty radio stations, both FM and AM, originating in both Canada and the United States. If an advertiser wants to reach a specific type of listener, it might have to advertise on several different stations. People cannot retrieve a radio ad (or a television ad) once it has been played. Information such as telephone numbers and addresses are hard to convey. Radio advertising can, however, be created quickly and changed within a few minutes. Radio advertising time is very cheap to purchase (a few hundred dollars for a thirty second spot on a top-rated station), and radio is a portable medium. People listen to a radio in cars, on boats, at the beach, in a gym, and so on. They can't do the same with television.

Direct mail involves a broad spectrum of advertising media, including flyers, catalogues, postcards, sales letters, folders, and booklets. It is difficult to measure the percentage of advertising expenditures for direct marketing as companies that exclusively used paper mail have converted to electronic mail. While many people call these solicitations junk mail, it may surprise you to know that 3-percent of people receiving a piece of direct-mail advertising decide to make purchases based on the information that this advertising provides. Direct mail allows an advertiser access to every home in a given area (it thus reaches even more people than newspapers do), thanks to Canada Post. It can provide a large amount of detailed information to a customer, yet the format of an ad can be changed easily and quickly should an advertiser so desire. At a slightly increased cost, target mailing lists (made up of people who have a common attribute) may be purchased allowing for a personalized message. Even though most direct mail is third class, the per-capita cost of postage makes direct mail the most expensive of all the media. The quality of a mailing list is also critical. If a database of addresses is correct today, six months from now 10-percent of the addresses will have changed. Mailing lists which are out-of-date lead to much undelivered mail. Maintaining an accurate database of addresses is both a difficult and expensive proposition.

Finally, there is outdoor advertising. Posters, billboards, electronic displays, signs on the sides of buses and taxis, and ads on transit shelters account for about 6.5-percent of advertising expenditures. If designed properly, outdoor advertising can effectively communicate short, simple messages. In high-traffic areas, it is possible to expose consumers to an advertising message repeatedly. Outdoor advertising is especially effective for notifying potential customers about nearby sales (just witness the proliferation of outdoor advertising for summer garage sales). Of course, the message must be brief. It is impossible to convey an advertising message, an address, and a phone number on a billboard. Environmentalists have begun to question the use of outdoor advertising, identifying it as a form of visual and spatial pollution.

It should be noted that, regardless of the medium, the advertising message changes over the product life cycle (see fig. 2).

Figure 2. *THE LINK BETWEEN THE PRODUCT LIFE CYCLE AND THE ADVERTISING MESSAGE*

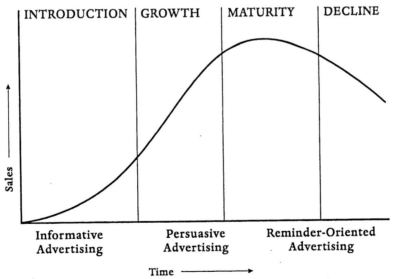

SOURCE: Dale Beckman, David Kurtz, and Louis Boone, *Foundations of Marketing*, 5th ed. (Toronto: Dryden, Holt, Rinehart and Winston of Canada, 1992), 509.

◊◊ The Field of Sales Promotion

When asked to define promotion, most people immediately begin talking about advertising. But the importance of advertising in the promotional mix has been declining of late. No doubt this is a direct result of the proliferation of new cable-television stations, greater reach of radio stations, and the growth in social media on the Internet. But advertising's loss has been sales promotion's gain. It is difficult to define exactly what is meant by a sales promotion. Some define it by what it is not. Sales promotion is not advertising, public relations, or personal selling. Others see sales promotion as an attempt to reach a very specific target market and motivate its members in very specific ways.

One of the most important sales-promotion techniques involves the distribution of samples, coupons, and premiums. Samples are products that are distributed for free. They are intended to build awareness, demonstrate a product's features, and eventually stimulate trial purchases. Distribution may be done through the mail or on a door-to-door basis. You may have recently received a sample of a new shampoo or a new laundry detergent.

Coupons offer a specific price reduction on the next purchase of a product. They are especially useful in stimulating trial purchases, and can help to overcome the perceived price barrier that prevents some consumers from buying certain premium products. Most retailers readily redeem coupons – which are distributed through the mail, in magazines, inside packages, and in newspapers – as they are not only reimbursed for the discounts but they also receive a handling fee.

Premiums are bonus items given free with the purchase of another product. As children, many of us begged our parents to buy a special brand of cereal because of the prize that could be found inside. In some instances, these premiums have become desirable in and of themselves. Witness the growth of sports cards, which were once used to sell bubblegum. Today the gum has all but disappeared from the packages. Premiums are used to stimulate trial purchases of a product and to initiate brand switching.

Another sales-promotion technique is point-of-purchase advertising. While many consumers enter a store with some idea of which brands they will purchase, it is often possible to influence them at the place where the purchase decision is made. Point-of-purchase advertising can be as simple as a small sign or sticker attached to a shelf or as complicated as a stand-alone display designed to show the product in a special light. Both types of promotion are designed to draw attention away from competitors' products.

Contests are a form of sales promotion that is usually intended to encourage repeat purchases. As the odds of winning a prize are fixed, the more times one enters a contest the more likely one is to win. Often contests offer significant cash or merchandise prizes to call attention to particular products. Just think of the millions that can be won in the Publisher's Clearinghouse contests. Contests may be regulated at the municipal, provincial, and federal government levels, so experts are often hired to guide a company planning this type of promotion. Generally, governments insist that the purchase of a product not be required to enter a contest, though this fact is not generally known to most consumers.

A subtle form of sales promotion is specialty advertising, which uses everyday articles to carry the name, address, and advertising message for a company. Look at the pen or pencil on your desk, the book of matches by the fireplace, the calendar on the wall, your key ring, a shopping bag, or the T-shirt you are wearing and you may find some form of specialty advertising. It turns common items into advertising media.

Finally, there are conventions, large gatherings where wholesalers, retailers, and, sometimes, the public have a chance to meet, discuss trends in a certain industry, and view displays and product demonstrations. You may have attended a car or boat show to marvel at some of the new technology. Other shows, such as those for the landscapers, retail fashion buyers, and personal-fitness-equipment-makers, are not accessible to the general public. While no significant cash-and-carry sales are made at such shows, wholesale and retail orders are often placed for the selling year ahead.

◊◊ The Personal Selling Process

While some are more gifted when it comes to meeting clients and pursuing sales, all people are salespeople at various points in their lives. We often try to sell ourselves, whether it is to get a job, get elected to an office, attract a mate, or seek a bank loan: selling is not an easy task. It involves seven distinct steps.

The salesperson begins the process by identifying potential customers. Prospecting for customers, he or she may have to consult databases, talk to friends, or networking through social clubs. Generating these lists is a difficult job, and the salesperson does not often receive an immediate payback for it. Identifying potential customers is a continual part of the life of a salesperson, and it can be frustrating. In the qualifying phase, salespeople must check their potential-customer lists to ensure that they are not wasting valuable time talking to someone who is not a customer and is unlikely to become one. He or she needs potential customers with not only a desire to purchase but also purchasing power and the authority to buy.

Next comes the challenging step of actually meeting with a potential customer. Making the approach is never easy, and the difficulty increases with the importance of the customer. In other words, a customer who might place an order for three million dollars of equipment is much harder to approach than a customer who might place an order for a few hundred dollars. To ease the tension, a salesperson is well-advised to learn as much as possible about these prospective customers and the environments in which they operate.

When the formalities and pleasantries of a first meeting are out of the way, a salesperson needs to give the sales message to the potential client. In making the presentation, the salesperson describes the product's major features, points out its strengths and benefits, and lists previous successes. Above all else, the presentation should be clear, concise and positive.

Because some product benefits are difficult to describe, it is sometimes necessary to supplement the presentation with a demonstration. The salesperson can also reinforce and supplement what he or she has said by showing the product in action. It is important for the demonstration to be unique. Anyone can throw some dirt on the floor and then vacuum it up. It is much more effective to show that the vacuum can remove spills of both liquid and dry material. However, many sales have been lost when a product malfunctions or the salesperson cannot demonstrate all the features. Clearly, careful planning and practice are the keys to successful demonstrations.

No salesperson can fully anticipate all questions a potential customer will ask. The presentation or demonstration may not lead to an immediate sale. The potential customer may have some questions about the product or some objections to making the purchase. Answering these questions and handling these objections should not be seen as a chance to remove barriers, but as the opportunity to present additional information. If someone says, "I don't like green," they are actually saying, "In what other colours is the product available?"

Every presentation inevitably reaches a point when the salesperson must ask the potential client to make a purchase. Closing techniques vary considerably from one salesperson to another. Some prefer to present potential clients with two equally acceptable (to the salesperson) alternatives, so that either outcome is good. Others prefer the higher risk strategy of silence, which will always force a customer decision – though not always the one a salesperson desires. Still others prefer to make appeals to emotion or guilt to swing a customer and make a sale.

But the sale is not the end point of the selling process. From psychology, there is a concept called cognitive dissonance. After making a purchase, customers may experience post-purchase doubts about the product or the size of the order. Left to themselves, these customers may well cancel the order or reduce its size. A good salesperson visits the customer after the closing, and makes certain that all is going well. The goal of a salesperson should not be to make one sale but, rather, to develop an ongoing relationship that leads to many sales. If the salesperson psychologically reinforces the customer's decision and handles any problems with delivery or order specifications, she or he will ensure customer satisfaction, and will increase the likelihood of further purchases.

Both personal and non-personal communications play important roles in the promotion mix. Studies have shown that leading up to and following a transaction, non-personal communications plays a relatively more important role. When the transaction is actually taking place, personal communications is much more important (see fig. 3).

DISTRIBUTION
STRATEGY

When engaging in polite dinner conversation, it is said, one should avoid three topics: politics, sex, and religion. To those add Canada Post. Few Canadian institutions can evoke such strong emotions at the mere mention of their name. Much of the ill will generated by Canada Post can be traced to its distribution strategy.

The cornerstone of any distribution strategy, or any marketing strategy, is the consumer. A company should set a standard of distribution upon which consumers can rely. Such standards normally include a time frame and a penalty clause, should the standard be breached. Some pizza-delivery companies have a standard that promises customers a free pizza if they are kept waiting longer than thirty minutes. A major road-equipment company guarantees spare-parts delivery within forty-eight hours or it pays the repair bill.

Canada Post, too, has a customer-service standard for correctly addressed mail. Within the same city, a letter should be delivered within two working days. Between cities in the same province, a letter should be delivered within three working days. Between cities in different provinces, a letter should be delivered within four working days. Do you notice anything missing from this standard?

There is no penalty clause. In 2007, Canada Post complied with its customer-service standard 85-percent of the time. By 2013, this had improved to 99-percent of the time. This seems an impressive change, until you realize that Canada Post handles nearly 9.0 billion pieces of mail each year – 4.0 billion pieces of letter mail and 5.0 billion parcels. Ten-percent of the mail originates with individuals; the remainder with businesses. Still, the 1-percent of mail delivered late is equivalent to ninety million pieces. Every year, one in two Canadians will have a piece of mail delivered to them late.

It is this uncertainty about prompt delivery that makes Canadians unhappy with their postal service. If delivery were slowed, few people would be upset as long as they could be guaranteed that the mail would arrive within the specified time frame. Canada Post's competition, the courier companies, back their guarantees with self-imposed penalties if they fail to meet service standards. To win us back, Canada Post may want to consider a similar gesture.

◊◊ Physical Distribution

We begin our discussion of distribution by focusing on the activities that move products from manufacturers to the ultimate consumer. After all, physical-distribution costs represent half of all marketing costs incurred by a firm. Logistics, or physical distribution, involves transportation companies, warehousing firms, financial institutions, insurance companies and marketing-research firms. It also involves customer service, inventory control, materials handling, order processing, transportation, packaging and warehousing (see fig. 1).

The starting point in logistics is defining a customer-service standard.

Too low a standard may mean dissatisfied customers and lost sales, while too high a standard may mean increased job stress and high distribution costs. A proper standard requires a trade-off between the customer and the manufacturer. Tied to the customer-service standard is the choice of transportation mode: train, truck, boat, airplane, or pipeline. Though these will be discussed as separate alternatives, companies must often combine them to meet customer needs. For example, shipping product to Prince Edward Island from an Ontario plant might require a truck, train, and boat.

Figure 1. COMPONENTS OF A PHYSICAL-DISTRIBUTION SYSTEM

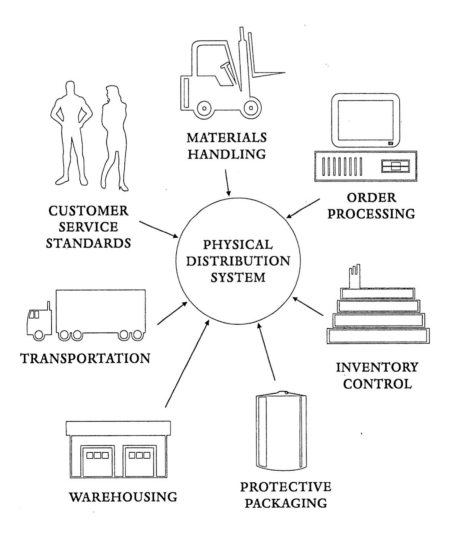

MATERIALS HANDLING

ORDER PROCESSING

CUSTOMER SERVICE STANDARDS

PHYSICAL DISTRIBUTION SYSTEM

TRANSPORTATION

INVENTORY CONTROL

WAREHOUSING

PROTECTIVE PACKAGING

Trains move the most product and have always been most efficient at moving large quantities of bulk goods over great distances. Their role has diminished over the last several decades due to two factors. First, every manufacturing plant used to be built near a railway so that a spur line could service the plant. Today, most industrial parks are built away from railways and close to roads. Second, the size of loads being shipped has declined. With just-in-time inventory systems, smaller quantities of products are being ordered more frequently. Half–filled railway cars are not efficient to move, and are often the cause of damaged goods and shifted loads. The fact that the railway has retained its lead can be attributed to its flexibility in moving liquids, raw materials, gases, grains, and finished goods very safely.

The trucking industry has grown at the expense of the railways. Due to the host of sizes (from panel vans to eighteen wheelers) and types (for example, refrigerated vehicles or tankers) available, there is great flexibility in the size and type of loads trucks can carry. They can reach any company that is on a road. They are excellent for quickly and frequently moving products short distances. Perhaps trucking's greatest failure is its human component. Drivers cannot drive twenty-four hours a day; they need to sleep and eat. Sleeper cabs allow for teams of drivers, and therefore improve productivity, but they are not a perfect solution. Trucks also need to be refuelled and maintained. Tires can go flat and, no matter what automobile drivers may think, trucks are constrained by speed limits. If a shipment of lobster must travel from New Brunswick to Alberta in one day, no truck can get it there on time.

Boats are best for moving large quantities of product over long distances. Most international trade requires the use of oceangoing vessels, whether it be to bring oil from the Middle East or cars from the Far East, or to take grain from western Canada to the rest of the world. Canada is blessed with excellent inland waterways. Smaller vessels move products through our Great Lakes and up our rivers. Boats tend to be the slowest mode of transportation, and thus are also the cheapest. Airplanes, of course, are the opposite. They offer the fastest way to move products and the most expensive. Planes are used when speed is crucial. They transport perishable products such as flowers and seafood; products needed in emergency situations such as spare parts for machines and human organs for transplants; expensive items such as gemstones and designer fashions;

and for important documents and parcels.

When one thinks of pipelines, oil immediately comes to mind. But pipelines can be used to move other liquids, gases and even some solids. Pipelines are not a common mode of distribution, yet much research is being conducted to see if pipelines can be more efficiently exploited. Pipelines generally provide a one-way movement of goods – from the source to the receiver. It is already standard operating procedure to place some items (for example, documents or test samples) in capsules that are then carried along the pipeline to the receiver. There have been experiments to determine whether two types of materials can be transported in the same pipeline (oil and water, for instance). Some people foresee a day when a reverse flow will be possible in a pipeline, thus allowing the two-way transportation of goods.

◊◊ Inventory Control

Manufacturers, wholesalers, retailers, and consumers are concerned with the question of how much inventory to have on hand. Again, this is a cost-trade-off question. Every time an order is placed, there is a cost. On one hand, assuming that the cost is fixed, that it remains unaffected by the size of the order, it makes sense for companies to place large orders. On the other hand, inventories are generally purchased with borrowed money. If its inventory can be sold quickly, a company's capital will be freed. It will be able to use it to repay the loan, and interest charges will be minimized. If the inventory moves slowly, interest payments grow, a company's credit rating falls, and the cost of borrowing rises. This suggests that perhaps it would be best to place many, smaller orders.

If the two costs are added, a parabolic total-cost curve is found (see fig. 2). As you may remember from your calculus classes, a parabola has a minimum point. After finding that minimum point, a company determines the economic order quantity – the amount that should be ordered at any one time to minimize inventory costs. If it knows what the approximate yearly demand for a product is, the company can also calculate how often it should place orders. Suppose the economic order quantity is five hundred cases per order, and the company knows it needs six thousand cases per year. Twelve orders would be placed annually, or approximately one per month.

Figure 2. *MINIMIZING INVENTORY COSTS*

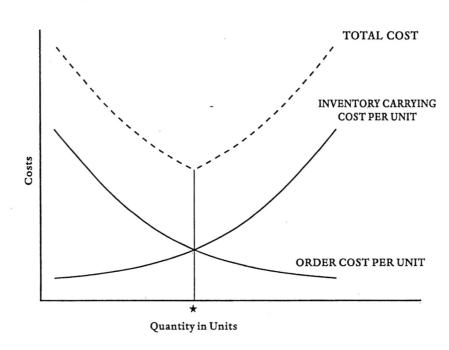

BOQ (economic order quanitity) formula, to calculate the minimum point of the parabolic total cost curve:

$$\sqrt{\frac{2RS}{IC}}$$

Where: R = the annual rate of usage
S = the cost of placing an order
I = the annual inventory carrying cost percentage
C = the cost per unit

SOURCE: Dale Beckman, David Kurtz, and Louis Boone, *Foundations of Marketing*, 5th ed. (Toronto: Dryden, Holt, Rinehart and Winston of Canada, 1992), 397.

◊◊   Materials Handling

In the 1940's, every case of every product was moved by hand. Imagine a truck reaching a dock and being unloaded by hand. Each case is passed from person to person and then reloaded, again by hand, onto a boat. Picture the weather as cold and wet. Finally, imagine the amount of damage, spoilage, and pilferage that could occur when products are handled in this way and under such circumstances.

Today, partly due to the costs of damage, pilferage, and spoilage and partly due to the cost of labour, human handling of products is minimized. Conveyor belts have been designed to move products across warehouses.

Stackers have been designed to place products on pallets (one-metre-square raised wooden platforms) and forklift trucks move the pallets onto trucks, railway cars, and boats.

Another important innovation has been the container. Shifting product from one mode of transportation to another (for example, from truck to boat) increases the risk of damage, pilferage, and spoilage, even if equipment is used. Special containers have been designed that can sit on the flatbed of a railway car, on the trailer of a truck, or in the hold of a ship. Once loaded, containers never need to be unloaded until they reach their destination.

◊◊   Warehouses

There are two ways to think about warehouses. One is to focus on the level of activity they maintain. In September and October, tomatoes are harvested in Ontario and taken to local canneries. At that time, all the tomato juice, tomato ketchup, tomato sauce, and tomato soup for the next twelve months is manufactured. If you buy a can of juice or a bottle of ketchup in July, it is probably several months old. This is not a very appetizing idea. Where has it been? A storage warehouse is designed to be a relatively inactive place where products are kept for relatively long periods of time – months. On a day-to-day basis, few trucks arrive and few orders are filled. A distribution warehouse, by contrast, is a very active place. Small quantities of all the products in a company's product line are stored there for only a few days. During this time, the products are sorted and prepared for shipping to fill orders received from wholesalers or retailers.

A second way to think about warehouses is as efficiency centres. Suppose a company in Montreal had orders to fill in Regina, Saskatoon, Edmonton, Calgary, and Winnipeg. It could load five different trucks, one for each city, and wait for them to make their deliveries. But that would not be very efficient. For most of the journey, the five trucks would cover the same route, only diverging towards the end. It would be more efficient to use a larger carrier, say a railway car, to ship all the product to a central site in the West. The warehouse at the central site would then break the order into the five smaller lots to be delivered by truck. This activity would occur at a ***break-bulk*** warehouse.

At a ***make-bulk*** warehouse, small shipments from several different producers destined for the same city are assembled for efficient transport by a larger carrier. If producers in Waterloo, Hamilton, Guelph, and Mississauga all have shipments bound for Halifax, it would be cheaper for them to put those shipments together on a large truck rather than using four smaller trucks.

◊◊ Marketing Intermediaries

Wholesalers and retailers operate between the producer and the consumer. Although they lengthen the distribution channel and slow the distribution rate, these intermediaries perform several essential functions.

They provide information to manufacturers about the reactions of retail stores and consumers to new products, about customer complaints, and about competitor activities. On behalf of a manufacturer, they can be a source of technical information, as well as information about price changes and industry trends to retailers and consumers. Intermediaries often provide financing for their customers. To encourage you to buy, **Sears**, **WalMart**, and **The Bay** offer you the convenience of a store credit card. A wholesaler often extends credit to a retailer. Should the retailer be able to sell its inventory, it can repay the wholesaler and claim the rest toward overhead and profit.

Wholesalers and retailers perform a storage function. Every retail store maintains an inventory of products both on its shelves and in its storeroom. Likewise, wholesalers need to keep a supply of product on hand to fill orders from retailers. These distributed inventories allow manufacturers to minimize their inventory costs. Intermediaries also perform a transportation function. Sears will deliver a new refrigerator to your home. Wholesalers will deliver orders to the door of retailers.

It is not easy for a manufacturer to make the decision to lengthen the distribution channel by adding intermediaries (see fig. 3). The decision can be influenced by the type of product being sold. Perishable products need short distribution channels. So do high-fashion products. Standardized products or low-unit-value products typically have longer channels. The type of market influences the length of the channel. Consumers like to purchase products from retail stores. Industrial customers often prefer to deal directly with manufacturers. In densely populated areas, a bakery can sell directly to consumers, but in low population-density areas, wholesalers and retailers are used.

Figure 3.   *FACTORS AFFECTING THE LENGTH OF A DISTRIBUTION CHANNEL*

❖ The Consumer/Customer
❖ Product Characteristics
❖ Manufacturer Characteristics
❖ Factors in the Business Environment

Certain characteristics of the manufacturer can have an impact on the channel.   Companies that want the control which comes from having their own wholesale and retail outlets must have large financial resources. Most small or new manufacturing companies have to rely on the kindness of intermediaries. A manufacturer may also desire total control over the presentation of its product. In that case, a shorter channel is used. Finally, the manufacturer must consider the types of channels allowed by law and those used by its competitors. **Molson** and **Labatt** would like to sell beer through corner variety stores in Ontario, but they must use the intermediaries provided to them by law. Mary Kay, of **Mary Kay Cosmetics** fame, claims that when she wanted to enter the cosmetics industry, **Max Factor**, **Maybelline**, and **Cover Girl** had a virtual lock on retail stores. She chose a more direct route, party selling, to give herself a competitive edge.

◊◊ Wholesaling

Wholesalers are companies that sell to retailers, other wholesalers, and industrial customers, but do not sell significant quantities to individual consumers.   A manufacturer may wish to forward integrate or a group of retailers may wish to backward integrate by acquiring a wholesaler, but most wholesalers are independently owned and operated.

Independent wholesalers can be divided into two groups: those that take title to, or own, the products they handle and those that do not.   The latter group is made up of agents and brokers.   One example of this group is an auction house. In London, England, one of the world's famous auction houses, **Christie's**, displays and sells precious art. While the art is stored at the auction house in the days leading up to the auction, it remains, at all times, the property of someone else. As an agent-broker, **Christie's** must bring buyers and sellers together, and for this it receives a commission (as much as 20-percent of the selling price). When agents and brokers are mentioned, many think of stockbrokers or real-estate agents. Agents and brokers may only work on one side of a transaction. I want my stockbroker to get the highest possible price for my stock. You want your broker to get the lowest possible price for the stock. If the broker worked for both of us, he or she would have an insurmountable conflict of interest.

Merchant wholesalers take title to the goods they sell to others. For example, a truck wholesaler takes title and possession of perishable products like bread, milk, vegetables, fruit, potato chips, candy, and eggs. This wholesaler arranges frequent, perhaps daily, deliveries to retailers to guarantee the freshness of the goods being sold. If the truck wholesaler miscalculates and buys more eggplant than is demanded by retailers, it must find a way to dispose of the excess at its own expense.

◊◊ Retailers

Retailers sell products and services to the ultimate consumer for his or her own consumption. Many different classification systems have been developed in an attempt to better understand the host of different retailers. An easy way to classify a retailer is to consider the amount of consumer shopping effort it demands. Convenience stores are designed for maximum accessibility. Long store hours, fast checkout service, ample parking, and easy-to-reach locations are hallmarks of the variety store, gasoline station, dry cleaner, grocery store and instant banking machines, all of which may be considered convenience retailers.

Shopping stores are designed to allow consumers to compare prices, brands, and product components before making a purchase. Typically, shopping retailers – for example, furniture stores, appliance stores, clothing outlets, and sporting goods stores – try to differentiate themselves through floor layouts, window displays, special merchandise or brands, and knowledgeable salespeople.

Consumers must work to shop at specialty stores. Often they have shorter hours of operation, no free parking, and less accessible locations. But consumers are willing to expend the effort because of a particular specialty store's unique combination of product lines, service, and reputation. Specialty stores often work to breed loyalty among consumers, so that repeat business is guaranteed.

There are some special decisions retailers must make (see fig. 4). The first concerns a store's image. The moment customers walk into a store, they form an impression about the type of shopping experience they will have there. Imagine yourself entering a men's clothing store. The staff offer you a cup of cappuccino or, perhaps, some sparkling water. You are invited to discuss your clothing needs while seated on a leather couch. The store's walls are covered in walnut panelling with brass accents. This is shopping at its best. Compare this to the worn linoleum tiled floors, chrome racks, and dark ceilings that you might see at a **Giant Tiger** discount department store. Image is a very powerful promotional tool for a retailer.

Figure 4. WHY CONSUMERS CHOOSE A PARTICULAR RETAILER

❖ Low Prices
❖ Convenience of Location or Hours
❖ Variety of Selection
❖ Perceived Product Quality
❖ Assistance from Salespeople
❖ Reputation for Integrity and Fairness
❖ Special Services Offered
❖ Sales/Special Value Offered

Equally important is a store's location. While shopping malls, which offer one-stop shopping, have grown in popularity, not every retailer is wise to locate in one. If a store's products appeal to impulse buyers, then a location that gets lots of walk-by traffic is the most desirable. What are traffic patterns like? Is there a bus stop nearby? What are the neighbouring stores? It wouldn't be wise to open a **Ralph Lauren Polo** shop beside a retailer called **Everything for a Buck**.

◇◇ Intensity of Distribution

If a manufacturer has chosen to include wholesalers and/or retailers in the distribution channel, it must decide how many of each it needs? This raises the question of market coverage or intensity of distribution. Exclusive distribution comes into play when the rights to sell a product are limited to a geographic region. In Winnipeg, there may be only one store that carries **Waterford** crystal, or **Royal Daulton** china, or **Mercedes-Benz** automobiles. In some cities, perhaps, no one carries a specific brand of product. Exclusive distribution is often used to enhance the image of a product and build its prestige.

Intensive distribution is designed to saturate the marketplace with a product. Everywhere consumers turn, they find the product. Windshield-washing fluid, for instance, can be acquired at a hardware store, an automotive-parts store, a grocery store, a gas station, a variety store, a department store, a feed-grains store, and a discount store. Clearly, intensive distribution is used to make a product easy to purchase, and is used most often for convenience goods.

There is also selective distribution. In this case, to reduce the costs of intensive distribution yet avoid making a product hard to find – as it can be when exclusive distribution is used – a small number of intermediaries are employed. If you wish to purchase a Sony television, there are probably a handful of retail locations in your community where you can find one. When you visit these different retailers, you can compare not only prices but also the availability of credit, service terms, and delivery charges. The selective-distribution strategy is most frequently used for shopping products.

THE CASE METHOD

Socrates, born in Athens, Greece, in 470 B.C., has long been considered one of the world's great philosophers. He founded a school of philosophy, which, in later years, influenced Plato and Aristotle. It required people to know themselves first. Socrates believed that goodness was based on wisdom, while wickedness was based on ignorance. No wise person would deliberately choose evil in the long run, but most people, through ignorance, might choose evil if it appeared to be good at a given time.

Why is Socrates of ancient Greece important to the teaching of marketing today? He employed a unique style to educate the young people of Greece. He didn't write books. We can find no trace of any writing by Socrates, and some scholars believe he wrote nothing. The only knowledge we have of Socrates comes from the writings of Plato. He preferred to wander the streets, marketplaces, and gymnasia. When he had gathered a few students, he would sit on a bench with the young people gathered at his feet. Socrates taught by questioning his students about their opinions and then asking further questions about their answers. By this means, he could show them how inadequate their opinions were. Then he helped them go beyond opinion and search out essential truths.

His approach to learning was considered dangerous. By asking questions of his students, he forced them to search for new meanings and to question the standard ways in which government and commerce were conducted. Inevitably, those in power brought charges against Socrates that he was corrupting the youth of Greece. He died in 399 B.C. after drinking a cup of poison hemlock before the state could execute him.

◊◊ The Case Method

This book is likely being used to supplement a textbook in an introductory marketing course. The goal of such a course is to give you a whirlwind tour of marketing – to show you dozens of concepts, get you comfortable with the jargon, and stimulate you to dig deeper. In most introductory courses, instructors will assume that students have no previous knowledge of the subject area. These instructors have a great quantity of information to share and little time in which to share it. Most instructors will use the tried and true lecture format. They will use visual aids and a chalkboard, or whiteboard. They will read from prepared notes. Having listened, you will take notes and, occasionally, when things are not clear, you will ask questions. While lecturing is an established form of teaching, there is some doubt about its overall effectiveness. Students listen for possible exam questions. If the instructor is not going to test them on the material, then they are not likely to try and master it. Even such mastery is a fleeting goal, for as soon as the exam has been completed, some students will forget the lecture material.

If mastery of marketing concepts is the ultimate learning goal, then learning by doing or learning on the job is the best approach. As you may have discovered from personal experience, it is one thing to talk about swimming, for example, and quite another to actually do it. In the last three decades, universities and colleges have instituted co-operative work-study programs and summer internships to allow students to learn on the job and apply their knowledge between academic terms. Equally popular are group projects where three to five students work with a client firm to study a problem and make recommendations. While these approaches work well for more advanced courses, for introductory courses enrolling many students, learning by doing is very difficult to coordinate.

The Socratic method allows us the best of both worlds. Using a case study, an instructor captures a real-world problem and brings it into the classroom. By assuming the role of decision maker, the student is forced to apply the knowledge being shared through the instructor's lectures. Through the questions posed by the instructor and the answers of classmates, students not only develop mastery of the material but also can begin to see the limits and artificialities of the theoretical concepts discussed. The Socratic method also builds individual communication skills, as students must logically argue and support, either in writing or orally, their positions. As students quickly discover, making decisions in the face of ill-structured problems, incomplete information, and the need to make assumptions is a messy, yet interesting, task.

The case-study method, or Socratic method, is the main feature of this book. Here, you will find contemporary case studies written about real companies from across Canada. Every case places you in the role of central decision maker. Some companies you will recognize by name. Others have been disguised to give the company anonymity. Some of the problems confront marketers every day, while others are unique. Some cases will require you to use structured, quantitative analytical techniques. Others will demand that you be more creative and qualitative in your analysis. Try to find some time to read additional case studies not assigned by your professor so that you can gain additional marketing insight.

Because these case studies present ill-structured problems, there are few set rules for their solution. In science, you are often given a series of equations that you master by solving problems. These problems are approached in the same manner. In marketing, it is not possible to find a template and apply it over and over again. With the case method, one of the frustrations you will encounter is seeing the instructor or a fellow student use a problem-solving tool which you had completely overlooked.

Worse still is watching the class discussion evolve towards a solution that is the exact opposite of the one you discovered. Don't worry about this. When acquiring any new skill, you get better and better with practice.

◊◊ Understanding Case Studies

Case studies are constructed along three dimensions: conceptual, analytical and presentation (see fig. 1). The conceptual dimension is the number and type of concepts to which you are exposed in a case study. At the low end of this dimension, you are exposed to one simple concept. At an intermediate level, you might be exposed to multiple concepts or a more complicated concept. At the high end, you see many difficult concepts.

The analytical dimension looks at the work expected from the student. Simple analysis clearly shows a problem and decision. Playing armchair quarterback with the help of hindsight, you decide if there was a correct match and then offer support for your opinion. At the intermediate level, the problem is presented but you must make a decision based on whatever criteria you see fit. The most difficult type of analysis only offers a situation. You must decide on the problem and a methodology for its solution.

The presentational dimension is the writing style of the case. A simple presentation style means the case is short, well-organized, and contains only the information that is most relevant to the situation at hand. At the intermediate level, bits of information may be omitted, and you will therefore be forced to make assumptions. Case writers may also introduce red herrings – misleading information. At the most difficult level, the case becomes quite long and wordy. It will be poorly- organized, much information will be missing, and what remains may be misleading.

As you can see from the case-difficulty cube, one can rate a case on each of these dimensions using a three-point scale. The simplest cases would receive a 1.1.1 rating, while the most difficult would receive a 3.3.3 rating. By adding the scores on the three dimensions, one will get a measure of overall case difficulty. The cases in this book are rated between four and seven on the overall case-difficulty scale; they are relatively short and straightforward, though here and there you will find exceptions to this rule.

Figure 1. THE CASE-DIFFICULTY CUBE

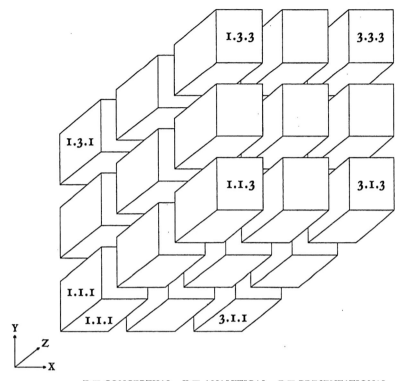

X = CONCEPTUAL, Y = ANALYTICAL, Z = PRESENTATIONAL

SOURCE: Michiel R. Leenders and James A. Erskine, *Case Research: The Case Writing Process* (London: University of Western Ontario, Research and Publications Division, 1989), 119.

Before beginning to analyse a case, you should remember that case studies are written to help you understand a concept or concepts. After your first reading of a case, it is worthwhile to take a minute and reflect upon the purpose of the case. What did the writer want you to learn from this case? Why did your instructor assign *this* case? If you try to get that overall sense of purpose, you can analyse the case more quickly and keep your organization logical. Occasionally, you may miss the point of a case and take your analysis in a completely different direction. Don't be concerned about this. Your ability to see problems will improve as you proceed.

◊◊ A Framework for Analysing Cases

No two instructors follow exactly the same framework for case analysis.

The one presented here is only a suggestion. It is to your advantage to ask the instructor about his or her approach. If possible, try to get a written outline of the instructor's expectations. Your analysis might also differ depending on whether the case is being discussed in class or submitted as a written assignment. Remember, the key to successful case analysis is maintaining a flexible approach.

Clearly, the first step is to read and re-read the case. During the first reading, try to get a feel for the situation and an understanding of the basic facts of the case. Keep an open mind as you are reading and avoid reaching too firm a conclusion about what the company should do next. You will want to differentiate between facts and opinions. In every situation, there is a certain amount of insider information which may or may not be correct. Every assertion should be supported with facts or data; otherwise it is suspect. People inside a company do not always see the problems they face in an accurate way.

During the second reading, you might wish to use several markers to highlight specific types of information – one colour for problems, another for environmental issues, another for marketing-mix variables, and so on. Carefully examine each exhibit of the case. Generally, the exhibits have been included with a purpose in mind. They contain some information that will be useful to you in analysing the situation. In some cases, the raw information may need to be processed using a special analytical technique – for example, product life cycle, breakeven analysis, and the BCG matrix. You should begin to think of various techniques and whether they are appropriate in this situation. With this initial reading completed, set aside the case and work on some other non-marketing problems. Your mind will continue to process facts and questions in your subconscious.

You are now ready to apply your instructor's case solution model. One approach is presented in figure 2. There are five steps required in the analysis. The first is to identify the problems or objectives facing the decision maker. In identifying a problem, you should be looking for root causes rather than symptoms. If the problem is a decline in sales, the root causes could be lack of product awareness, consumers having bad experiences with the product, competitor activities, problems with distribution or changes in consumer behaviour. Students complain that companies don't always have problems. A case study involving a problem-free company might focus on a new corporate objective. Perhaps the company would like to expand to new markets or develop new products. Some case problems/objectives will be simple, others will be complex. Though this first step constitutes only a small part of the analysis, do not rush it. To quote an old cliché, a well-defined problem is half-solved.

Figure 2.   *CASE-SOLUTION MODEL*

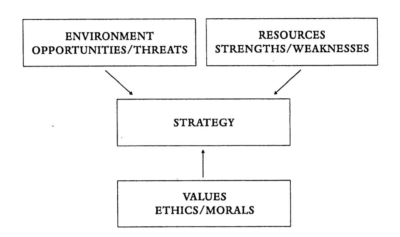

The second step requires identification of the *current* marketing strategy. More specifically, you should identify the current company policies involving each of the four P's of marketing and the target market for the product. Before you try to solve problems and change strategies, it is important that you determine the current strategy – you cannot plan a journey if you do not know the starting point.

The third step is to identify the strengths and weaknesses of the company and the opportunities and threats in the environment. Before one makes any attempt to change the marketing strategy of a company, one needs to understand the capabilities of the company and the peaks and valleys in the playing field. Students often have trouble separating environmental issues from company issues, but this separation can, in fact, be made quite easily: an issue falls into the environment if the company cannot control it. Companies cannot control governments, suppliers, consumers, and competitors: they may be able to influence them, but they can't control them. Some students also have trouble with the word *opportunities*. Students frequently will tell me that a given company has the opportunity, for instance, to expand into Mexico. That is not an opportunity or threat in the environment. What the company has, most likely, is an alternative to pursue. When considering the strengths and weaknesses of a company, look at the functional areas of finance, information systems, production, human resources, and labour relations, along with marketing. Though it may be taught as a separate course, marketing is part of an integrated company effort to satisfy consumers. At this point, no changes to the marketing strategy have been discussed.

The fourth step is to develop and analyse changes to the previously identified marketing strategy. The key to good decision making is to generate as many alternative courses of action as possible. Some will not be workable, match the environmental constraints, or fully use the capabilities of the company, and can be quickly eliminated. However, three to five major strategic directions should begin to emerge. Evaluating these alternatives to see which best solves the problems or meets the objectives, which were first identified, is critical. One method of analysis is to list the strengths and weaknesses of each option. Consideration should be given to the effect of each alternative on revenue and profitability, meeting consumer needs, and on the other products manufactured by the company.

It is here that learning occurs. Some students may feel that they don't know enough about the industry or a problem to make good decisions. While this may be true, it is important for such students to bear in mind that marketing courses are designed to help them acquire this skill. In analysing an alternative, make certain that the company on which you are focusing is operating from a position of strength. Use the company's strengths to: block threatening actions in the environment; improve weak areas of the company's business; or take advantage of opportunities in the environment. Another common problem in analysis arises when the problem solver tries to do too many things at once. A fire department in a small town cannot hope to extinguish ten fires simultaneously. It chooses the most important building to save. If the fire in that building is extinguished quickly, the department moves to the second most important building. By the next day, seven buildings might be destroyed, but three remain standing. Some of the greatest business blunders have occurred when companies try to take advantage of too many opportunities when their resources are already stretched too thin.

The last step is to make a recommendation and lay out an implementation plan. Based on your analysis, try to recommend one or two alternatives. Sometimes students try to find a way to delay or defer a decision. One delaying tactic is to suggest a search for more information. Such tactics rarely work and can be fatal to an organization. You will need to sort through the alternatives presented and logically support a decision either by showing why your decision is better than the other alternatives or showing why the other alternatives don't solve the situation at hand.

The recommendation is not a conclusion. One does not guarantee the success of a strategy merely by recommending it. It has been said that a brilliant strategy poorly implemented becomes a bad strategy, while a poor strategy brilliantly implemented becomes a great strategy. For the alternative(s) recommended, you should develop a brief tactical implementation plan. Tactical plans list, in order of priority, the specific actions that are required to make the strategy happen. If the recommended strategy is to develop a new product, some of the specific tactics will be to develop a working prototype with the help of research and development, to develop packaging alternatives, to work with an advertising agency to create a series of radio advertisements and to alert retailers to the need for additional shelf space. Timing should also be specifically discussed. It is not good enough to distinguish between short- and long-term tactics; use specific time periods such as a week, a month, or a year. Tactical plans also include control points. In journeying from Toronto to Charlottetown, a traveller not only has a planned route but also intends to be in Quebec City by the end of the first day. If the traveller has not reached the control point of Quebec City after one day's travelling, the plans for the remainder of the trip may need to be altered.

◊◊ Some Additional Tips

In a case study, you will be confronted with useful information and misleading information, and some information will be missing. You will need to make some assumptions. While it is not possible to make precise assumptions given your lack of marketing experience, try to state clearly and support the assumptions you are able to make.

Many may think they are unable to make assumptions. How is one to know how much money it takes to introduce a new brand of beer into the market? Is it more than a dollar? Is it less than one billion dollars? If you think both are true, we have now established a lower and upper bound. Granted these limits cross ten orders of magnitude, but they are limits nonetheless.

Maybe we can refine them. Would the cost be more than ten dollars? More than one hundred dollars? More than one thousand dollars? More than ten thousand dollars? More than one hundred thousand dollars? More than one million dollars? Move in the other direction. Less than one hundred million dollars? Less than ten million dollars? From ten orders of magnitude, we have reduced the problem down to one. A likely estimate on the cost of introducing a new brand of beer is between one million and ten million dollars. With a little work, that estimate could be refined further.

Another problem is the excessive repeating and summarizing of the case. It is true that the current marketing strategy, the strengths and weakness of the company, and the opportunities and threats within the environment must be summarized from the case. But a rehash does not demonstrate analytical thinking. Your instructor will not require a summary of the case. Instead, extract only those facts which help lay the foundation for your analysis.

Try to avoid stating a conclusion without providing any reasons for it. Though your argument may seem clear to you, your instructor may see your conclusion as a snap judgement without any connection to earlier evidence. A student could claim, for example, that one weakness of the company is that it is undergoing a profit crisis and lacks funds for investment purposes. The student could then recommend that the company open two additional plants. However, the second idea does not follow from the first. Similarly, some arguments are not brought to their proper conclusion. In such cases, the reader is left in the dark, baffled by dangling statements.

◊◊ Written and Oral Communication

When submitting a written analysis, plan on writing two versions of the report. The first is a rough copy. Proofread (don't just use a computer spell-check program) and edit this one. Attempt to do a perfect job of preparing the second copy. While instructors are looking primarily for high-quality solutions, reports submitted with coffee cup rings, small corrections in pen, and no page numbers will not be impressive. It should go without saying that the final version of your report must be double-spaced; have one-inch margins at top, bottom, and sides; and include a title page. Imagine that the report you are submitting is being given to a superior in a company. Would that person be impressed with the look of the report? If it was intended for you, would you be happy with it?

After completing the first version of your report, have other people read it and suggest changes. Have them pay special attention to spelling, grammar, sentence structure, and the flow of logic. Even if they have never taken a marketing course, they should be able to understand the material being presented. You know the report is well-written when these readers ask questions and offer advice on the content being presented.

Avoid generalizations. Some people believe that a *specific* statement is either right or wrong while a generalization is always partly right. This is not so: generalizations weaken your arguments.

Avoid using special marketing terms, especially if you are trying to impress an instructor. You might be tempted to sprinkle your case solution with terms such as *demographics, psychographics,* or *family life-cycle stages*. However, only use these special terms if you know what they mean. If you misuse and misspell them, you will damage your argument.

There is no single correct solution to any case situation. Still, there are many wrong solutions. In class, an instructor will press for a solution that will best enable the decision maker to deal with the problems presented in the case. If you are asked to submit a written report, you will not have the benefit of classroom experience. You can, however, simulate that experience by joining an informal working group. By meeting before class, you can share your ideas and be exposed to other points of view. The result of a group discussion should offer you the chance to explore issues and provide a better understanding of the case situation.

Part of the instructor's task is to facilitate discussion by means of intensive questioning. Through the dynamics of the classroom, ideas can be developed and fully explored by drawing on the different points of view held by different students. Along with helping to manage the class process and to ensure that the class achieves an understanding of the case situation, the instructor helps students develop oral- communication skills and thinking capabilities.

Most courses are designed to build week by week on material already covered and discussed. Class attendance is necessary if learning is to occur under the case method. But while listening to the discussion might give you some insight, it is critical that you become a participant. It is natural to fear talking in front of the class but it is a fear you must overcome. After you graduate, you will find that the people who can present their ideas and convince colleagues and superiors of their merit will advance more easily and quickly within a company.

◊◊ Some Final Thoughts

You are encouraged to deal with each case study as it is presented. You should put yourself in the role of the decision maker profiled and look at the situation through her or his eyes. As many of the cases happened in the past, it is tempting to use today's hindsight to make yesterday's decision. Don't do that. Analyse each case using the material available at that time; this way you will confront the dilemma on the same terms as the initial decision maker did. Using hindsight is not an effective way to develop your skills at marketing strategy.

Some students may try to make contact with the company or decision maker. This practice should be discouraged. Companies have kindly donated their time to the creation of a case with no expectation of further commitment. Additional information about a case could also thwart teaching objectives. The facts of the case and its mode of presentation have been chosen to facilitate learning. While it may be necessary to present general information about the period during which the case occurred (for instance, you may be told that there was a recession in 2008-09, or that the Trans-Pacific Partnership was signed in 2015), additional information will not necessarily improve your solution.

Though it may seem daunting, the case method is an enjoyable and stimulating learning tool. Now that you have been briefed, try the first case study assigned. Good luck!!

MARKETING
RESEARCH

You are sitting at home watching television when a commercial break begins. In one commercial, a consumer is confronted with two soft drinks and asked to taste Brand A and then Brand B. When asked which soft drink he or she prefers, the consumer chooses Brand A. Then the narrator adds the tag line: "Research has shown that half the consumers who participated in a similar taste test also chose Brand A."

We have all seen commercials, for a host of products, that have a similar plot line. The interesting question is: What message should someone watching television receive from that commercial? An erroneous conclusion is that Brand A is preferred to Brand B. Given two choices, one would expect people to randomly choose Brand A half the time. The faulty conclusion lies not in the research, but in the inferences drawn from that research.

If the marketing concept involves finding out what people want and giving it to them, then marketing research is of primary importance to that concept. Marketing research **is** the art of finding out what people want. It is an ongoing process of information gathering and analysis. Today that process is known as a marketing information system. But rather than examine an ongoing process, we should try to understand the process of conducting a single research project.

◊◊ The Research Process

As is so often the case, the need for a specific research project is triggered by the identification of a problem or market opportunity. (See fig. 1) Care must be taken at this stage to define the research project; it has often been said that a well-defined problem is half-solved. Research should address not the symptoms of the problem but the problem itself. Suppose the triggering event for the research project is a decline in sales. This is just a symptom. The problem could be caused by the actions of a competitor, shifting consumer tastes, currency fluctuations that make cross-border shopping more attractive, changes in tariff rates, and so on. Before a company begins to design a questionnaire or choose a research method, the problem needs to be fully explored and understood.

Part of that understanding leads to the development of some very specific hypotheses, which can be tested through research. Men consume more of the product than women. Older people use the product more often than younger people. People with university educations purchase more of the product than people with high-school educations. These specific hypotheses are critical when it comes to designing an experiment or questionnaire and choosing a research method.

Another critical decision is the type of data that will be gathered to test the hypotheses. Secondary data has been gathered and published by someone else. It could come from internal company records, financial reports, or salesperson meetings, or it could come from such external sources as Statistics Canada, A.C. Nielsen, Environics, Gallup, university research, or government departments. While secondary data can be found in the public domain, a company will generally have to pay a fee for its use. However, that fee is often less than what it would cost the company to gather that information itself. Time can also be saved using secondary data. A research project could take a minimum of ten days to complete, while secondary data could be available in a few hours.

Figure 1. THE MARKETING RESEARCH PROCESS

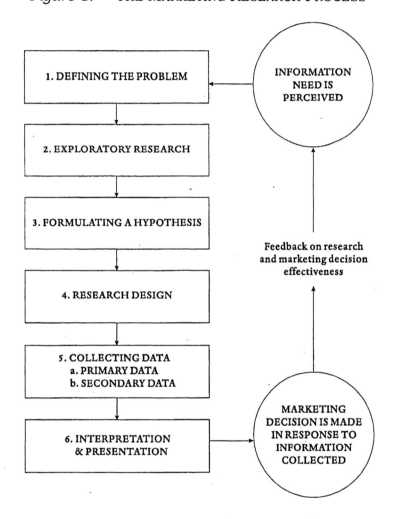

SOURCE: Dale Beckman, David Kurtz, and Louis Boone, *Foundations of Marketing*, 5th ed. (Toronto: Dryden, Holt, Rinehart and Winston of Canada, 1992), 107.

A company may be forced to gather primary data if secondary data is outdated. For example, secondary data on the ownership of smartphones from 2006 is not much use in 2017. Sometimes the method by which secondary data is classified makes it unusable. A company might want to know about the brands of soft drink purchased by those people sixteen to twenty-four. Many studies divide consumers into age groups with ten-year spans – say from ten to nineteen and twenty to twenty-nine. Such categories would not be of much help. The most common reason for undertaking primary-data collection is that secondary data is simply not available. Reaction to a politician's speech on Monday or a change in a pricing policy on Thursday is not available from previously published sources.

◊◊ Methods of Data Collection

An experiment is an attempt to establish a cause-and-effect link between variables. Here is a simple experiment: Hold a pen at arm's length and let it go. I guarantee that it will fall to the ground. If we were to take some measurements under controlled conditions, we would determine that the pen was exposed to a constant force that caused the speed with which it fell to increase by 9.86 metres/sec^2. We know that force to be gravity. While science deals primarily with inanimate objects like atoms or planets or compounds, marketers deal with people. As people do not always react the same way to the same stimuli, marketing research experiments are much more difficult to undertake. This explains why experimentation is one of the least used methods of gathering marketing information.

Experiments can be conducted in a laboratory setting or in the "real" world. In the laboratory, the experimenter can control all extraneous variables to make sure that variations in the dependent variables are being caused by manipulations of some independent variable or variables. Unfortunately, most consumers do not make decisions or buy products in a laboratory. In the "field," an experimenter has less control over the experiment, but consumers are able to respond in a realistic setting. One of the most often used field experiments is test marketing. In this procedure, a new product or new promotional campaign is introduced to a medium-sized city such as Lethbridge or Guelph. The proposed marketing plan is reproduced on a small scale in the city – from the number of coupons delivered to the shelf facings in the store to the amount and type of advertising used. The marketing plan becomes the independent variable, and the experimenter measures the sales and consumer reaction to the product as the dependent variables. If a product does not generate the desired sales level, or is not well-received by consumers, it is withdrawn from the market. Though a test market could cost several hundred thousand dollars, it is an excellent insurance policy against the millions that national introduction of a product to the market would cost.

A second technique is to view the actions of respondents. Observation studies could include counting the traffic which passes a potential site for a new mall, watching shoppers as they make their way through a grocery store, and monitoring the lengths of the lines at checkout counters. If we observe the actions of consumers, we are not obliged to rely on their capacity to remember or their desire to answer in a socially acceptable manner. Watching the patrons of a bar to see if any drink to excess and then attempt to drive home gives us a much more accurate picture than we would get if we questioned the same people about their behaviour. Observing people may also be the easiest, or the only way to gather information. How could you really determine computer users' responses to a new keyboard design if you did not watch them trying to use it?

A major drawback to observation is the difficulty of interpreting what you have seen. A child picks up a toy, plays with it for thirty seconds, cries out, and then runs to mother. What does that mean? Is there something wrong with the toy? The child? The room? Also, we all bring our biases to what we are seeing. A man in his mid-twenties arrives at a store dressed in an old T-shirt with the sleeves torn off, a pair of jeans with holes in the knees, and a baseball cap worn backwards on his head. Some people would see a man with a low income. Some would see a man who had been working around the house, had used the last bit of some product, and was there to buy more. Others would see a trendily dressed, average student.

The final technique, and the most commonly used, involves the structured answering of questions and recording of answers. Survey research can easily provide the answers to questions such as: Who? What? When? Where? How? As you have gathered, Why? is always the most difficult question for the researcher to answer. In survey research, people can be asked why they do something and they will give a response. But the answer is often meaningless because consumers really don't know why they do something.

There are three primary methods of conducting survey research. The first is to distribute a self-administered questionnaire to respondents to complete at their own pace. The questionnaire may be delivered by hand, mailed, or sent by electronic mail. A major drawback of this method is the response rate. Between twenty-five and fifty percent of self-administered questionnaires are completed and returned. Incentives such as a lottery ticket or a two-dollar coin are sometimes used to improve response rates. A researcher is always concerned that there may be some form of systematic bias that prevents some people from responding. For instance, self-administered surveys require fairly good language skills. People who, for any one of a number of reasons, have problems reading and/or writing in the language of the questionnaire are less likely to participate. Even if people will respond, the questions put to them must be carefully worded. Ask someone where he or she was born, and you might get answers as diverse as "Medicine Hat," "Mexico," "Europe" or "in a hospital."

A second method of conducting survey research is by telephone. When calls are to be made locally, phone surveys can be cheap and quick. If long-distance calls are required, WATS lines (whose numbers typically begin with 1-800) may be used to reduce costs. On the phone, it is difficult to ask long questions – reading someone a list of twenty brands of peanut butter so that she or he can identify the one they purchase most frequently is very tedious. Some people can't easily be reached on the phone – those with unlisted numbers, those who have moved since the phone book was published, and those who do not have a telephone. In many cities, one-quarter of the population is not listed in the telephone directory. Gathering personal information over the phone can also pose difficulties. If a male researcher asks a female respondent about her marital status, her annual income, where she lives, and her hobbies, it is not unusual for her to hang up. People administering a survey over the phone are complete strangers whose motives are always suspect.

The final method of conducting survey research requires an administrator to ask questions and record answers in a face-to-face situation. Personal interviews are a means of obtaining more detail by probing and clarifying a respondent's answers. Because of this detail, personal interviewing is a very slow method of collecting data. Also, the increased human involvement adds substantially to costs. Personal interviews easily accommodate the skipping of questions as well. For instance, if someone has purchased shoe polish in the last month, the researcher might want to ask a question concerning brands or colours. If shoe polish wasn't purchased, the follow-up question might involve a completely different product category.

While most studies attempt to generate quantitative answers that can be analysed by a computer, personal-interview studies are especially useful when qualitative market research is the goal. One qualitative technique is the focused group interview. Here eight to twelve people are assembled in a special room equipped so that the discussion can be either audiotaped or videotaped. Such rooms often have one-way mirrors, which allow an observer to view the session without intruding. With the help of a moderator, the group discusses a topic, in a very non-structured manner, for one to two hours. In the end, the researcher will have developed a better "feel" for the subject being studied.

◊◊ Closing the Loop

When a design and method are chosen, the researcher then needs to talk to consumers. In some cases, the number of consumers is so small that each can be contacted. That process is called a **census**. Generally, it is only possible to conduct a census when dealing with industrial customers. For convenience and economic reasons, a subset of the consumer population must be chosen. This sample can be generated in one of two ways. If every member of a population has an equal chance to be chosen, the technique used is called probability sampling. For instance, if the names of all students enrolled in the third-year business program are placed into a drum and one hundred are randomly drawn, every student will have an equal chance of being selected. For a probability sample, the presence of a master list is critical. When such a list is not available, some members of the group in question will, for whatever reason, have no chance of being selected. Consider the task of talking to families who have at least one child under the age of five. No master list of these families exists. To study them, one might visit a day-care centre or a pre-kindergarten and attempt to talk to parents as they drop off their children. However, some families do not or cannot use these facilities and they will have no chance to participate in the study.

Once the questions have been asked and the data gathered, it must be analysed. You probably have some familiarity with statistical computer-software packages and the difficult task of data analysis. Results must be assembled into a written and/or oral presentation. The presentation of the results of statistical analysis is an art that lies beyond the scope of this book.

.

Creating graphs, charts, tables, and text that both convey information and keep a report interesting is not easy to do. You will no doubt have a chance to practise this art during your course of study.

◊◊ The Ethical Dilemma

Though ethics is an important consideration in all aspects of business, it is especially important in research. One of the common complaints about marketing research is that it invades consumer privacy. Most people would not mind being asked how many cups of coffee they had consumed in the last week. Similarly, most would not mind being asked if they had any problems registering for academic classes. But imagine being asked how many bank accounts you have or if you have ever undergone lipo- suction. You would likely say that these questions are an invasion of privacy. Why? The answers to both sets of questions help a company satisfy consumer needs. The questions in the second set, though, touch on subjects that most of society considers too personal. Ethics are, after all, influenced by societal norms of behaviour.

If you intend to offer money to consumers to induce them to complete a questionnaire, should you give it to them before or after they complete the questionnaire? If identifying your client could bias the results, are you under any obligation to tell respondents who that client is? While one requires permission to survey consumers on private property (say in a mall), is it ethically correct to survey people on the public sidewalk just beyond that property? If a questionnaire will take twenty minutes to complete, is there anything wrong with telling a respondent that it will only take five minutes? You may explore the answers to these questions with your class- mates and instructor.

You will encounter three different levels of ethics in your life. These are: individual ethics, institutional ethics, and professional ethics. Individual, or personal ethics constitute the moral code by which we live our lives. This code would cover issues such as premarital sex, abortion, our views on killing, lying, and so on. When you join a company, you will encounter a set of institutional ethics. While this rarely deals with the issues just presented, there will be policies on the rights of co-workers, harassment, proper business practices, environmental pollution, and workplace safety. As well, some career paths might bring you into contact with professional ethics.

Doctors, lawyers, and priests all have codes of ethics that govern their professional behaviour. So, too, do marketing researchers, sales promotion company employees, and those who work for advertising agencies.

Where there is no overlap, there is no conflict. But what happens when you personally abhor environmental pollution and are working for a company that has no corresponding institutional ethic? What happens when your employer asks you to conduct some research in a way that is inconsistent with your professional ethic? You now have a problem. Do you blow the whistle? Do you change your personal code of ethics to keep the job? Ethical dilemmas are never easy to answer and can arise several times a day.

CONSUMER
BEHAVIOUR

When Bill Clinton was elected president of the United States, saxophone sales and lessons skyrocketed. Why? When Roberta Bondar became Canada's first woman in space, why did enrollment by women in university science and engineering programs increase? When the television series "The Big Bang Theory" became a hit, stars Johnny Galecki and Jim Parsons set a fashion trend with their superhero T-shirts. Why?

The answer lies in psychology and sociology. If companies are waging a battle for consumers, the battleground is the mind. Many marketing concepts have been borrowed from these disciplines. Quantitative marketing research can easily characterize consumers; it can determine when and where they shop, what they purchase, and how often they shop. A good working knowledge of psychology and sociology can help us understand why consumers buy.

In answering the questions posed earlier, we may find that the psychological concept of self is helpful. There are three aspects of self. The first is our real self: the objective view of oneself as one really is. The second is the looking-glass self, which is one's interpretation of how one is seen by others. Finally, there is the ideal self, which represents the way one would like to be. Parts of all three selves combine to form self-image – the way one sees oneself. Why is this important to marketers? Because we know that people buy products that move them closer to their ideal selves.

Consumer behaviour is the series of actions in which individuals engage to obtain and use goods and services. Decision processes are influenced by two major factors: personal influences, which are self- generated; and interpersonal influences, which come from family and friends.

◊◊ Personal Influences on Consumer Behaviour

Our purchasing actions can be traced to four theoretical concepts which have been inferred from psychological studies (see fig. 1).

Purchases begin with a need, a lack of something useful. That lack must be so powerful that it impels you to satisfy it. For instance, you lack a Barbie doll. That lack does not, however, have the power to make you do anything about it. You don't **need** a Barbie doll. Motives are intimately linked to needs. They are internal mental states that direct us toward satisfying a felt need. Suppose you have a need for food (a very powerful lack). Motivators might include a growling stomach, a feeling of weakness, a headache, or a sudden craving for a chocolate-chip cookie.

Abraham Maslow proposed a hierarchy of needs based on two premises: our needs are based on what we already possess; and once one need has been almost satisfied, another will emerge (see fig. 2). The most basic needs are physiological: food, shelter and clothing. In some developing countries, people spend most of their lives trying to satisfy these needs. Once satisfied, a series of safety needs emerge: protection from physical harm and shelter from the unexpected. In places where guerilla warfare rages, people struggle daily for security and safety. At the third level, we face social needs; we must belong to, and be accepted by, groups and family. In Maslow's original writings, he claimed that most North Americans were able to reach this level of the hierarchy, but few could progress beyond it.

Figure 1. PERSONAL INFLUENCES ON CONSUMER BEHAVIOUR

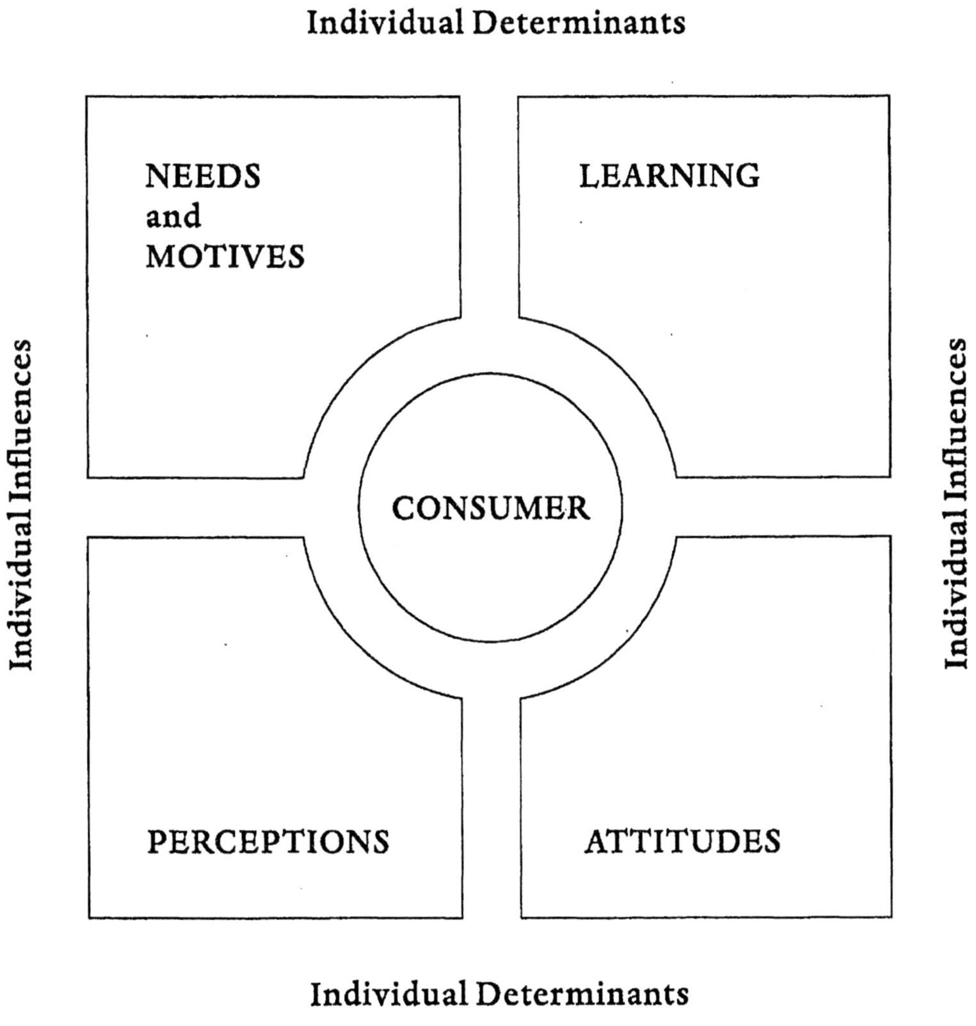
Individual Determinants
NEEDS
and
MOTIVES
LEARNING
Individual Influences
CONSUMER
Individual Influences
PERCEPTIONS
ATTITUDES
Individual Determinants

SOURCE: Adapted from C. Glenn Walters and Gordon W. Paul, *Consumer Behaviour: An Integrated Framework* (Homewood, IL: Irwin, 1970), 14.

Near the top of the hierarchy are esteem needs: status, praise, recognition by one's peers. Though linked to social needs, esteem needs arise from the desire for respect from groups or family members. Maslow suggested that only a few people reach the top of the hierarchy, where self-actualization needs are situated. Self-actualization refers to a feeling of using one's talents and capabilities totally, of realizing one's full potential. Perhaps people such as the Pope, Mother Teresa, Martin Luther King, Albert Schweitzer, and Bishop Desmond Tutu have been able to reach a state of self-actualization.

A couple of problems arise in applying Maslow's hierarchy. First, there is a North American/Western European cultural bias. In Southern and South-east Asia, social needs may come before both safety and physiological needs. Second, Maslow's hierarchy applies to groups of people and not individuals. I doubt that consumers in a supermarket will tell you that they purchased a jar of Kraft peanut butter because it fulfilled their social needs.

Figure 2. MASLOW'S HIERARCHY OF NEEDS

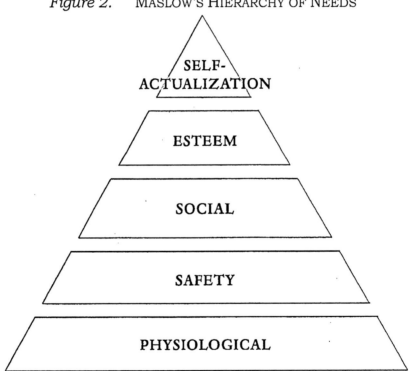

SOURCE: Adapted from A.H. Maslow, "A Theory of Human Motivation," in *Motivation and Personality*, 2d ed. (New York: Harper & Row, 1970).

A second set of influences is perceptions – the meaning we attribute to stimuli received through the five senses (touch, taste, sight, smell, and sound). From psychological studies, we know that two people confronted with the same sets of stimuli will interpret them differently. Just ask police interviewing eye witnesses to a crime. Descriptions of the perpetrator vary widely, even when it comes to aspects such as gender and dress. Hence, as marketers, we need to know that a consumer's perception becomes his or her reality.

As you read this book, you are being bombarded by dozens of stimuli – the sound of air moving, the drip of a faucet, the rustle of your clothes, an aftertaste from breakfast, music off in the distance. If your brain allowed you to be conscious of every stimulus received, you would soon go crazy. As a defense mechanism, you develop filters, or screens, to block out background noise. Only unusual stimuli will break through the screen. This concept can be applied in advertising. Marketers know that people watch nearly an hour of commercials during an evening of television, yet the next day they will consciously remember only a handful of ads. These are the ones which were most unusual, made them laugh or in some way touched a nerve.

◊◊ Attitudes and Learning

A third set of influences is attitudes – the favourable or unfavourable feelings, actions, and knowledge – we have toward an object or idea. We cannot measure attitudes directly. The question "Do you have an attitude about ice cream?" does not elicit usable answers on a survey form. Instead, we measure three components of an attitude. Think of them as the ABC's of attitudes: affections, behaviours, and cognitions (see fig. 3).

Affections are your subjective emotions or feelings about an object or idea. Consider the snake. Most people *feel* that snakes are dangerous and slimy. They don't like them. People don't think of snakes as friendly or playful. Affections toward them are generally negative. Cognitions are the objective facts and knowledge you have about an object or idea. All but one variety of Canadian snakes is non-poisonous. They eat insects, frogs, grasshoppers, and rodents. Their skin is scaly and dry. They grow to be about half a metre to a metre in length, and are usually a dark brown or green colour. Objectively, cognitions are generally positive for snakes.

Behaviours represent our tendencies to act in a certain way when confronted with an object or idea. If I threw you a snake, you would probably shout or scream and then run away. This is not a positive behaviour. Though it is an over-simplification to simply add the three components to

Figure 3. THREE COMPONENTS OF ATTITUDES

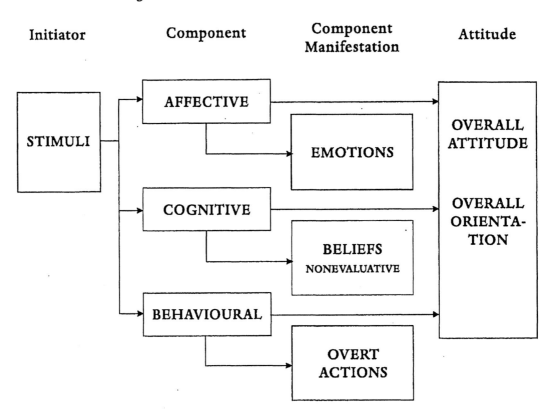

SOURCE: Del I. Hawkins, Kenneth A. Coney, and Roger J. Best, *Consumer Behaviour: Implications for Marketing Strategy* (Dallas, TX: Business Publications, 1980), 334. The figure is adapted from M.J. Rosenberg and C.I. Hovland, *Attitude Organization and Change* (New Haven, CT: Yale University Press, 1960), 3.

determine an overall attitude, from this analysis it is easy to see why society in general has a negative attitude toward snakes.

A marketer's worst fear is that consumers will develop a negative attitude toward a product. When that happens, it is always easier to change the product to match prevailing attitudes than it is to change the prevailing attitudes. In my example, snakes cannot easily be changed so you would have to try to change attitudes. This is a difficult task. There are only three courses of action to try, and these mirror the three components of attitudes.

For instance, if cognitions are negative, new, positive cognitions could be introduced to educate consumers. If affections are negative, the product could be linked to something emotionally positive. Hence, the reason for so many products being linked to physical attraction: sex sells. Finally, if behaviours are negative, consumers could be asked to engage in attitude-discrepant behaviour. By distributing free samples or coupons, or by doing blind taste tests, consumers would be encouraged to try the product, even those who say they don't like it.

A final personal influence is learning, which is defined as changes in behaviour as a result of experience. The learning process begins with a motivator or drive which impels some action. Cues are objects in the environment which help determine a reaction to the drive. These cues might be advertisements, shelf positions in a store, billboards, or free samples. The drive and cues create a response that, for a marketer, is generally the purchase of a product. This successful combination then needs to be reinforced positively so that it occurs again when the same set of drives and cues are present. Of course, a response could be a refusal to purchase the product. In that case, reinforcement is designed to show this as an incorrect behaviour and to stimulate a different response when the same drives and cues occur. As the process of drive, cue, response and reinforcement is repeated again and again, the response becomes automatic. This model is really better suited to the training of animals. It neglects the effect of human free will in the decision process. Nonetheless, it gives insight into the learning process.

◊◊ Interpersonal Influences on Consumer Behaviour

In much the same way as the four P's of marketing operate within a business environment, personal influences on consumer behaviour operate within a sociocultural environment that can also shape behaviour. Three major factors come into play here (see fig. 4).

The group with the strongest influence on behaviour is the family. It shapes our behaviour when we are young in ways that do not manifest themselves until adulthood. As children, our influence on purchase decisions is limited, yet when our parents become elderly, we may be asked to take responsibility for the decisions that affect them. Families have changed much in the last seventy years. In the 1940's, it was common to have three generations living under one roof. Today, both the old and the young seek independent living alternatives. The divorce rate of over fifty percent has triggered an increase in single-parent households. Men are being awarded child-custody rights, which were once given almost exclusively to women. More women are working, yet the average work week has shrunk to less than forty hours. Men are more likely to be involved in shopping, though they still do less of it than women.

Figure 4. INTERPERSONAL INFLUENCES ON CONSUMER BEHAVIOUR

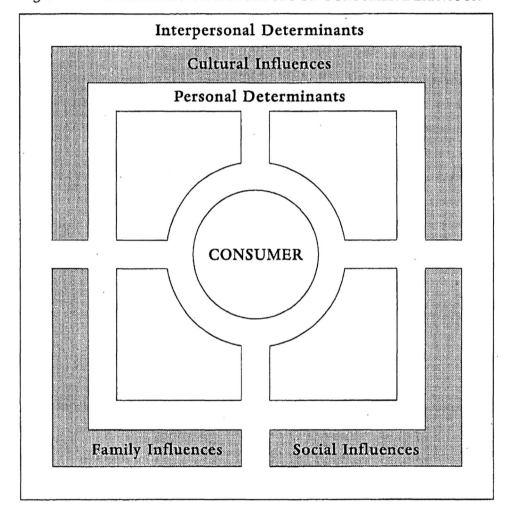

SOURCE: Adapted from C. Glenn Walters and Gordon W. Paul, *Consumer Behaviour: An Integrated Framework* (Homewood, IL: Irwin, 1970), 16.

Married heterosexual couples can make decisions about which products to purchase in four different ways. Decisions can be male dominant (for example, the decision to purchase a car or insurance policy) or female dominant (the purchase of food, kitchenware, or children's clothing). They can also be made jointly (the purchase of a home, vacation, or furniture).

Finally, decisions can be made equally by either the husband or wife (the purchase of milk or non-prescription drugs whenever they are required).

A second important influence is social groups. From these groups, we acquire both status (a position in relation to others) and a role (expectations of others about our actions). In class, your instructor has a specific status and you expect her or him to act in a certain way. As students, you are subject to behavioural expectations as well. Groups that can influence behaviour are called reference groups. You do not need to formally join such a group for it to have an influence on you. You might choose to dress like a racing cyclist in lycra shorts and aerodynamic shirt even if you don't own a bicycle or belong to a cycling club.

Reference groups can influence you to purchase a product or a specific brand. For instance, a particular reference group might influence you to buy a telescope or a motorcycle. It might influence your choice of magazines or music. We also know that this influence is quite strong. People like to conform to the norms that are established by group leaders. Within a group of cyclists, there is probably one who is the first to test each technological advance and then either encourage or dissuade others in the group from making a purchase. It is important for marketers to identify these opinion leaders and to gauge quickly their reactions to new products.

A final interpersonal influence is culture, which includes the values, beliefs, attitudes, and institutions created by a group of people. These values and institutions shape human behaviour not only today but also in generations to come. In Canada, which has a rich cultural mosaic, there are many subcultures that represent opportunities for the marketer. The largest subculture is that of French Canadians. We know that this group has a sweeter tooth, has a greater joy of food and drink, and is much more family-centred. Subcultural groups can be defined by ethnicity (Italian, Pakistani, Ukrainian), religion (Catholic, Jewish, Islamic), and social group (skinhead, preppy, biker). A uniquely Canadian government policy encourages sub-cultures to retain their values and institutions rather than be assimilated into the general Canadian culture.

In an internationally context, cultural differences are very significant. Chevrolet's plans to introduce the Nova to Latin America came to an abrupt halt when someone finally realized that in Spanish "no va" means "won't go." In an Arabic country, an appliance manufacturer displayed a billboard showing dirty clothes, a washing machine, and clean clothes – a clear implication that the washing machine worked well. However, Arabs read from right to left. The implication of the ad in the Arab world was that the washing machine was good at making clean clothes dirty. In parts of Europe, the main gift-giving occasion is not Christmas Day (December 25); gifts are presented at varying times throughout January. Clearly, a marketing program that works well in one country or with one culture will not necessarily do the same in another setting.

◊◊ The Consumer Decision Process

As demonstrated by figure 5, the consumer decision is the series of steps that a consumer takes in determining a need for a product and choosing the brand to purchase. Both personal and interpersonal influences affect the consumer at every step of the process.

The process begins with the recognition of a need. It may be that a person has consumed her or his supply of a product or is bored with the brands on hand. It may be that a consumer has had a bad experience with a brand or simply wants a greater variety of options. A consumer might have come into some money, become unemployed, or recently married, and is thus looking for different types of products. With a recognized need, consumers begin to search for background information to help them make a decision. Searches can be internal (recalling what he or she already knows) or external (visiting libraries, talking to others, obtaining brochures). A search can be fast (the micro-second firing of a synapse) or slow (many years) but when it is completed, the consumer has determined a set of products or brands from which to make a final choice.

This set of brands is then logically evaluated. This evaluation may also vary in duration. The criteria used may be objective (for example, the price, colour, or size of the object), or subjective (the reputation, flawlessness, or feel of the product). While it may appear that dozens of criteria are required to purchase a complex product such as a house or car, studies show that most consumers use at most seven criteria to guide their decision making. With multiple criteria, the results on one dimension may be used to compensate for deficits on another dimension. For instance, a consumer choosing between two cars may prefer the black one but discovers that the yellow car is twenty-five percent cheaper. In other cases, no compensation is allowed –

the consumer only wants a black car, regardless of its rating on other criteria. Consumers make decisions using their own models and judgement, but at the end of this stage a definite purchase decision has been made.

Figure 5.   THE CONSUMER DECISION PROCESS

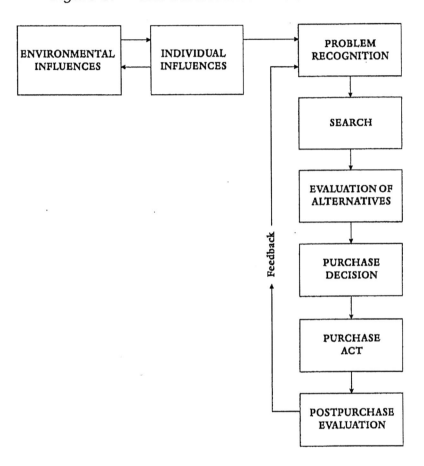

SOURCE: Adapted from C. Glenn Walters and Gordon W. Paul, *Consumer Behaviour: An Integrated Framework* (Homewood, IL: Irwin, 1970), 18; and John Dewey, *How We Think* (Boston: C.C. Heath, 1910), 101–05. Similar steps are also discussed in Del I. Hawkins, Roger J. Best, and Kenneth A. Coney, *Consumer Behaviour: Implications for Marketing Strategy*, rev. ed. (Plano, TX: Business Publications, 1983), 447–606.

The next stage involves the purchase act. The product purchased may or may not be identical to that decided upon earlier. For example, you may have decided to purchase a bag of Oreo cookies, but when you get to the store the shelf is bare. Though you decided you wanted Oreos, you may leave the store with Fudgee-O's.

Having completed the purchase, you may feel some anxiety. Did I buy the right product? Did I pay too much? This psychologically unpleasant state is called cognitive dissonance. It is most likely to occur when the decision is major (choosing a university to attend), represents the expenditure of many dollars (buying a house), or when the rejected alternatives are not clearly inferior to the item purchased. The marketer from whom you purchased the product will want to help you reduce the dissonance by providing personal reassurance and by sharing supportive information. Of course, a marketer representing the competition will attempt to increase dissonance so that you regret your decision and will consider making a different decision, should a similar need arise. The latter was the premise behind the immensely successful "Wow! I could have had a V-8" advertising campaign.

INTERNATIONAL MARKETING

The North American Free Trade Agreement. The European Union. The Trans-Pacific Partnership. The General Agreement on Tariffs and Trade. The World Bank. The International Monetary Fund. The G-8 countries. Unless you have been hibernating for the last decade, these names should be instantly recognizable. While few of us know, in detail, what they mean, we realize that trade and marketing are becoming an increasingly prominent global concern.

It has not always been thus. Seventy years ago, few countries were able to produce enough goods to satisfy internal demand. Transportation options were few and fairly unreliable. The world standard for currency was gold and that was difficult to carry.   Communications with home offices took days, so it was not possible to check the credit worthiness or legitimacy of a buyer from another country.   In those early days of inter- national trade, crooked dealings and illegal activities were quite common.

Perhaps that, in part, explains the sluggishness with which Canada and the United States have pursued international trade.   As North America was one of the first areas to develop substantial surpluses, it was also one of the first to suffer through the problems and pitfalls of international trade.

But the technological advances of the last few decades have closed the loopholes and made international trade more possible and desirable and less difficult than ever before.   Increasing affluence around the world, the need for technology transfer to developing countries, mass and instantaneous access to communication media, an unprecedented period of world peace, and a rapid realization that Earth is a much smaller planet than first imagined have brought the world's markets closer together.

◊◊   Some Terminology

When a country produces goods for sale outside of its domestic market, it is engaging in exporting.   Importing occurs when a country purchases goods from outside its borders for use internally.   For every billion dollars of exports, a country can generate thirty thousand to forty thousand jobs.   Not surprisingly, a dependence on imports can cause an increase in national unemployment.

The Balance of Trade may be thought of as an interesting relationship between exports and imports.   If exports exceed imports, a country has a trade surplus or a favourable balance of trade.   When imports exceed exports, a country has a trade deficit or an unfavourable balance of trade. For most of the last decade, Canada has had a trade surplus while the United States has had a trade deficit.

Another measure looks at flow of cash between nations.   Starting with the balance of trade, one adds or subtracts spending on tourism, the military, foreign aid, and foreign investment to arrive at the balance of payments. Primarily because of the interest payments on the national debt that Canada must make to foreign countries, and because Canadians love travelling outside the country, Canada has an unfavourable Balance of Payments.   In essence, this means that cash is leaving the country.

Because business and financial transactions take place around the world, exchange rates are a major consideration. These are the rates at which one nation's currency can be exchanged for other currencies. Francois Mitterand, the late President of France, once performed a startling experiment. He had the equivalent of one hundred dollars in French francs converted to local currency as he toured the twelve founding nations of the European Union. When he returned to France, he had less than half the money with which he started, yet he had made no purchases. Mitterand used the results of this exchange-rate experiment to help convince members of the Union to adopt a Euro dollar as a common currency.

◊◊ Trade Restrictions

The simplest trade restriction is called a tariff. It is a tax levied against imported products. Tariffs or duties may be imposed by a country as a source of revenue. Tariffs on tobacco products in Canada are mainly levied to raise money for the federal government. Tariffs may also be imposed to protect domestic products from cheaper imports. As Canada does not produce cotton, textile manufacturers face higher costs and thus produce higher-priced goods. The government has imposed a tariff on imported textiles to protect Canadian manufacturers and improve their chances of economic survival. Tariffs may be levied as a fixed amount (fifty cents per item) or as a percentage of the value of the product.

The General Agreement on Tariffs and Trade was established internationally to encourage freer trade and reduce tariffs. This agreement makes levying either a new revenue or protective tariff very difficult. To be allowed to levy a new revenue tariff, a country has to show economic need. To levy a new protective tariff, a country has to demonstrate that competitive harm is being done to its domestic industries. The most often cited example of harm is dumping, or the selling of products at significantly lower prices in foreign markets than in a country's domestic market. In recent years, Canada has been accused of dumping cedar shakes and shingles, steel, beef and lumber. In turn, Canada has claimed to be the victim of other countries, which have dumped toothpicks, shoes, steel, computer chips, and wine.

If competitive harm is so great that tariffs have no effect, a country may impose an import quota. By setting limits on the volume of a product which may be imported, the country hopes to minimize damage to its domestic industries. In the 1980's, sales of Japanese automobiles grew dramatically in North America. To protect national car manufacturers, steep tariffs were imposed often increasing the price of a Japanese automobile by over one thousand dollars. This had little effect on sales. Both Canada and the United States imposed import quotas on the number of Japanese automobiles brought into North America. Such restrictions are not in place today, as Japanese car makers responded by building plants in North America and assembling the cars here, thus protecting the jobs of Canadian and American auto workers.

The most extreme form of an import quota is an embargo. This is a total ban on importation of a product, and is most likely to result from political or legal, rather than economic, pressure. To force governments to change their policies, in the last fifty years, Canada has imposed embargoes on all products from South Africa, Iraq, Iran, Syria, and Bosnia. If sanctions are to be fully effective, all nations have to participate. The United States imposed an embargo on trade with Cuba in the early 1960's, yet Cuba survived by trading with Communist countries and others, such as Canada, that did not join the United States in its action.

◊◊ Levels of Involvement in International Marketing

There are five levels at which a company can be involved in international marketing: casual exporting, active exporting, sales offices or branches, foreign licensing, and foreign production and selling. Casual exporting is the lowest and most passive level. In essence, it is what happens when a company exports goods only when it has a surplus or, in some cases, without even meaning to export product. For instance, a visitor from Italy may come to Canada and develop a fondness for maple syrup manufactured in Quebec. That visitor may then decide to purchase, through a relative, four litres of maple syrup each year and have them shipped by that family member to Italy. The manufacturer will have no knowledge of the export. Clearly, casual exporting requires no sustained effort on the part of a manufacturer.

When a firm is prepared to make an ongoing commitment to selling its merchandise in other countries, it is involved in active exporting. The ongoing commitment can vary from regularly filling a few orders from one country to setting up a structure to process orders from around the world. For most Canadian firms interested in international marketing, this level represents the extent of their commitment.

Once demand for a company's product outside the country reaches a certain level, it may make economic sense for that company to become more committed to international markets by establishing a sales office or sales branch in another country. A sales branch collects orders through sales-people and fills those orders from stock held on site. A sales office does not carry stock; orders are filled from stock held in Canada.

Another level of international involvement is attained when a company shifts some production from its home base to a foreign country. This may be accomplished, for example, through licensing. This involves a domestic firm allowing a foreign company to produce and distribute its products. In exchange for the production technology, the licensee agrees, in a formal contract, to pay a royalty – usually some combination of a lump-sum payment and a percentage of sales revenue. The licensee also contributes its knowledge of local markets, distribution channels, local laws, and advertising media. Nearly half of all licensing agreements end in failure. It is possible for the licensee to learn about the technology, improve upon it in some way, and then cease paying royalties. For that reason, technology that is nearing the end of its useful life span is more likely to be licensed. Licensors may also err by not providing full technical help to overcome production headaches that arise when there are variations between the raw materials used by the licensee and those used by the licensor itself, or when there are problems with environmental conditions.

By combining out-of-country manufacturing with out-of-country selling, a company reaches the highest level of international marketing involvement. A firm can engage in foreign production and selling by building its own facilities in another country, by buying an existing foreign operation and adapting it, or by entering into a joint venture with another company. In a joint venture, a company joins with a foreign counterpart to create a new company jointly financed and managed.

While few companies reach this final level, multinational companies are becoming more important in global markets. These companies view the entire world as their market, and can service this market through their plants located in many different countries. Coca-Cola, General Motors, Nestlé, McDonald's Restaurants and Disney are just a few of the multinationals at work in the world today.

◊◊ Multinational Economic Integration

In the last forty years, the world seems to have become a smaller place. With instant communication links, exposure to mass-media coverage, access to travel, and better access to information, the peoples of the world know much more about each other's histories, cultures, and economies. Seventy years ago, the world saw political alliances designed to either increase or balance military power. Today, rapidly forming economic alliances prevail. Clearly, few countries have access to the raw materials and technology required to produce enough goods and services to satisfy all their internal needs. The need to trade is a starting point for integration.

One of the simplest forms of economic integration is free trade, whereby participants agree to remove tariffs on the goods they trade among themselves. A free-trade agreement may not cover all goods produced, nor will it be implemented instantaneously. Normally, there is a phase-in period, which gives firms a chance to adjust to the new trading opportunities and threats. The North American Free Trade Agreement and the Trans-Pacific Partnership are two examples of this form of economic integration. Rather than forging a wide-ranging agreement, some countries establish free-trade zones. In these zones, products may be imported with no duty. Often these products are component parts which are assembled into finished goods destined for other countries. Tariffs are paid only once: when the finished good enters the country that is its final destination. The establishment of free-trade zones can bring jobs and investment, possibilities that, if tariffs had been imposed, might not have occurred.

A stronger form of economic integration is a customs union. This has all the elements of a free-trade agreement but adds a uniform tariff policy for trade with non-member nations. When the European Union was formed, the member nations sought to establish a uniform tariff structure so that free-trade gains would not be undermined. Suppose there was no uniform tariff policy. Countries A and B have a free-trade agreement. Country A imposes a tariff of ten percent while Country B imposes a tariff of twenty percent. Outside manufacturers will ship products to Country A, and then use the free-trade agreement to move the product to Country B, thus avoiding the higher tariff. Unfairly, Country A will reap most of the economic benefits of trade with non-member nations.

The strongest form of economic integration is an economic union. It has all the features of a customs union, but includes additional agreements that allow free flow of capital, services, and workers. Many people have suggested that the North American Free Trade Agreement should be expanded to an economic union with ancillary agreements concerning pollution standards, workers' rights, rules on sexual and racial discrimination, minimum-wage standards, and so on struck between Canada, Mexico and the United States. In 1992, the European Union was formed between twelve member nations (Belgium, Denmark, France, Germany, Great Britain, Greece, Ireland, Italy, Luxembourg, Portugal, The Netherlands and Spain) - an amazing feat considering that many of these countries were at war only fifty years prior.

◊◊ Global versus International Concepts

Recognizing the trend toward the formation of multinational companies and toward closer multinational economic integration, educators are placing a greater emphasis on teaching marketing from an international perspective. But what does this mean?

In teaching the concept of cost-plus pricing, an instructor could internationalize the discussion by citing costs in rupees or yuan, adding an appropriate mark-up, and determining the final selling price for India or China. But is this internationalization? No. The concept of cost-plus pricing is global, and can be universally applied. Changing the currency does not really change the application of the concept.

However, as marketing students, you have probably been exposed to Maslow's hierarchy of needs. Let me recap the first three levels. The most basic level involves physiological needs: food, water, shelter, and clothing. On the second level are safety needs: protection from physical harm, protection from the unexpected. Finally, on the third level are social needs: the need to be accepted by family and friends. Is this a global concept? No. The hierarchy outlined applies best to North America and Western Europe. In much of the Southern and South-East Asia, social needs precede safety needs. Some people have argued that social needs even precede physiological needs there. This is an example of an international concept – one that varies from one culture to another.

It is difficult to estimate how much of marketing is global rather than international. Some people believe the split is eighty percent to twenty percent. Some feel it is just the opposite. As a student, you may, at first, find this confusing. But you should see it as a challenge. You should always be asking yourself and your instructor if the concepts you are being taught have global acceptance or if there are subtle variations of which you should be aware.

Thompson Brothers Funeral Homes

Pritt Andersen, General Manager of Thompson Brothers Funeral Homes, was reviewing the operations of the Mount Hamilton Chapel location. In 2013, he had planned on the chapel performing 90 services for the year but with the June figures in front of him, that location would now be lucky to do 70. Something had to be done to improve the performance of that location. As funerals could be an expensive service, he wondered if emphasizing a different method of pricing would help. He was concerned, though, about how customers and the other funeral homes in the area would react.

Company History

One hundred and forty-five years ago, brothers Alexander and Samuel Thompson opened one of Hamilton's first funeral homes. By 2013, in the Greater Hamilton area, five locations comprised the Thompson Brothers Funeral Homes company. The most recent change for the company was the 2007 sale of the firm to Trillium Funeral Service of Toronto, a subsidiary of Arbor Capital Inc. – one of the largest funeral home companies in Canada.

Trillium Funeral Service strongly believed in newspaper advertising and so encouraged Thompson Brothers to place its first ads in The Hamilton Spectator. These one column by three inch ads ran every other week for the nine non-summer months in the "Lifestyle" section of the newspaper. Outside of notices in church bulletins, the firm did no other form of mass media advertising or social media. All Hamilton funeral homes did some small display advertising in the Yellow Pages. In 2004, the company launched a website featuring all five locations. Page view tallies showed the two most popular sections of the website were pages giving driving directions to the funeral homes and an online condolences book where people could post words of sympathy for the family to view. While the website described in general terms the services offered by the funeral homes, no specific prices were given. People were encouraged to call and speak to funeral home representatives to arrange any funeral service.

Geographically, the five locations were well-positioned with one location in Ancaster, two in the downtown Hamilton core, one location in Burlington and one location on Hamilton "mountain." Pritt Andersen noted that, "as Hamilton grew, many people moved out of the downtown core and onto the mountain. Business at our downtown locations and those of our competitors has dropped by 30% over the last fifteen years. The two mountain locations of our competitors have nearly doubled business."

This case was written by Marvin Ryder. Case material is prepared as a basis for classroom discussion only. Copyright 2015 by Marvin Ryder, Assistant Professor of Marketing and Entrepreneurship, Michael G. DeGroote School of Business, McMaster University. This case is not to be reproduced in whole or in part by any means without the express written consent of the author.

This trend was the primary reason why Thompson Brothers opened a location on the mountain. The location it acquired had an interesting past. In the mid-1950's, Thorpe Funeral Home was started but in the mid-1970's the owner passed away. His widow disliked the idea of selling the home so she leased it to the Legacy Group of funeral homes. That company had little success at the location never doing more than 35 funeral services annually. In 1992, the Legacy Group decided not to renew its lease and Mrs. Thorpe sold the property to a firm dealing in insurance and real estate. That firm had plans to renovate the location for offices. However, with the high interest rates at the time (nearly 12% per annum), the company decided not to carry the mortgage and sold the building. In 1997, Thompson Brothers purchased the abandoned funeral home site on Upper James Street in the central mountain area. At a cost of $1 million, acquiring and renovating this location was much cheaper than spending $2 or $3 million to buy land and construct a new facility.

Thompson Brothers completely renovated the site. Car ports were removed. Interlocking paving stones were installed in the driveway. A new parking lot was constructed. Inside, a special glass-enclosed foyer was constructed to give the home a proper ambience. Still, in its first full year of operations, the home was the site for only 48 funeral services. When Thompson Brothers was sold to Trillium in 2007, the new owners had even replaced the low granite sign with a much larger metal sign, with brown lettering on a beige background, and a clock. Even with the changes, this location only completed 46 services in 2012.

Some people blamed the poor performance on the location which was between two strip malls. "I've heard people say that they don't like the idea of a funeral home located near a Harvey's (fast food restaurant) or beside an Alexanian's carpet store," stated Pritt Andersen. "Others say that there is retail clutter and, though the new sign is large, people just aren't paying attention as they drive along. Still Upper James Street is one of the busiest in terms of traffic volume in Hamilton. We even have a bus stop right in front of the funeral home. How much more exposure can a funeral home get?"

Consumer Approach to Funerals

From 1991 to 2011, the average life expectancy for Canadians increased from 77 to 82 while the annual death rate per thousand people had increased (from 6.9 to 8.3). Pritt Andersen commented, "millions of Canadians had never experienced the death of someone close to them. Many had never been to a funeral or even seen a funeral procession. A great number had never seen a dead body except on television or in a movie. Even where people had been directly involved in the arrangements of a funeral service there was often confusion or doubt about the role of the funeral director and the cost for his or her services."

The word "funeral" came from an old Sanskrit word of northern India which meant smoke. Funeral services could be traced to several thousand years before the birth of Jesus Christ. Early Romans originated the customs of wearing black, funeral processions and burial mounds. Early Egyptians pioneered embalming practices while the people of early India refined the process of cremation.

In Canada, the funeral director had been a provider of goods and some services. They were originally casket builders and sellers. Frequently, they were furniture dealers or cabinetmakers who began to sell caskets because of their carpentry skills. By 1850, some casket builders had begun to add some services, such as restorative art and livery. Basically, though, they were sellers of caskets until around 1900, when the modern concept of the funeral director became fairly well developed. A casket was purchased and all other services provided "free." Funeral directors were still judged, however, by the type of clientel to which they catered and the breadth of casket selections they offered.

As the "baby boom" generation (born from 1946 to 1964) began to face their own mortality, funeral directors were seeing more requests for customization of funeral services. Caskets and funeral urns were one source for customization. Pritt heard from an American funeral director that a "self-professed hippie" was so stuck in the 1960's that he ordered a casket with an exterior that looked tie-dyed. In brochures, Pritt had seen motorcycle-themed items – urns that look like motorcycle gas tanks that could be custom painted to match a bikes. He had seen pictures of caskets with hot rod flames. One of the things identified at industry conferences was the notion that one's life is individual and personalized, and your funeral should be also.

The casket was not the funeral service, nor was the funeral service the casket. The failure of some funeral directors to accept this fact and explain it to those they served was in some ways responsible for much of the concern over funeral practices and prices today.

Funeral Costs and Pricing

In 2013, the funeral homes in Hamilton conducted a total of 4,600 services at an average price of $8,500. The average wholesale cost of merchandise sold was $1,900, broken down into $1,500 for the casket and $875 for the vault. The costs of the casket and vault were multiplied by an average of 4.5 and 2.0, respectively, to arrive at the selling price of the funeral service. Average variable expenses per funeral were $550. Average national operating expenses for funeral firms are shown in percentages in Table 1.

Table 1   Operating Expenses for Funeral Firms

Revenue	100%
Expenses:	
Salaries	30%
Vault	6.7%
Casket	14%
Automobiles	5.4%
Facilities	12.2%
Cemetery/Flowers	11.1%
Administration	6.7%
Miscellaneous	2.8%
Promotion	2.8%
Taxes	4%
Profit After Tax	4.3%

Source: Ohio Funeral Directors' Association, "A Factual Guide to Funeral Costs"

The pricing system used by early funeral directors was obtained by taking three times the cost of the casket. One-third was for the cost of the casket, one-third for the extra services offered by the funeral director, and one-third for overhead and profit.

Thompson Brothers used two alternative pricing systems: unit pricing and complete itemized pricing.

Unit Pricing

In unit pricing, one price covered all the costs of the funeral except cash advances and optional extras. This method was the most widely used in the industry at that time and was frequently based upon some multiple times the funeral director's cost of the casket. The value of the multiple varied with a higher multiple used for lower-cost caskets than for more expensive ones. The unit price usually included such items and services as:

1. Removal of remains to the funeral home;
2. Complete preparation of and dressing of remains;
3. Securing necessary certificates and permits;
4. Use of the funeral home staff;
5. Assistance of the funeral home staff;
6. Transportation of the remains to the cemetery;
7. Fixed amount of additional transportation to cemetery;
8. Acknowledgement cards and memorial register; and
9. Casket selection.

Complete Itemized Pricing

Complete itemized pricing went to the other extreme, adding a separate price for each element of the funeral service. This method was most popular with the ten to twelve percent of business resulting from people pre-paying a funeral. These people were either 55 to 65 years old and living on their own with no nearby relatives or were 75 to 85 years old and came to discuss pre-paying a funeral with children who were 40 to 50 years old. The itemized system provided a separate price for each of the following:

1. Removal of remains;
2. Embalming;
3. Dressing, casketing, and cosmetizing;
4. Use of chapel;
5. Use of other funeral home facilities and equipment;
6. Staff assistance;
7. Funeral coach;
8. Additional vehicles;
9. Casket;
10. Memorial register; and
11. Acknowledgement cards.

Competition

While funeral homes were considered an essential service, business for any one home was not certain because of competition. Three other funeral home companies along with three independent funeral homes were operating in the Hamilton area. While Thompson Brothers had 20% of the market, its largest competitor was the independent Markey Dermody Funeral Homes which had 26% of the market while operating at only two locations. One of these was the successful Cresmount funeral home operating on the east side of the mountain and doing 450 services per year. The other location in the east end of Hamilton was only three years old and had replaced two smaller, older locations in the downtown core.

Third largest was Marlatt Funeral Homes which served seventeen percent of the market from two locations. One location, in Hamilton's downtown area, serviced 500 funerals per year and was the largest home in terms of funeral services in the greater Hamilton area.

Just behind was the Legacy Group of funeral homes with sixteen percent of the market served from four locations. On the mountain an independent, M.A. Clark Funeral Home, did 275 services per year. Like Cresmount, it was located on the east side of the mountain area. Another important independent was Friscolanti Funeral Home which did 275 services per year from its downtown location. This home was of little competition to Thompson Brothers as it catered to the large Catholic Italian and Portuguese community in Hamilton.

The final company was only three years old and was born from Markey-Dermody's decision to build at a new location. The Dermody family re-opened the two older, smaller locations left by Markey-Dermody under the name of P.X. Dermody Funeral Home. Both homes catered to the Catholic community and did fewer than five percent of the funeral services in the downtown area.

All of these homes used a pricing system similar to Thompson Brothers', with the price of a funeral service based upon a multiple of the funeral home's cost for the casket plus a charge for services. Prices were difficult to compare, since each funeral home represented several different manufacturers of caskets and carried a wide range of casket styles and qualities. Few customers made any attempt to check a competitor's price due to the nature and timing of the purchase decision.

Changing Role of the Funeral Director

Fifty years ago, when the church, the family, and the neighbourhood were all tightly knit groups, they helped the surviving family members adjust to changes in their lives and relationships brought about by a death. All that was required of funeral directors was an adequate casket and a few simple arrangements. Over the years, the funeral director's role and involvement in the community changed. Funeral homes took on the status of an essential service much like fire and police departments, hospitals, schools and churches. Most of these latter services were government run and subsidized through taxes. Funeral homes had remained independently run yet were expected to provide twenty-four hour service, seven days a week.

In the 2010's, funeral directors served the living, and their professional reputation rested upon their ability to assist the survivors in the transition process. They were counsellors upon whom the survivor relied. This emphasis on services was consistent with the general rise in the use of services in other sectors of the economy.

To operate successfully within this environment, funeral directors provided comfortable facilities, developed sound technical skill for the restorative process and sanitary control, had legal know-how to cut through government and insurance red tape, and possessed the psychological knowledge to instill confidence in their judgement during the adjustment process.

Three other trends were noted by Pritt Andersen. Cremation was growing as an alternative to traditional burial. While still only 40% of the business in Hamilton, cremation made up 60% to 70% of the business in Oakville and Burlington. In Ontario, 46% of funeral services involved cremation. Urban areas were home to a shifting, nearly nomadic population base which was less attached to the permanence of park-like cemetery plots and granite memorials. He also noted that people from traditional "blue collar" backgrounds were less price-oriented than the people in the "white collar" segment. Not only did they spend less on funerals but the "white collar" segment complained more about the services provided.

A final trend he noted was shifting ethnic and religious traditions in the area. Hamilton was no longer a strictly Judeo-Christian community. In certain religions, such as Hinduism, Sikhism and Buddhism, cremation was mandatory. In some countries around the world, cremation dominated funeral practices: Japan 99.8%, Taiwan 92.5%, India 85%, Denmark 76%, England 73%, Sweden 70%, New Zealand 70%, Australia 65%, China 46%, United States 44%, Norway 36%, and France 33%.

The Need for Change

Pritt Andersen had discovered a recent marketing research study found that the majority of consumers would prefer to have more information concerning funeral prices. When offered a choice between the two common methods of funeral pricing, 40% stated a preference for unit pricing while 60% voiced a preference for itemized pricing. These responses implied that a change to itemized pricing could bring in more business for the Mount Hamilton Chapel.

While Trillium Funeral Service had been quite patient with the Mount Hamilton Chapel's performance, that goodwill was running thin. As Pritt looked at the problem, he was certain of some details. "I know it's not the building. The decor and architecture of that funeral home is as good if not better than all the others in Hamilton. I know it's not a lack of parking as that home has more parking than any two of our other homes. I know it's not the manager. He's doing all we ask of him and even more. I know it's not the quality of our services. Our traditional funerals and cremations are run flawlessly. I'm so desperate, I have begun considering social media. Should we have a Twitter account? Pinterest? Instagram?"

"To be honest, Mount Hamilton Chapel should be doing two to three times the business that it is currently doing. Something needs to be done soon!"

HURON CANVAS CLOTHIER

Nicole Reynolds was examining the sales performance for a line of children's clothing at one of her stores. She owned three Huron Canvas Clothier franchises in Saint John, Fredericton and Moncton, New Brunswick and she was bothered by the relatively low sales of the clothing designed for children aged eight to thirteen. It was October, 2013 and she was about to place her order for spring. She had to decide if she could increase sales of this line or ask head office if she could discontinue carrying the line.

Company Background

The first Huron Canvas Clothier store was opened on May 24, 1995 in Port Dover, Ontario by Suzanne Mitchell. The village had a population of 5,100 who were mostly employed in the fishing, tourism, shipping, and hospitality industries. She was 28 years old at the time and was tired of working for other people. Her store was filled with canvas duffle bags, pillows, sailing gear and some clothes in bright, solid colours made from 100% cotton canvas. When the doors opened that holiday weekend, the clothes sold out first! Back orders stretched into weeks of production. With limited resources, Suzanne cut all the fabric herself and called upon several local women who were good sewers to help keep up with production.

Money was tight in the first year. Suzanne received a $30,000 bank loan with the help of a co-signer and in its first year, the single store generated revenue of $64,000. An independent business consultant encouraged Suzanne to expand Huron through franchising, a method which would inject cash into the struggling parent company and would lessen her risk by using other people's capital for expansion.

Design of the clothing was kept basic, simple and uncluttered while the colours chosen were bright and striking. Two distinctive lines were planned for the two main seasons each year – winter and summer. Newspaper reporters and fashion critics loved this original Canadian clothing concept and the novelty of using people sewing in their homes. The additional media coverage attracted more customers and potential franchisees excited by the enthusiasm and energy of the founder.

In the second year, two additional franchises were opened in London and Toronto. By 2013, there were 48 franchises located in major Canadian cities from all provinces save Newfoundland. In the first five years, sales grew by 1,000 per cent. In 2002, sales topped $11 million and the Ontario Ministry of Industry, Trade and Technology recognized the company with the Provincial Business Achievement Award.

Recognizing the importance of publicity, Huron was a sponsor for the 1999 and 2003 Canadian entry in the America's Cup yachting championship. Also wearing the cotton clothing

----

were the hosts of "*Canadian Sport-fishing*" on TSN-The Sports Network, canoeists Gary and Joanie McGuffin who paddled across Canada and cyclist Brent Walters who raced in Europe. The story of the Huron Canvas Clothier was also broadcast into thousands of homes as part of TV Ontario's "*Frontrunners*" series.

Nicole Reynolds Involvement in Huron

In 2003, Nicole Reynolds was looking for an outlet for her entrepreneurial energies. She had some experience in retail sales and had considered starting her own clothing store when she heard of Huron. She was very interested in getting the franchise rights for the area near her home – Saint John, New Brunswick. These rights, however, were tied up in a legal dispute between the parent company in Port Dover and the first franchisee in Nova Scotia. Instead, she was offered the franchise rights for two other New Brunswick cities – Fredericton and Moncton – with a promise that if the other franchise rights became available she would be given the first opportunity to purchase them.

Nicole decided to accept this offer and, in March 2004, she opened a Huron store in Fredericton. It was located in a downtown pedestrian mall of boutique-like shops which used some old renovated homes. It made a profit in its first year of operation and continued to show strong performance every year.

As a condition of her purchase, Nicole had to open a store in Moncton within five years. This was accomplished in 2008 when a store was opened in Moncton's only downtown shopping mall. The day before it was set to open, a water pipe broke in the ceiling and damaged the store. It was an omen of problems to come as in the first year the store suffered a break-in and theft. Traffic patterns were not as high as expected and there was much wasted space in the store layout. This led to a move to the middle of the mall in a store half the size of the first. With rent set at $39 per square foot per year, the move saved a lot of money. The head office was quite concerned about her success as the Moncton store had the highest start-up costs of any franchise opened by Huron.

Nicole was nicely getting the problems ironed out in franchise number two when she received word that the legal battle was over and she could have the other franchise rights if she wanted them. Nicole jumped at the chance and opened a third franchise in a strip mall (containing four other stores) in Saint John during November, 2011.

As a franchisee, Nicole had certain obligations to head office. First, her store layout was basically predetermined for her. She had to use the standard pine shelving, clothes racks, counter tops, dressing rooms and decorative signage designed in Port Dover. All items sold had to be wrapped in brown paper and tied with a string. She was only able to carry Huron clothing in her store. She did have flexibility to decide what lines she would carry and the colours, sizes and amounts that she would order.

The Children's Clothing Line

Shortly after Suzanne Mitchell opened her first shop, she was asked to make children's versions of her popular clothes. (See Exhibit 1) She quickly developed a five-item line of clothes designed for children eight to thirteen years of age. They were essentially the same design but in smaller sizes. Each item was available in six colours. She also developed two items which had special appeal for children – pencil cases and canvas wallets.

Nicole Reynolds had not had great success with the line in any of her three stores. In her 920 square foot Saint John store, she found that children's clothes only accounted for 1% to 2% of her annual sales. (See Table 1 for a list of prices and units sold) She felt that there were two markets for the clothes: 1) small adults, like teenagers and petite women, who found the regular Huron sizes too large; and 2) people who genuinely bought the clothes for children. The second group could be further divided into: 1) grandparents who bought the clothes for their quality and didn't mind higher prices as they wished to "spoil" their grandchildren; and 2) "young professionals" who bought the clothes because they had snob appeal and were trendy. The "young professional" market also shopped for children's clothes at Roots, Old Navy and The Gap stores and bought clothes for the label that came with them. A few people also liked the idea that the parent and child could dress alike.

Table 1   Comparison of Prices and Saint John Store Sales for Children and Adult Clothing*

Clothing Item	Price Child	Price Adult	Annual Sales Child	Annual Sales Adult
Bush Pant	$38	$58	120	1,600
Godet**	$35	$47	70	1,100
Deck Shorts	$16	$24	60	1,080
Long-Sleeve Shirt	$36	$55	20	1,240
Short-Sleeve Shirt	$32	$45	40	1,280
Pencil Case	$ 5		1,500	
Canvas Wallet	$ 8		750	

* There were many other items in the adult clothing line but they are omitted here.
** A Godet was a heavier canvas pullover which could double as a shirt or jacket.

While the children really liked the clothing, they didn't have the money to purchase items. Nicole felt that price was probably the single factor holding back the "average" consumer. Children's clothing at chain and department stores was approximately half the price of Huron. Of course, these clothes were made from cheaper fabrics and polyester blends rather than 100% cotton canvas. At the other end, exclusive children's stores often charged higher prices for designer clothing. While the quality of this clothing was only marginally better, prices were 50% to 100% higher than at Huron. At the Saint John location, there were two large department stores (Sears and The Bay), a junior department store (Wal-Mart) and one exclusive children's shop (Children's Heritage) located nearby. There was no other competition in the immediate area for children's clothing.

Nicole was quick to point out that head office "couldn't be making much money on this line. It took about the same amount of labour and thus cost about the same amount to make a children's pair of bush pants as an adult's but it had to be priced lower." Not only was head office forced to sell the clothes to franchisees at or below cost but the clothes also depleted limited raw materials. One hundred percent cotton canvas was always in short supply at Huron. Many times adult clothes were back-ordered because of a lack of canvas to produce them. Yet Suzanne Mitchell was firm on her desire to make available a line of children's clothing.

To get a retail price, Nicole marked-up the wholesale cost of all clothes by 100%. She did this to cover her basic selling costs along with the costs of alterations and returns. While she did not lose money on the sale of children's clothes, she felt that they were occupying valuable store space that could be devoted to other items. It also took management and sales time that could be better spent.

Nicole felt that she had three basic options: 1) Continue to carry the children's clothing line; 2) Drop the line from her three stores; or 3) Develop a specialty store around the concept of children's clothes.

Continue to Carry the Children's Clothing Line

If she were to continue carrying children's clothing, sales for the line would have to increase to 5% to 10% of total sales. For instance, she would need to sell 300 to 400 pairs of children's bush pants annually at each of her stores for her efforts to be properly rewarded. One method of doing this would be to advertise more. Huron had a general policy of doing little promotion. It only had one sale each year, in January, to clear end-of-line merchandise and last year's fashions. She had wondered about using some "Back-to-School" promotions. She could also participate in children's fashion shows. She had even considered giving a couple of popular children some Huron clothes in hopes of starting a fashion trend. Neither head office nor any of the franchisees had a website. No one in the company used Facebook, Twitter, Instagram or other social media.

Drop the Line From Her Three Stores

Sales of the children's clothing line were about the same at Nicole's three stores even though each faced a slightly different portfolio of competitors. She had an intuitive feeling that she should not continue to offer the children's line but that decision would raise new problems.

While carrying or not carrying certain items was left up to the store owner, Nicole wondered what head office would think of her decision? After all, her three franchises represented about 6% of Huron's annual gross clothing revenue. She was also worried about maintaining consistency within franchises. Someone who was used to finding children's clothing in another franchise would be disappointed to find that she was not carrying that line. That disappointment could hurt adult clothing sales to that person.

Open a Specialty Children's Clothing Store

Nicole felt that people expected to pay more when they visited a children's specialty store than in a store predominantly oriented to adults. She reasoned that a "Huron for Kids" would eliminate the pricing problem she was currently facing.

Opening a fourth store was really more work than she had originally intended. She had little time available after her commitments to the three stores and financing another opening now would be difficult. As well, she wasn't sure what reaction head office would have to this idea. She had heard of other stores developing a children's specialty shop (Old Navy for Kids, The Gap for Kids) but she had never heard that any of them had been very successful. There were no stores like this operating in New Brunswick. A new store would require selection of a location and the design of some special promotional material. In fact, a children's specialty shop might have to be run quite differently from a regular adult store.

The Decision

The past few years had presented many opportunities and challenges. The Saint John store was about to break even on sales of about $525,000. Perhaps she was making a mountain out of a molehill. Still she had to make a decision about the children's clothing line within the week as her spring order was due to be submitted.

Nicole reminded herself that there was no real competition for the clothing in the price range she offered. No competition could mean one of three things: 1) no one had properly exploited the market; 2) people had tried to exploit the market but hadn't developed the proper approach; or 3) there really wasn't a market at all. In helping to make her decision, she reviewed some population and income figures for the Moncton/Fredericton/ Saint John areas.

Table 2 Relevant Population Statistics for Moncton/Fredericton/Saint John

Group	2006	2011	% Change
Male: 0 to 4 years	8,795	9,775	+11.1%
5 to 9 years	9,355	9,540	+2.0%
10 to 14 years	10,570	10,195	-3.5%
Female: 0 to 4 years	8,395	9,495	+13.1%
5 to 9 years	8,800	9,335	+6.1%
10 to 14 years	10,535	9,585	-9.0%

Year	Total Population	% Change
1976	260,036	
1981	276,841	6.5%
1986	289,105	4.4%
1991	307,992	6.5%
1996	318,146	3.3%
2001	322,702	1.4%
2006	335,039	3.8%
2011	360,673	7.7%

Exhibit 1   Some of the Children's Clothing Offered by Huron

Table 3   Moncton/Fredericton/Saint John Individual Income Statistics*

Amount of Income	Number in Population
No Income	12,365
Less than $10,000	47,055
$10,000 to $19,999	51,395
$20,000 to $29,999	44,395
$30,000 to $39,999	38,960
$40,000 to $49,999	29,245
$50,000 to $59,999	20,895
$60,000 or over	51,270
Total Population over 15	295,580

Average Income for the Population = $37,747

* Income statistics for 2011 are only compiled for those people 15 years of age or older

E.D. Smith and Sons Limited

Lee Ann Gentry of E.D. Smith and Sons Limited reviewed the history of the firm's line of jam products. As Product Manager, she determined the company marketing plan for the product line. The 135 year old company based in Winona, Ontario would have to respond to the declining consumption of jam and jelly, and trade rumours that retail store shelf space for all jam, jelly, and marmalade products was about to decrease. Three years ago, advertising support for the product line was cut. As she gazed at the lush agricultural lands of the Niagara Escarpment on a warm June day, the plan of action for the remainder of 2016 was far from certain.

Company Background

In 1882, Ernest D'Israeli Smith was a fruit farmer in the fertile Niagara Escarpment area of Ontario known as Winona. Growing raspberries, black currants, grapes, apples and cherries, E.D. Smith was dissatisfied with shippers taking part of the grower's profit. His solution was to ship his own fruit directly to the wholesaler. He was so successful that demand overtook his own farm's supply. He began buying and shipping other farmers' fruit as well. In 1900, Smith was faced with a glut of fruit in successive seasons which had caused a price drop and excess fruit left unsold. E.D. Smith decided to start making jams and jellies.

Up to 1903, all pure jams sold in Canada were imported from England. E.D. Smith's was the first pure jam ever produced commercially in Canada. Starting in the basement of the fruit house, the first products were so great a success that in 1905 a factory was built and the company went into full scale jam production.

In 1910, the company expanded production into tomato ketchup and puree. In the depression of the 1930's demand for fruit products declined. Tomato puree grew to become an important product especially in export markets. One company with whom it had a contract, H.P. Sauce Limited of Great Britain, responded by allowing E.D. Smith to sell its products in Canada. In 1942, the Second World War reduced commercial trans-Atlantic shipping to a trickle and H.P. sales were severely reduced. H.P. licensed E.D. Smith to make its sauce in Canada using a secret formula – a deal sealed with only a handshake. In 1948, H.P. acquired Lea and Perrin's which, in turn, allowed E.D. Smith to manufacture the famous Worcestershire Sauce.

In that same year, E.D. Smith died at the age of 95. Among his achievements was a ten year term as Member of Parliament for Wentworth South and a seat in the Senate granted in 1913. He fought for, and won, better transportation facilities for fruit on railways and steamships. He also inspired improvements to mechanical loading and unloading of ships at dockside. He was a strong advocate of women's rights, in particular, a woman's right to vote.

Returning from active service in World War II, Armand Smith, E.D. Smith's son, became President of the company. The return of servicemen and the increased flow of immigrants to Canada brought a renewed demand for processed food products. Plant operations had to be expanded to process fruit pie fillings and a host of new tomato-based products. Armand Smith remained as President until 1956 when E. Llewellyn G. Smith, grandson of the founder, succeeded him.

From 1956 to 1981, the company went through a major expansion plan that enabled it to compete with multi-national food corporations in the Canadian market. A company organization based on the functional areas of business – marketing, sales, manufacturing, finance and data processing – was adopted. Diet products, bulk pie fillings and, in 1969, Garden Cocktail vegetable juice were all introduced. In 1968, E.D. Smith purchased Ware Foods Limited of Hamilton which produced a broad line of institutional products for the growing food service industry. In 1976, the company acquired McLarens Foods Limited of Hamilton whose olives, pickles and selected specialty products had an excellent reputation within Canada.

In 1986, a fourth generation of Smith's became President with the appointment of Llewellyn S. Smith. E.D. Smith remained, over 135 years later, a wholly Canadian controlled and operated company.

Company Operations

The company had kept pace with changing markets and new taste trends by means of a modern, efficient manufacturing capability, progressive management, and a dedicated group of over 200 employees. With the exception of sales offices, the entire E.D. Smith company operated from Winona, Ontario. The company continued to handle its own shipping. Products were carried by rail to Atlantic and western Canada while in Ontario and Quebec, the E.D. Smith fleet of transport trailers handled deliveries.

Grocery products accounted for a major proportion of the Food Division business. Not mentioned previously, E.D. Smith sold chili sauce and relish under its own name. It continued to sell H.P. Sauce and Lea & Perrins. Sales of these products were handled primarily by the 20 person National Grocery Sales Force who worked in all provinces except the Atlantic where a broker was retained. Although the company's markets were mostly domestic, the firm had limited sales outside North America.

In manufacturing, whenever possible, Canadian raw materials were purchased. Raspberries from British Columbia, blueberries from the Maritimes, rhubarb in Quebec and apples and cherries from Ontario were examples of Canadian sourcing. In fact, the company was working to establish a Canadian source of strawberries that met its specifications better than Mexican or American fruit.

People were a key ingredient to E.D. Smith's success. A team spirit was promoted and an open door policy was maintained to ensure good labour relations. Employees were encouraged to participate in "speak-up sessions" and in the company newsletter – The Homestead – offering a forum for suggestions on maintaining and improving company standards. Employees were also encouraged to participate in subsidized courses both on and off the premises.

Automation and innovation had streamlined the production process. Modern methods preserved the products' natural goodness and ensured quality standards while maintaining stable prices. Computers assisted management in controlling operations from receipt of ingredients to order assembly for customer deliveries. While the company was busiest in the fall, production continued year-round with frozen and fresh fruit imported from the United States, British Columbia and Europe. The seasonality and variety of products necessitated a complex scheduling system to ensure maximum efficiency and cost control.

The Jam, Jelly, and Marmalade Market

Marketing research indicated that when consumers were asked what image the name E.D. Smith conjured in their mind, the answer most often given was jam. After all, E.D. Smith was the first company to sell "pure jam" in Canada. Any product called "pure jam" had to contain a minimum of 45% fruit. The remainder of the product could contain sugar and natural preservatives such as citric acid. No additives, no artificial colours and no chemicals could be added to "pure jams."

E.D. Smith sold 85% of its pure jams in Ontario. Sales in Quebec were negligible due mostly to Quebecers liking of sweeter, less thick jams. Likewise sales in Canada's west were nearly negligible due to the high cost of shipping a heavy product sold for a low price. The Maritimes accounted for the remainder of E.D. Smith's jam sales. Due to the concentration of sales in Ontario, Lee Ann decided to narrow the focus to this market.

In Ontario, the top six brands of jam, jelly and marmalade accounted for 53.7% of the sales. (See Table 1 for a comparison of the top six companies) This was a highly fragmented market with many companies vying for market share. Only two of the top six brands were made in Canada. The products of many smaller companies were not classified as "pure" jams and either contained less fruit or large quantities of pectin (a natural substance used to "solidify" a jam, jelly or marmalade). Yet heavy competition was surprising since demand for both jam and jelly had not grown in the last five years (annual changes in demand fluctuated between +1% and -1% for both dollar sales and volume) and demand for marmalade was declining at a rate of 8% per year.

Theories to explain the competition were plentiful. Perhaps more and more people were not eating breakfast, or at least not eating breakfast in the home, but breakfast cereal and microwaveable breakfast sales were growing. Perhaps consumers had turned away from jam, jelly and marmalade in favour of honey, peanut butter and other breakfast spreads. Dollar sales of peanut butter grew 3% in the last year though the volume sold did not change. While fewer children were eating peanut butter, consumption by people over 45 was growing. 70% of Canadians ate peanut butter weekly. Lee Ann had noticed that a former market leader in the jam, jelly, and marmalade sector – Kraft – had dramatically changed its strategy. It still made available a few flavours of jam (raspberry and strawberry) in 500 ml. jars but its emphasis had shifted to its line of peanut butter even adding a whipped and an "all natural" peanut butter line. Honey was a different matter with year over year dollar sales growing by 9% due mostly to volume increases. While some people had a nut allergy, no one was allergic to honey. Not all consumers ate honey at breakfast; some people used honey as a natural sweetener in baking or in a cup of tea.

Table 1   Comparison of the Top Six Jam, Jelly and Marmalade Producers

	Smucker's	St. Dalfour	E.D. Smith	Greaves	Welch's	Bonne Maman
Market Share	15.7%	10.5%	9.3%	7.6%	5.3%	5.3%
Where Made?	USA	France	Canada	Canada	USA	France
Typical Retail Selling Price	$3.49 (250 ml.)	$6.19 (225 ml.)	$3.99 (250 ml.)	$4.99 (250 ml.)	$4.49 (500 ml)	$5.49 (250 ml.)
Jam Strawberry	X	X	X	X		X
Raspberry	X	X	X	X		X
Blackberry	X					
Apricot	X	X				X
Cherry	X	X	X			X
Peach	X	X				
Seedless Rasp	X		X			
Seedless Straw	X		X			
Black Currant		X	X			
Blueberry	X	X		X		X
Other Jam Flavours	Pineapple	Four Fruit Cran/ Blueberry	Fieldberry	Threeberry Straw/ Rhubarb		Straw/Rhubarb Four Fruit Caramel Spread
Jelly Strawberry	X					
Apple	X					
Marmalade Orange	X	X				
Orange – No Sugar	X					
Flavours Available in 500 ml jars	Raspberry Strawberry Apricot Grape Jelly Orange Marmalade $4.49			Raspberry Strawberry Apricot Fieldberry $4.99	Grape Jam & Jelly	

Certainly, people had not turned to making their own jam. The amount of homemade jam produced in Canada had been on a steady decline for the past 40 years. One other theory was the decline in consumption of toast at breakfast. In 2006, the average Canadian ate toast and jam 36 times per year. By 2016, that had declined to 29 times per year.

The top selling brand in Ontario was Smucker's with 15.7% of the market. In fact, it was the best selling brand in Canada. Typical consumers of Smucker's products were children who used the spread with peanut butter in a sandwich. Smucker's was a large, diversified, processed food company. It entered Canada in 1988 – shortly after the Canada/US Free Trade Agreement was signed. With a large advertising budget, it was able to establish and maintain the brand name in the consumer's mind. Its position, as the only producer of jam, jelly and marmalade, was soldified by a product relaunch in 2011. Smucker's had changed the labelling (giving new emphasis to the fruit).

The number two brand was St. Dalfour with 10.5% of the market. It only sold "pure" jams and marmalade. It entered the Canadian market in the early 2000's making it the newest market entrant. Typical consumers of St. Dalfour jams were "discriminating" shoppers. They were looking for a better product with a better taste. Independent taste tests indicated St. Dalfour's flavour was better than Smucker's and equal to E.D. Smith's. Being made in France, gave the brand some "snob" appeal which compensated for giving consumers 25 ml. less in jars.

E.D. Smith was third in the market with 9.3% of the market. Like St. Dalfour, typical E.D. Smith consumers were looking for a better product with better flavour. In 2010, the company re-positioned its diet line of jams as "no sugar added" and, by 2016, accounted for 33% of E.D. Smith's sales. These jams contained no sugar but were sweetened with Sorbitol – a natural sweetener suitable for use in a low sugar diet. The "no sugar added" product line, including Apricot, Fieldberry, Raspberry and Strawberry, had recently been reformulated using juice concentrates as sweeteners. The only competition in the "no sugar added" line was Smucker's. The two companies split the market equally.

One-quarter of the jam packaged at E.D. Smith was private labeled – the packaging of E.D. Smith product using another firm's jars and labels. Typically, private labeling was done for a grocery store which possessed a house brand (like President's Choice, Selection, Irresistibles, Blue Menu, Yellow label, etc.). In recent months, private label sponsors had requested a change in the glass jars from the cylindrical shape used by E.D. Smith to a squarer shape. None of its competitors had ever engaged in any private labeling.

The number four brand was Greaves with 7.6% of the market. This company made its jams forty minutes down the Queen Elizabeth Way (QEW) highway in Niagara-on-the-lake. In some ways, Greaves was a regional player serving the greater Toronto and Hamilton area along with Niagara. It operated a boutique store in the historic town of Niagara-on-the-lake which was a favourite stop for tourists. Expanding into grocery stores allowed those tourists to re-stock Greaves jam without having to travel back to the town. Greaves was perceived as a brand to be savoured by adults and not "wasted" on children.

Tied for fifth position was Welch's and Bonne Maman at 5.3% of the market each. Welch's competed in a narrow market niche – grape jams and jellies. In fact, Welch's was the number one seller in that niche. The Welch's family brand extended to grape juice and grape drinks in frozen concentrate, glass jar and tetra-brick (cardboard box) forms. It only sold grape jam and jelly in 500 ml. jars. In that size category, it only saw competition from Smucker's and E.D. Smith. Only Smucker's produced a grape flavour. Bonne Maman was also made in France. It entered the market in the late 1990's. The labeling and appearance of the jars seemed quite rustic – like it was made by someone's mother. Lee Ann wondered if the brand had adopted a more professional approach whether it would sell more units.

The Situation at Hand

In 2010, E.D. Smith sold 250,000 cases of jam and jelly in Ontario – a $6.2 million business. By 2016, that figure had declined to 163,000 cases – an annual sales decrease of 7%. Without realizing it, E.D. Smith had been "milking a cash cow" for, at one time, E.D. Smith had been the market leader. The steady decline had been halted only twice during the last twenty years – the introduction of "no sugar added" jam in 2010 and a relaunch of the product in 2005. That relaunch consisted of a change in label design (emphasizing the fruit) accompanied by a couponing campaign in a newspaper/magazine insert. In recent years, the jam line was given no advertising support as E.D. Smith had focused advertising dollars on other product opportunities.

During the recession of 2008, E.D. Smith undertook cost-cutting moves which saw the amount of fruit used in the pure jam reduced to the minimum. Only a small quantity of fruit could be supplied by the E.D. Smith farms so, with purchasing budgets cut back, the quality of the imported fruit also suffered. A final cost-cutting measure saw the substitution of cheaper fructose sugar for glucose sugar – a savings of thirty-six cents per case of twelve jars. A side effect of using fructose in cooking the jam was a slight browning of the mixture. Glucose sugar not only improved the colour of the mixture but improved the flavour as well.

The market was highly price sensitive and E.D. Smith was a price taker or follower. Its strategy was simply to price 50 cents above Smucker's. When Smucker's changed its price to $3.49 for the 250 ml. container, E.D.Smith charged $3.99 at the retail store. Occasionally, to help move a volume of product, one of the two firms would use a "sale" price 50 cents lower at the retail store. However, it was not unusual to find the other brand moving its price once one took the lead. E.D. Smith expected the regular price set by Smucker's to increase soon as there had been no price increase during the previous three years.

Lee Ann was concerned with rumours/suggestions from wholesalers and retailers that the amount of shelf space devoted to jam, jelly and marmalade in retail stores was about to be reduced. The argument made by the trade was that sales of these products had been declining and thus did not deserve as much exposure as they currently had. This meant either that the number of varieties carried by each store of each type of jam, jelly and marmalade would be reduced or some brand(s) would have to be eliminated. Both Greaves and Bonne Maman appeared to be vulnerable.

The Possibilities for E.D. Smith

Lee Ann could take a defensive posture and eliminate some of the varieties of jam and jelly produced by E.D. Smith. Two varieties (strawberry and raspberry) accounted for nearly 70% of sales. These two could be kept in two sizes (250 ml. and 500 ml.). A different approach would be a flanking maneouver which positioned the jam and jelly line as a product used in cooking/baking rather than as a breakfast spread. Jam could be used in cakes as a filling, in jelly rolls, on ice cream, over waffles, in tarts, in dessert treats, in Christmas baking, as a sauce ingredient, or in muffins. Before Lee Ann joined E.D. Smith, the responsibility for two products from the jam line – Lemon Spread and Mint Jelly – were internally transferred to other units. Many consumers viewed mint jelly as a condiment – like ketchup or mustard – and served it exclusively with lamb dishes. Similarly, many consumers viewed lemon spread as a tart or cake filling. Though these products could be found in the jam, jelly, and marmalade section, they were not Lee Ann's responsibility.

A different flanking manoeuver would be to focus on "peculiar" or unique flavours of specialty jams and jellies. At a current average price of $27.00 per case, a new flavour had to generate sales of at least 4,000 cases to break-even. Coupled with this could be a price increase to establish a more premium image. Though sales volume would likely fall, the profit margin on each jar would be greater and, presumably, profits could rise. A more offensive move would be to relaunch or even reformulate the product. In a relaunch, a company could change the packaging, the labeling or the promotion of the product in such a way that it had a fresh, new image. Reformulation would mean a change in the basic product itself either through a new jam recipe, a change in fruit or a change in sugar. If a relaunch or reformulation were undertaken, how similar or dissimilar should the packaging, label, promotion or recipe be to the other products on the market? Should the price be changed? Should E.D. Smith try to become the price leader?

Another offensive move would be to launch jams/jellies in the United States. Informally, E.D. Smith liked to concentrate the firm's efforts within an 80 mile radius of Winona. Shipping costs increased price to a nearly non-competitive level outside of that area. Nonetheless, including the United States, 160 million people lived within an 800 mile radius of Winona.

Thirty years ago, E.D. Smith stopped selling Orange and Three Fruit marmalade. Perhaps the line could be revitalized. The ultimate offensive move would be the launch of a second E.D. Smith jam and jelly line. E.D. Smith could have a regular and premium/old-fashioned line of jams and jellies – E.D. Smith Classic? These two lines would have different price points, packages, labels and recipes and would require separate promotional support to build awareness and separation in the minds of the consumer.

The Decision

The costing of the many options would have to come later. For now, Lee Ann was screening the alternatives from a strategic viewpoint. Equally of concern was the tactical plan that would have to be developed for any chosen strategy. Lee Ann took off her jacket and slipped off her shoes. There was plenty of work to be done.

LIME LIGHT CINEMA

In January 2014, after nine months of operation, Lime Light Cinema of Victoria, British Columbia, was still not generating satisfactory revenues. To attract larger audiences, Head Office in Montreal had made two major changes to the marketing strategy in the last year: it changed the programming format and the pricing strategy. Olga Siroonian, the new Manager, was faced with the responsibility for successfully implementing these changes and increasing local profitability by at least 25%.

Company History

The theatre had operated as a pornographic film house under the name "The Cosmopolitan Cinema" for twenty-five years. In January, 2013, Phoenix Theatres of Montreal purchased the business as part of an expansion plan. To reposition the theatre as a first run art film cinema featuring two films per evening, major renovations were undertaken in late February. In March, Phoenix reopened the theatre as "The New Cosmopolitan Cinema."

From the beginning, the new cinema encountered problems with image. Even though the concept had changed, association with the previous name still branded the cinema as a place to see pornographic films. In October, the name was changed to "Lime Light Cinema" (an homage to Charlie Chaplin's silent film "The Lime Light") and a new marquee was erected. In November, the owners fired the Manager and promoted the Assistant Manager (of four months), Olga Siroonian, to the position. Prior to becoming Assistant Manager, Olga had worked for five months as one of the theatre's ushers.

Company Problems

After the name change and under Olga's new management, business improved slightly. In March and April the average audience size had been about 60 people per show, well below the 375 seat capacity. Attendance in December was 60 to 70 people per show. Olga remarked that "As we will be receiving an average admittance fee of $5.00 per head, we will pretty well have to pack the place every night to break even."

In Olga's opinion, the theatre had two problems: 1) people did not know much about the theatre; and 2) people did not know much about the films being shown. "People don't know what they are getting when they go to see an art film," stated Olga.

After eight months of operations, Phoenix finally realized that Victoria did not have the population size or audience interest to support a "first run art film cinema." (Available cost data is outlined in Exhibit 1).

Recent Changes

Responding to low attendance figures, the theatre's concept was changed again. Beginning in mid-December, Lime Light Cinema became a repertory theatre featuring two different movies every night (one shown at 7:00 p.m. and the other at 9:15 p.m.). Features would include second-run commercial films (movies shown two to three months after their premiere), occasional premiere films, classic movies, foreign films, and first-run art films. Olga explained, "Most of the films shown will have been in Victoria already. People will know the films and that will make our promotion job a lot easier." The variety of films and reduced prices were key elements in the new strategy.

As well, in mid-October, Lime Light moved from a straight admission fee of $6.00 for students and $8.00 for adults to a membership basis. Company management felt the old prices were not low enough to attract enough people to come to see a film with which they were unfamiliar. Members would pay $10.00 a year to join the cinema and $4.00 per show admission fee. For non-members, the fee would be $6.00. At these prices Lime Light Cinema would be offering lower prices than the other repertory theatre in town which charged a $15.00 membership fee, and $5.00 and $7.00 for admission. Initially, Lime Light Cinema had ordered 2,500 membership cards.

There was one bright spot – in the last two weeks of December, Olga had increased theatre revenues and profits by making changes in the candy bar operation. She added/deleted products and adjusted prices on soft drinks and popcorn. The average receipt per patron had increased from about $2.50 to $3.00. The theatre generated a high contribution margin, and thus profit, from the candy bar operation, so these changes were important.

The Theatre Industry

There were eight commercial theatres and one repertory theatre in Victoria. (See Exhibit 5 for Population data) Originally, Lime Light Cinema was not directly competing with either type of theatre. However, with the changes, it would be competing directly with the other, very well established, repertory theatre in town. Olga expected to have some initial difficulty competing for business but believed that there was room for two repertory theatres in Victoria.

Besides the other theatres, another source of competition was home DVD or DVR machines along with Netflix. The latter allowed an unlimited number of movies or television shows from an immense library to be streamed to a computer or internet-enabled television in exchange for a monthly membership fee. By the time second-run commercial films were shown at Lime Light Cinema, they were available on DVD's or online. People could purchase or rent these media for home viewing. Premiere films would not be affected by DVD sales or online services. Art films were generally not available to the public on DVD or online. Only with concerted effort could some of the exotic art or foreign film titles be located. Olga had read predictions for new technologies. Consumers had a choice between computers and tablets, iPod's and iPad's, and even smartphones as sources of entertainment. The future would likely see other new devices to compete with watching a movie in a theatre.

A variety of customers patronized the cinema. Olga estimated that 35% of her customers were students from the University of Victoria. Customers could be categorized as follows:

1) regular movie-goers who could afford to go to commercial theatres;
2) avid movie buffs, including film students from the University of Victoria;
3) people who wanted something off-beat and different; and
4) people who were just looking for an inexpensive night out.

She believed the theatre was targeting and promoting to everybody.

Promoting the New Concept

Approximately $30,000 had been allocated to promotion for the year. In the past, most advertising had been allocated to newspapers. Lime Light Cinema placed a seven-line ad daily in the Victoria Times-Colonist and an occasional sixty-line ad in The Martlet, the university student newspaper. (See Exhibits 2 and 3) Olga felt that radio advertising was generally too expensive but would use it occasionally to promote premiere films. In addition, bi-monthly tabloid-type printed program schedules were distributed to potential customers through all record stores and donut shops in the city. These schedules were provided by Head Office (Information on media costs is provided in Exhibit 4). Lime Light had a Facebook page. It was mostly used by patrons to discuss movies. She had wondered if she should launch a website or maybe get a Twitter account to also promote the theatre. Olga did not really know if any of the advertising was effective. She did know that the future promotional strategy for the repertory concept had to be successful or she was out of a job.

The objective of the new promotional program was to make people aware of the repertory format, the new prices, and to sell memberships. So far, Olga had purchased a sixty-line ad in the Victoria Times-Colonist to announce the opening and had arranged an interview on a CHEK-TV entertainment program to talk about the new concept. She was thinking of trying to arrange a couple of radio interviews as well, but she knew more had to be done.

Exhibit 1   Theatre Cost Information

Film Rental Per Showing	$200.00
Estimated Management Salaries	$45,000 per year
Estimated Theatre Lease (building & utilities)	$5,000 per month

Estimated Gross Margin on 'Candy Bar' operation - 65%
(i.e., 65 cents of each dollar spent at the 'Candy Bar' was profit; 35% covered variable costs)

Average Staffing Per Night (average of 3.5 hours per person at minimum wage)
    One Cashier
    One Candy Bar Person (Two on Friday and Saturday nights)
    Two Ushers
    One Doorman
    One Projectionist – 4.5 hours per night at $20.00 per hour

Exhibit 2   **Daily Ad in the Victoria Times-Colonist**

Exhibit 3   **Weekly Ad in The Martlet (University of Victoria Newspaper)**

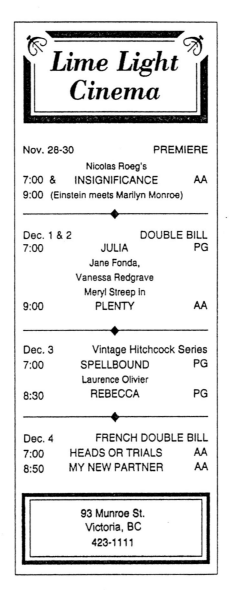

Exhibit 4   Advertising Rates

NEWSPAPER	Circulation	Line Rate (per column)
Victoria Times-Colonist	88,796 (total paid daily)	$5.16 $4.61 (over 10,000 lines per year)
TV Plus (Victoria edition) (free distribution)	42,913 (weekly) (26 week schedule)	1/4 page - $310.00/week
The Martlet	10,000 (weekly)	$2.62 $2.48 (rate for weekly contract)

RADIO	AAA	AA	A	B	
CFAX (#1 station in Victoria area - reach 28% of homes)	$55	$43	$35	$28	60 Seconds
	45	34	29	23	30 Seconds

AAA - 6:00 am to 10:00 am weekdays   AA - 4:00 pm to 11:00 pm weekdays
A - 10:00 am to 4:00 pm weekdays and Saturdays   B - all other times

Reach plan $35 per spot for 21 sixty-second spots
Made up of four AAA, six AA, six A and five B spots

CFUV University of Victoria - 60 Seconds - $10.00

Exhibit 5   Population Statistics

Metropolitan Victoria
    Population   344,615*
    Rank in Twenty Largest Canadian Census
    Metropolitan Areas   15th
    Age Groups

14 and under	45,190	
15 to 24	42,535	
25 to 34	45,200	
35 to 44	42,825	
Over 44	168,865	

    Average Household Income per week $1,525.96
    Rank in Twenty Largest Canadian Census
    Metropolitan Areas   9th

* Student population
    University of Victoria 19,500

Source: Statistics Canada, Canadian Census, 2011

TREMCO LTD.

Paul Sagar, Marketing Manager, felt that a full re-examination of Mono Foam was in order. He had been with the company for three years and had not participated in the first business plan for this insulating spray foam product. His objectives were to: 1) grow sales volume and market share for Mono Foam; 2) improve Mono Foam's profitability; and 3) increase the total market for insulating foams. The latter was a risky move. If he was able to cause consumers to buy more insulating foam, they could decide to buy one of his competitor's cheaper products rather than Mono Foam.

Product Background

Tremco Ltd. manufactured and distributed protective coatings and sealants for consumers. It also sold industrial applications including roofing and flooring systems for building maintenance and construction, autobody sealants, and adhesives. The company was founded in 1928 by William Treuhaft of Cleveland, Ohio. Over time, the company grew internationally coming to Canada during 1962. In 1979, Tremco was sold to BF Goodrich which maintained it intact as an operating division. In 1997, RPM International purchased Tremco for $230 million. Today, the company employed 2,000 people in Canada with manufacturing sites in Toronto, Montreal, and Quebec City. It also had an extensive Canadian distribution network with centres in Montreal, Calgary, Edmonton, Halifax, Vancouver, Toronto, and Winnipeg.

The Consumer Products Division was unique to Canadian operations. No consumer products were sold in the United States and only limited numbers of consumer products were available in Australia and Sweden. The first consumer product in 1962 was Tremclad rust paint which could be applied directly to metal surfaces and effectively controlled rusting. Later that decade, the company added Instant Patch - a consumer roof repair product. In 1981, it launched Mono caulking products. Each of these was a successful product in the Industrial Division applied to a consumer market.

Annually a small executive delegation from Tremco attended the North American Hardware Trade Show in Chicago, Illinois, looking for new product ideas and monitoring competitor innovations. A few years ago, while touring the cramped lower floor of the show where small companies hope to win sales of recently developed new products, Tremco's Canadian executives discovered the booth of Foam-o, a manufacturer from Norton, Ohio. It had created an insulating spray foam. Foam-o was primarily a private labeller (i.e., it had no brand of its own opting, instead, to place the labels of other companies on its products). Executives quickly discovered that Foam-o had no Canadian presence and that the company would agree to give Tremco exclusive rights to distribute the product in Canada. Foam-o was even willing to add a non-competition clause which ensured that it would not try to enter the Canadian market either directly or indirectly (i.e., through an

----

American reseller). Knowing that no Canadian firm manufactured insulating spray foam, all of these terms excited Tremco executives. The product would not be available in the Industrial Division making it the first exclusive product for the Consumer Products Group in Canada.

Though insulating spray foam was first introduced to Canada ten years earlier, today there were four companies selling expanding insulating foam in an aerosol format. Insulating spray foam was used to seal drafts behind baseboards, around wall vents for dryers and fans, and fill cracks around window installations. When sprayed, the sticky foam expanded to fill empty spaces and then dried to form a semi-rigid barrier to air flow. Three brands, Great Stuff, Foam-it, and Touch 'n' Foam, were imported from the United States while the fourth, Sista, was imported from Germany. Tremco had followed the progress of this product line as it was given limited shelf facing in the caulking section of hardware, building supply, and mass merchandising stores. This placed it near Tremco's number one selling caulking product – Mono. However, unit volumes compared to caulking sales were less than one to twenty.

The plan was quite simple. Tremco would import Foam-o's product. The Mono brand name was extended and the product was called Mono Foam (Mono Mousse in Quebec). This line extension was supported by a limited amount of advertising in trade publications. Distribution in retail stores was gained through Tremco's national sales force and on the strength of the Mono brand name. For Tremco, this was an easy decision. Tremco had an excellent warehousing and distribution system. It did not incur any new product development costs. There was no additional overhead other than working capital required for inventory.

Using a premium pricing system, Tremco was able to achieve a 30% contribution margin. This meant that Mono Foam sold for about $8.00 a can at retail – about the same price as Sista and twice the price of Great Stuff, Foam-it and Touch 'n' Foam. If consumers were not willing to pay the premium price, Tremco was prepared to withdraw from the market. Nonetheless, the chance of losing money on the project was low.

The Situation

For Mono Foam, sales peaked two years ago and then remained unchanged. Apart from some modest trade advertising and sales force support, there had been no promotional investment in the product. Communication with the consumer consisted of exposure only – through an attractive rack and an available information brochure. This approach was not unusual as no competitor supported its brand with anything more than infrequent trade discounts common to the industry. Foam-It and Touch 'n' Foam supplemented their low price approach with a manufacturer's agent who targeted smaller independent hardware stores. Sista and Great Stuff were larger competitors which were new and unknown to Tremco. Both had succeeded in getting exposure in chain hardware stores – most notably Canadian Tire.

Although positioned as the quality leader, Mono Foam placed third in market share. (See Figure 1) As a result, Mono Foam's performance was seen as little more than a line extension that generated only a limited operating income. The market size, measured in number of cans sold, also remained stable and was virtually unaffected by the introduction of Mono Foam. Perhaps the biggest problem for Mono Foam was the unwillingness expressed by Canadian Tire to put the product on its shelves. By not achieving full retail distribution, the product was not exposed to all potential customers. Canadian Tire accounted for 25% to 30% of all hardware sales to consumers in Canada.

Figure 1   Market Shares – Consumer Insulating Foa

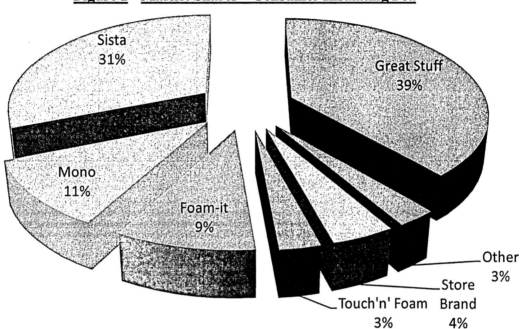

As part of the re-examination of Mono Foam, Paul Sagar's first step was to visit Foam-o in Ohio. He discovered that in Europe insulating spray foam had a forty year history though in North America the product was barely fifteen years old. Based on his knowledge of the use of caulking, one would expect no difference in demand for spray foam between North American and European consumers. However, Europeans were consuming five to ten times the volume of product. Foam-o convinced Paul that the market had a need for the product and that, in North America, the product could be in the primary stages of a growth cycle.

His second step was to gather market information. Sales to consumers acting as "do-it-yourselfers" accounted for 90% of volume. The other 10% was sold to small contractors. No market research was gathered on this group. Last year, 3.9% of Canadian households bought an insulating foam product. This translated into 1,642,000 containers with a retail value of $13 million. Canisters came in three sizes: small – 350 grams (45% of sales); medium – 620 grams (37% of sales); and large – 935 grams (18% of sales). (See Table 1 for details) Based on some European data, Paul believed the consumer market for foam could grow at a rate of 15% per year. Future growth would be directly related to the market's incidence of purchase. If 30% of households purchased the product each year, the insulating spray foam market would be bigger than the caulking market.

Insulating spray foam was purchased year round but sales peaked in October, November, December and January – the months when consumers were most interested in "winterizing" their homes. Consumers also tended to purchase and then use an entire can of insulating spray foam regardless of its size. This was partly due to the product as once the can was opened, insulating spray foam had a three month shelf life. But this was also partly due to the multi-purpose nature of the product. Once homeowners began filling cracks and blocking air leaks, they were able to find enough to empty an entire can.

Table 1   Market Size - Consumer Insulation Foam

Product Size	% of Households Purchasing	Total Households Purchasing *	Average Units Per Purchase	Total Units Sold
350 gram	2.9%	380,000	1.93	733,400
620 gram	1.7%	230,000	2.63	604,900
935 gram	0.9%	120,000	2.53	303,600
All Sizes	3.9%	520,000	2.45	1,641,900

* Assumes approximately 13,300,000 households in Canada.

Although Great Stuff had the highest market share, it had no product in the 620 gram market and finished second behind Sista in the 935 gram market. Its sales were concentrated in the small 350 gram market. Great Stuff was positioned as the low price foam with the same performance attributes as Mono. Sista was the first insulating spray foam in the Canadian market and Sista dominated the 620 gram market and had half the sales of Great Stuff in the 350 gram market. Sista also enjoyed a dominant position in the Quebec market while Great Stuff fared better in the rest of Canada. Tremco identified these two companies as its key competitors.

Last year, Mono added a 935 gram package to complement its 350 gram size. As the total number of cans sold remained constant, one could assume that some cannibalization had occurred. Nonetheless, a bigger volume of Mono Foam was sold. Revenues for last year were approximately $624,000 with a contribution margin of $187,000. If the market grew as anticipated, Mono Foam's sales volume would be most affected by its market share. If it could aggressively acquire share then, with its margins, it could benefit the most.

Paul's third step was to talk directly with consumers. No competitor was undertaking any primary or secondary marketing research. Most viewed insulating spray foam as a mature product and a commodity. One competitor was quoted as likening the industry to fasteners. After all, "nails are nails."

Paul's research provided some interesting findings. Only 20% of consumers showed awareness of insulating spray foams. Awareness meant they could know the product well, have a vague idea of the product, or have no idea about the product other than recognizing the name. Approximately 25% of those aware had purchased the product. (See Table 2 for Mono Foam sales) These people were very satisfied with the product and would purchase again if a similar need arose. They had not purchased it instead of caulking and, in fact, saw the product as being completely different from caulking. They were also loyal indicating that they would buy and had bought other Tremco products.

Table 2   Mono Foam Sales Volume (in cans)

Product Size	Year 1	Year 2	Year 3
350 gram	100,700	110,300	84,600
620 gram	-	-	-
935 gram	-	-	21,900
Total	100,700	110,300	106,500

For the unaware group, researchers explained the product, how it was used, and the benefits it could offer. Consumers were asked to use a five point scale to indicate how likely they would be to purchase the product. "Very likely" and "Likely" responses comprised 50% of the sample. This "top box" score was the highest of all previous products researched by Tremco. When asked what the most important factors were when buying an insulating spray foam, the top five consumer responses were: 1) high insulation/"R" value – 22%; 2) easy to apply – 19%; 3) provides a tight seal – 11%; 4) seals air leaks – 11%; and 5) seals cracks – 6%. Given the small sample size, Paul had to make the dangerous assumption that buying behaviour would be the same in Quebec as in the rest of the country.

Paul's final step was to visit with key retail accounts. (See Figure 2) One in four cans of insulating spray foam were acquired at Canadian Tire. This retailer was concerned about Mono's relatively high selling price. It also preferred to carry products supported by mass media advertising. In particular, it reacted better to products support by television advertising as Canadian Tire was a heavy user of this medium. Given the small volume of insulating spray foam sold, Canadian Tire did not feel it could justify a third product listing on its shelves. A listing was important to Tremco as once granted, a product would be guaranteed exposure in all Canadian Tire stores. The retailer might be interested in private labelling Mono Foam with the Canadian Tire name. Paul was given assurances that Tremco was seen as a key supplier to Canadian Tire and there was a willingness to continue the dialogue if any major new promotional effort was expended.

Next Steps

Paul tried to synthesize this information. "Mono" was a reputable and established brand name which represented well-made products to consumers. Tremco had a good understanding of the consumer insulating spray foam market as well as access to worldwide foam knowledge. Unfortunately, Mono Foam was not significantly different from its competition. Given the need to import from the U.S., the high American dollar, and the need to maintain a 30% contribution margin, Mono Foam would have to be premium priced thus eliminating a certain percentage of price-conscious consumers from the market.

One solution was to begin an aggressive campaign to expand the market to match European consumption trends. Marketing research seemed to support Paul's belief that a lack of consumer communication and awareness were at the heart of the problem. If Tremco could launch a major communications initiative it could increase the size of the market and with it, Mono Foam's market

Figure 2   Where Consumers Are Purchasing Insulating Foam

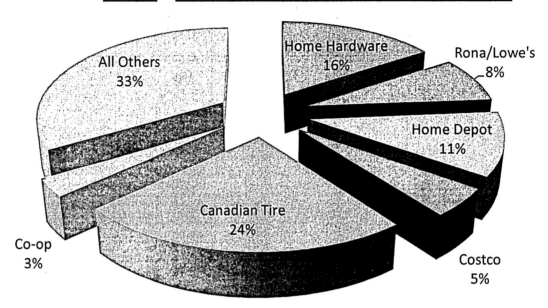

share. This strategy was not without its risks. Increasing demand for the product would undoubtedly benefit lower priced competitors as price-sensitive consumers turned to alternatives cheaper than Mono Foam. More of a concern, Tremco was betting that competitors would not comprehend its actions and would not change any of their marketing tactics. In particular, Tremco hoped its competitors would not launch any major communications campaigns.

A key question for Paul was how to communicate. He was limited to $100,000 for the coming year by company executives. He considered many options. Given the complex nature of the product, he could provide free samples to home owners. This would necessitate filling small trial aerosol cans with the product. These were expensive to purchase and he would be limited to 25,000 given his budget. Another possibility was in-store demonstrations. A representative could visit a retail hardware store with a small booth and, during store hours, visit with customers and show them how the product worked. This approach would cost $250 per day. A variation on this would be attendance at retailer trade shows where no homeowners would be allowed. Rona/Lowe's, Home Depot, and Home Hardware, to name a few retailers, held these two day trade shows twice a year. It allowed companies, new and established, a chance to speak one-on-one with local retailers and dealers. Booth rental was only a few hundred dollars but the big cost was the time of those who would staff the booth. Bigger retail trade shows, like the one held in Chicago, could cost tens of thousands of dollars to attend.

As the product filled a mass consumer need, Paul considered mass media advertising. Radio was a portable medium but lacked a visual element. Magazines or newspapers could get the message across but were relatively inefficient. By having to purchase space in dozens of publications, there could be message overlap and wasted dollars. Television had broad appeal and had been used successfully with its Tremclad line of paints and Mono caulking. Unfortunately, there were few network television shows devoted to home renovation. If television was used, sports-oriented programming would have to be targeted. He could try cable television. For example, the Home and Garden Television Canada (HGTV Canada) channel offered lots of home renovation programs but the audience was one percent of those watching sporting events on the networks. Finally, Paul considered in-store advertising. He had seen small television sets equipped with a built-in video player. A short video could be created which would play continuously in the store to attract attention. To be successful, salespeople would have to get permission from store managers and convince them that this set-up would not be a nuisance to their operations. A past trial of this expensive system ($600 per store) indicated that only 1% of managers would permit placement.

A different approach would be to look for other elements of the marketing mix which, when manipulated, would lead to share gains. Paul considered two additional sizes – medium and very small. He wondered about dropping the branded product and moving into private labelling for Canadian retailers. He could also reduce the contribution margin and lower the product's price. One key to future success seemed to be getting a listing at Canadian Tire.

JULIUS SCHMID OF CANADA LTD. – BOB WALLACE'S MOST IMPORTANT DECISION

Bob Wallace had been the Marketing Manager at Julius Schmid of Canada Ltd. for the last thirty years. Julius Schmid was Canada's largest seller of condoms. At his retirement party, a recent hire into the Marketing Department was chatting about Bob's career. "Looking back, what was the most important problem you ever had to face while working here?" she asked. Bob paused to reflect on the question. "I suppose it happened about ten years into my career. We were considering repositioning some of the products within the firm's condom line. With the prevalence of sexually transmitted diseases including HIV/AIDS, and with more women purchasing condoms, we felt new markets were opening. My dilemma was deciding what to do, if anything."

The Condom Market in the mid-1990's

The condom first appeared in the 16th century when the physician, Gabriel Fallopius, designed a medicated linen sheath for the purpose of preventing venereal disease. By the 17th century, the condom was also used as a contraceptive.

In the 1980's, unit sales of condoms in Canada had declined at an annual rate of three percent but the dollar volume of sales actually rose at an annual rate of two percent because of compensating price increases. When initial fears of an HIV/AIDS epidemic surfaced in 1990, a dramatic reversal in sales was seen with double-digit growth for the first half of the 1990's. By 1995, the condom market was a $38 million a year business in Canada growing at six percent annually.

There were four major condom manufacturers in the Canadian market. The market leader was Julius Schmid with about 63 percent of the market. While none of its product was manufactured in Canada, it did maintain electronic testing and packaging facilities in the country. Its condoms were manufactured in the United States and Germany. Ortho Pharmaceuticals was a distant second with about 22 percent of the market. Ortho had been a wholly-owned subsidiary of Johnson and Johnson Inc. but was recently purchase by Ansell Laboratories. Otho specialized in contraceptives and, by far, its largest product line was oral contraceptives. Ortho's condoms were imported fully packaged and tested from Brazil.

With only seven percent of the market, Akwel Pharmaceuticals held third place. Its condoms were manufactured and packaged in the United States. In fourth place, with about three percent of the market was Trojan. A few other companies accounted for the remaining sales.

The situation was quite different in the United States where Trojan was almost a generic name for a condom. Trojans accounted for 68 percent of the American market. Schmid Labs (the

----

American sister company of Julius Schmid) was in second place with about 16 percent of the market and Ansell held third place with 14 percent market share. The American market was about ten times the size of the Canadian market.

Condoms were primarily used by men 16 to 29 years engaging in pre-marital sex. A second user group was married men who reverted to using condoms during the two to three month waiting period between the time a woman stopped taking birth control pills and the time she could safely conceive a child. Estimates were that seven percent of couples, aged 15 to 44, engaging in intercourse, used condoms as a contraceptive method.

While men were the main users of the product, it was estimated that between 40 percent and 45 percent of all condoms were purchased by women. It was theorized that women had historically been the person in the relationship to think about contraceptive methods. Buying condoms for a lover would be a natural extension of that concern.

Seventy percent of condom purchases were made for contraceptive reasons. As such, the condom competed with the diaphragm, the intra-uterine device and the birth control pill. The condom was the only form of birth control, besides abstinence, that a man could use. The other forms were directed specifically at women. The remaining thirty percent of condoms were purchased to prevent sexually transmitted diseases (STD's). These diseases included: chlamydia – the fastest spreading STD; gonorrhea; herpes – an incurable STD that re-appeared two to three times per year; syphilis; vaginitis; and HIV/AIDS.

Company Background

Julius Schmid Inc. was founded in New York city by Julius Schmid who served as President of the company until his death in 1939. In 1936, Julius Schmid Inc. moved into Canada at the request of Drug Trading Company, one of the largest Canadian wholesalers of pharmaceutical/over-the-counter products, which was concerned with the then poor quality of condoms sold in Canada. The first condom brands sold in Canada by Julius Schmid were Sheik, Ramses, Cadet (in Quebec) and Fourex.

In 1965, the Toronto-based company became a wholly-owned subsidiary of the United Kingdom company London International Group PLC and began importing rubber gloves for sale in Canada. By 1995, the company employed 65 people. Sales could be broken down by product line: condoms (68 percent); rubber gloves, both industrial and consumer (25 percent); and some over-the-counter pharmaceutical products (7 percent). Sales of the company's condom line had been relatively stagnant. (See Table 1)

Table 1   Condom Sales for Julius Schmid of Canada Ltd.

Year	Quantity (in gross*)
1992	477,200
1993	484,000
1994	466,400 estimated
1995	488,400 estimated

* A "gross" was defined to be twelve dozen units.

Julius Schmid was unique in that it was the only competitor in the condom market to advertise. With an annual budget of approximately $500,000, advertising was confined mainly to magazines. The company appealed to both men, through magazines such as Cycle Canada and University Life, and women, through magazines such as Chatelaine and Flare. (See Exhibit 1 for two typical magazine ads) Julius Schmid spent part of the advertising budget on informative pamphlets and posters that were sent to secondary schools, health clinics and sexual counselling centres along with thousands of condom samples.

The AIDS Crisis

AIDS (Acquired Immunodeficiency Syndrome) was caused by a virus that attacked the body's immune system, leading to its collapse and thus left the person vulnerable to a number of infections or cancers. The virus which caused AIDS, Human Immunodeficiency Virus (HIV), was found in the blood, semen or vaginal fluid of an infected person, and was spread when any of those substances entered another person's bloodstream. The virus had also been isolated in tears and saliva of some infected individuals but not one known case of AIDS was caused by these bodily fluids.

Infection with HIV did not always lead to AIDS. However, even though some people infected with HIV appeared to remain in good health for a long time, it was not known how many people would go on to develop illnesses, some fatal, in the years to come. The U.S. National Academy of Science estimated that between 25 and 50 percent of those infected with the virus would develop AIDS eventually. The Centers for Disease Control in Atlanta, Georgia estimated that between 10 and 30 percent of those infected would go on to the final stages of AIDS within the next five to ten years.

AIDS was a world-wide phenomenon. The World Health Organization (WHO) conservatively estimated that there would be 38.6 million adults and 3.2 million children infected with HIV/AIDS by the end of 1995. In the year before, 5 million new HIV/AIDS infections were reported and 3.1 million people died of the disease – a higher global total than any year since the beginning of the epidemic. In Canada, it was estimated that 49,000 people would be infected with HIV/AIDS and 400 would die in 1995. (See Table 2 for a comparison of diagnosed HIV/AIDS infections and deaths by country).

In theory, anyone could get AIDS – it depended on one's behaviour. Homosexual and bisexual men who engaged in the practice of anal intercourse without precautions were at great risk and represented the highest percentage of AIDS cases. In Canada, this group represented over 82 percent of all reported cases, while in the United States, it represented 66 percent of reported cases. Through a better understanding of how AIDS was transmitted and an aggressive campaign for safe sex, the gay community hoped to see a decrease in HIV infections.

Intravenous drug abusers who shared contaminated needles or syringes were the second group to be most concerned and represented 17 percent of the AIDS cases in the United States. This group, however, only represented 0.4 percent of the AIDS cases in Canada. This low rate was probably due to a smaller drug abuse problem in Canada and the ready availability of clean needles and syringes at most pharmacies. Other risk groups included: those who had relationships with people who might be in the high risk group; those who received transfusions of infected blood

Table 2   Number of People Living with HIV/AIDS and HIV/AIDS Deaths by Selected Country in 1995

Country	People Living with HIV/AIDS	HIV/AIDS Deaths
Canada	49,000	400
South Africa	4,200,000	250,000
India	3,700,000	310,000
Ethiopia	3,000,000	280,000
Nigeria	2,700,000	250,000
Kenya	2,100,000	180,000
Zimbabwe	1,500,000	160,000
Tanzania	1,300,000	140,000
Mozambique	1,200,000	98,000
Congo	1,100,000	95,000
Zambia	870,000	99,000
United States	850,000	20,000
Thailand	755,000	66,000
Brazil	540,000	18,000
China	500,000	17,000
Mexico	150,000	4,700
Dominican Republic	130,000	4,900
France	130,000	2,000
Russia	130,000	850
Italy	95,000	1,000
Pakistan	74,000	6,500
Guatemala	73,000	3,600
Germany	37,000	600
United Kingdom	31,000	450
Australia	14,000	100
Japan	9,000	150

or blood products; and children who contracted HIV from an infected mother, before or at birth.

To minimize the risk of contracting or spreading AIDS, the Surgeon-General of the United States, recommended abstinence from sex. Since this was unlikely, maintaining a mutually monogamous relationship with a partner who had not been exposed to HIV would also eliminate risk. Many people did not practice mutually monogamous relationships, thus it was recommended that the proper use of a condom during sexual intercourse would decrease the risk of AIDS.

Researchers proved in laboratory tests that condoms could stop HIV. The virus could not penetrate the condom material of latex rubber condoms unless the condoms were ruptured. Regardless of the precautions taken, all sexually active people with multiple partners were advised to exercise safe sex practices. The use of condoms was statistically considered 95 percent effective.

Bob Wallace's Most Important Decision

"Sure. I had been Marketing Manager for nearly ten years but I wasn't sure what I should do. For instance, I could recommend that Julius Schmid reposition some of its condom products to appeal directly to the AIDS high risk group. Different names, different packages, different advertisements and different distribution channels would be needed. While this approach made some sense, I was worried that Julius Schmid would be seen as 'cashing in' on the AIDS problem. Also, Julius Schmid liked maintaining a low media profile. The firm tried to stay away from anything which could be seen as controversial. I was worried that designing a condom product especially for the gay community might be seen as condoning homosexual behaviour and that stance could create a backlash from our more conservative, heterosexual customers. Another consideration was the gay community itself. Many of its members did not wish to be identified – the term was 'being in the closet.' If Julius Schmid developed a condom for the gay community, would they risk buying the product and thus identifying themselves to the cashier and other people in a store?" Bob paused for a moment hoping the new hire understood the gravity of the situation that confronted him.

Bob continued. "I also wondered whether Julius Schmid should develop a condom product targeted specifically to female purchasers. Some industry experts considered them to be the largest single market as the 55% of men who were purchasers were made up of both homosexual and heterosexual males. Again different names, different packages, different advertisements, and different distribution channels would be needed."

"I knew we were talking about relatively larger markets (see Table 3) and the changes I was considering could have been the biggest change in condom marketing in nearly half a century," Bob shared.

Bob's words had clearly captured the attention of the new hire. "So … what did you do?"

"Ha. You're new here. I think you should think about it and see if you can figure out how to handle this issue," Bob said laughing. "I'm not going to tell you my solution." He paused and then added, "I will tell you this much. What I decided to do was contrary to what every professor had ever taught me about marketing!"

Table 3   Selected Canadian Population Statistics for 1995

Age Range	Number of Single Women	Number of Single Men
15-19	1,019,559	1,076,030
20-24	1,050,644	1,094,105
25-29	1,055,573	1,083,359
30-34	1,126,916	1,147,675
35-39	1,286,179	1,309,077
20-24	1,341,234	1,345,859

Though difficult to determine, estimates were that between 5 and 10 percent of the population was gay.

Exhibit 1   Selected Julius Schmid Magazine Advertising

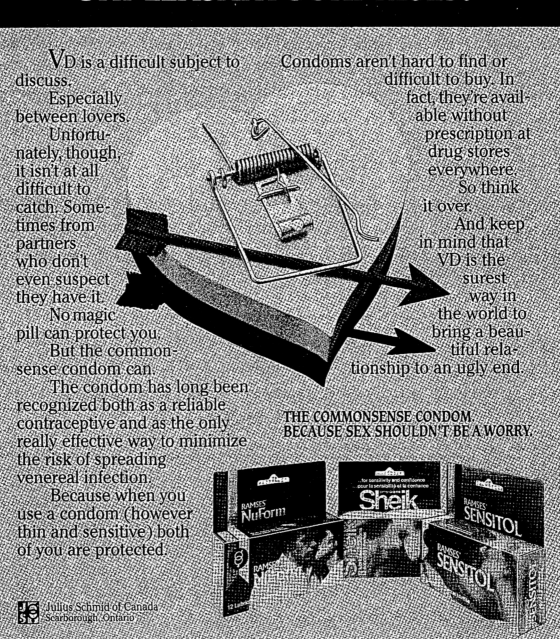

SEX IS BEAUTIFUL. BUT IT SHOULDN'T INCLUDE UNPLEASANT SURPRISES.

VD is a difficult subject to discuss.

Especially between lovers.

Unfortunately, though, it isn't at all difficult to catch. Sometimes from partners who don't even suspect they have it.

No magic pill can protect you.

But the commonsense condom can.

The condom has long been recognized both as a reliable contraceptive and as the only really effective way to minimize the risk of spreading venereal infection.

Because when you use a condom (however thin and sensitive) both of you are protected.

Condoms aren't hard to find or difficult to buy. In fact, they're available without prescription at drug stores everywhere.

So think it over.

And keep in mind that VD is the surest way in the world to bring a beautiful relationship to an ugly end.

THE COMMONSENSE CONDOM. BECAUSE SEX SHOULDN'T BE A WORRY.

Julius Schmid of Canada Scarborough, Ontario

Exhibit 1   Selected Julius Schmid Magazine Advertising

MORE AND MORE WOMEN ARE SERIOUSLY THINKING OF CHANGING TO A SPECIAL MALE CONTRACEPTIVE.

You've probably been relying on your own contraceptive ever since you first discussed birth control alternatives with your doctor.

And that can get to be worrying as time goes by.

The idea of relying on a combination of a male condom and vaginal spermicide may have seemed bothersome then.

But now there's Ramses Extra.

Ramses Extra is a fine quality latex condom which is already coated inside and out with a lubricant containing Nonoxynol-9. And Nonoxynol-9 is the spermicidal agent found in most vaginal contraceptives.

So some of the bother is gone* along with most of the worry.

You can forget about side effects, because Ramses Extra does absolutely nothing to interfere with the way nature meant your body to function.

Maybe it's time you called your doctor or your family planning clinic for another chat.

RAMSES EXTRA.
MORE PROTECTION AND A LOT LESS WORRY.

 Julius Schmid of Canada Ltd.
Scarborough, Ontario

*Ramses Extra is available without prescription at drug stores everywhere. While it should not be considered a complete substitute for the use of a condom and a separate vaginal spermicide, it does offer an important extra measure of protection without extra trouble.

Goof Proof Car Battery Boosting System*

Gordon H.G. McDougall

In early January 1994, Frank McLennan and Dean Joannou, two Ottawa-area partners had just received the feasibility study for their product, the Goof Proof battery boosting system.

"I think we should go full speed ahead and try and cover the entire market. The report shows we have a great product that is miles ahead of the competition. Let's strike while the iron is hot," said Frank.

"I agree that we have a great product," responded Dean, "but I think we should be a little more cautious. Why don't we continue to target the road service companies like the Canadian Automobile Association, see how it goes, and then decide what to do next? We don't have a lot of experience in marketing."

The product, a car battery boosting system, was designed by Dean Joannou to eliminate the problems of existing boosting systems. If a boosting system was not hooked up correctly (i.e., if the cables were placed on the wrong battery terminals), a number of problems could occur, ranging from sparking and shocks to blowing up the battery, burning out the alternator, and/or burning up the automobile's computer system. Goof Proof eliminated all these problems through several special features, which Dean Joannou had patented.

After some discussion, the partners decided to review the report and talk the next day. The report had been prepared by Alistair Macleod, an M.B.A. student, at the request of the two partners and as a favour to his father-in-law, Dean Joannou.

THE INVENTION

The evolution of the invention was based on a chance meeting between the two men in 1991. Dean Joannou, age 60, had always been an "inventor" since he graduated with a degree in electronic engineering from the University of Toronto in the late 1950s. Although he had worked with an electronics firm after graduating and for 15 years at Algonquin College as a lecturer in electronics, much of his spare time was devoted to designing/inventing products. While at the college he designed electronic air filters, assembled them in his basement and sold them to small contractors who installed them as part of a home furnace system.

In 1982, Dean Joannou left Algonquin College to devote himself to his business full-time. He took on a business partner and they set up a plant in Carlton Place, a suburb of Ottawa, to produce electronic air filters. Joannou spent most of his time on the design and engineering of a line of electronic filters while his partner handled the "business" end of the company. Their major product was an electronic air filter which was attached to a home furnace, had excellent cleaning ability and was superior to most filters on the market. It was sold only through Canadian Tire and listed in their catalogue. In 1988, Joannou and his partner had some serious disagreements over financial matters and Joannou sold his shares to his partner and left the business with a small amount of capital.

He immediately started another business to produce a series of electronic air filters which, relative to existing products, were smaller, more compact and more efficient. In the early 1990s, the business, CIMATEC, ran into financial difficulties and Joannou sold 50% of the business to venture capitalists who essentially "ran" the business while Joannou focused on research and development and producing the air filters. As of January 1994, CIMATEC had annual sales of around $2 million, 24 employees (mainly low-skilled assembly workers and 3 engineers), and small profits.

In 1991, Dean Joannou met Frank McLennan by chance through a business acquaintance. McLennan, age 55, had worked for a number of companies through the years, primarily in an accounting role. At this time,

he was looking at various options as his previous employer had gone bankrupt. When McLennan discovered Joannou was an inventor, he mentioned that his last employer had been importing a battery boosting system from Korea but the Korean manufacturer had stopped making the product. McLennan thought there was a good market for a boosting system that eliminated the "wrong hook-up" problem.

Joannou immediately set to work to design a new battery boosting system and within a month had developed a prototype. At the same time, he sold a further 20% of CIMATEC to the venture capitalist group for $100,000 and set up a separate company to handle the new product, now called Goof Proof. He and McLennan established a "gentleman's agreement" where Joannou would finance the venture and produce Goof Proof units while McLennan would invest his time and focus on marketing the product. The profits would be split 50–50 between the two partners.

Testing of the prototype identified a few "bugs" (i.e., the initial unit was so sensitive that if the clamps touched wet concrete, it would show a charge) and, after several revisions were made, Goof Proof was patented in 1992.

Goof Proof was initially designed for the industrial market, such as automobile service clubs (Exhibit 1). The system utilized "self-polarizing" technology to produce an error-free, battery boosting switch unit. Existing booster systems could cause car damage and human injury due to sparking, boosting frozen batteries, and connecting the cables in reverse polarity. Modern vehicles had sophisticated and delicate electronic components to support automotive industry standards such as electronic ignition and on-board computerization systems. This also included optional accessories such as cellular phones, computers, fax machines, and stereo systems. Reverse polarity or voltage spikes which could occur during traditional battery boosting situations could cause significant damage to these types of electronics, and repairs were often very expensive. Attempting to charge a frozen battery could result in battery explosion, thus resulting in severe operator injury. Existing boosting systems were not able to detect frozen battery conditions, which occurred approximately 0.1% of the time.

Goof Proof eliminated all of these problems through its unique design which offered several special features. The eight-pound box, approximately 175 cubic inches in size, consisted of an electrical device used to determine the polarity of a dead battery. One of its unique components, which was patented, was a reversing relay which "effects" the correct transfer of power. Likewise, the unit automatically "disconnected" the cables from the service battery when the clamps were removed. This meant the cables were not "live" before or after the boosting operation. Other features were a built-in over-voltage protection against power over 15 volts, a sounding device which let the user know when the power was on, and a safety feature that prevents the unit from "charging" a frozen battery.

Initial Marketing Efforts

In the summer of 1992, Joannou made 30 units (at an estimated cost of $45 per unit) in his basement while McLennan began marketing the product. Together they prepared a brochure (a portion of which is shown in Exhibit 1), had 3,000 printed, and got an 800 number for sales inquiries. McLennan focused his efforts on the Canadian Automobile Association (CAA) and began calling the regional offices (e.g., Ottawa, Toronto, Hamilton, Kitchener, etc.) in Ontario. While the people contacted expressed some interest, most said they were happy with their existing battery boosting system which was made for the CAA by a manufacturer and sold to the regional offices at a price of $280 per unit. McLennan did get the Kitchener office of the CAA to use one on a trial basis (at no cost) and, over the next six months, the Kitchener office purchased 4 units. McLennan then began contacting CAA offices in Manitoba and the Winnipeg office agreed to purchase six units for $280 a unit.

McLennan continued his efforts with CAA offices across Canada and also talked to various government agencies about Goof Proof. Over the next eight months he sold 6 units to the CAA in Ottawa and 3 units to the City of London at $280 per unit. He also sold 11 units to the federal Ministry of Transport at $475 per unit. As well, in the fall of 1992, he attended a road service industry show (i.e., firms that were involved in providing roadside assistance such as towing firms and those involved in supplying those firms) in Chicago and sold 16 units (the number he brought with him) at the show, at $280 per unit. The purchasers were particularly impressed when McLennan demonstrated the product and showed its "fail-safe" features. He also developed a list of possible distributors in the U.S.

In spring 1993, the Winnipeg CAA office contacted the partners and explained that, while they really liked the units, the metal case had rusted. They asked if the units could be fixed, and if they could, could the partners please sell them 12 more units. As well, some of the other units sold were sent back with the same rust problem. None of the units had ever failed in boosting batteries.

To solve the rust problem, Joannou developed a new epoxy resin case which was riveted shut. The case required the purchase of moulds at a cost of $15,000 which were provided to a plastics supplier who made the cases at a cost of $6 each. Although the new case was more expensive, Joannou redesigned the basic system so that it used cheaper components and was easier to manufacture. With the new case, the cost to produce a unit increased to $50. The rusted units were fixed and returned and Mr. McLennan began selling the new units for $297 each.

In September 1993, McLennan attended a road service industry show in Waterloo, Ontario. During the three-day show he conducted numerous demonstrations of Goof Proof. After finishing each demonstration for an individual or small group, he asked those present to complete a questionnaire. As an incentive, everyone who completed a questionnaire would be entered into a draw to win a Goof Proof unit. Over the three days, 70 questionnaires were completed and the results are provided in Exhibit 2. McLennan was encouraged by the results of the survey and thought that future prospects were promising. He sold 15 units at the show.

In September, Goof Proof received some public relations exposure through a newspaper interview (Exhibit 3). In addition, *Towing* magazine approached McLennan regarding a feature article on battery boosting in an upcoming issue. By the end of September, McLennan

EXHIBIT 1
Goof Proof Switch Unit

GOOF PROOF BOOSTING

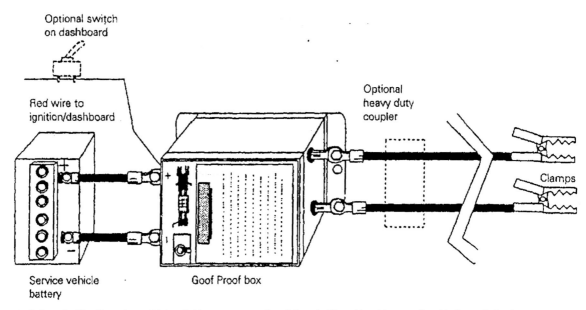

Optional switch
on dashboard

Red wire to
ignition/dashboard

Optional
heavy duty
coupler

Clamps

Service vehicle
battery

Goof Proof box

Easily installed in all service vehicles. Add remote control and detachable cables. Very easily added to existing booster carts.

Eliminate Your Boosting Liability
Install The World's First Error-Free,
Automatic Boosting System

GOOF PROOF BOOSTING SYSTEMS Inc. introduces a radically new, **SELF-POLARIZING** system that will become a new standard for service vehicles and boosting carts. It is error-free, simple to use, very quick to operate and provides complete safety to the operator and vehicles.

This ingenious system boasts an electronic device which makes the correct connections. What results is the world's first "goof proof", **AUTOMATIC battery boosting.**

The Goof Proof system has these advantages:

1. **Both clamps are the same colour.** The service mechanic does not have to worry about making the right connections.
2. The mechanic's **safety is increased** because a rugged relay connects a few seconds after both clamps are attached. Also there can be no sparking because the first electrical contact is made inside the unit.
3. Much **time is saved** in setting the clamps and in storing the equipment after boosting.
4. The unit automatically disconnects the cables from the service battery when the clamps are removed. Therefore **the cables are not "live" after the boosting operation.**
5. The mechanic is forced to use the automatic feature.

6. The sensitive electronics ensures that **all batteries can be boosted.** Even the ones that have very little charge left in them. (about 1/50 volts)
7. High current capacity — **600 amps for 30 seconds.**
8. A sounder is activated when power is delivered to the clamps. This makes the system **very user-friendly.**
9. There is a built in **over-voltage protection** against power over 16 volts.
10. The unit is in a splashproof box that can be mounted on all types of service vehicles.
11. Using the system results in **50% saving in boosting time.**

LOWER OPERATING COSTS:

Lower operating costs result because even inexperienced personnel can operate this system quickly and safely. Service staff, service vehicles and client vehicles are better utilized. **Very expensive errors are avoided automatically and quickly.** Wear and tear on cables and clamps are reduced.

To purchase this new technology, please contact GOOF PROOF BOOSTING SYSTEMS Inc.
Phone: (613) 253-4140, Fax: (613) 253-0407

EXHIBIT 2
Win a "Goof Proof"
Questionnaire

1. Do you feel that Goof Proof's self-polarization feature is of value to you and your business?

   YES 69 (98.6%)   NO 1 (1.4%)

2. Boosting is what percentage of your service calls?

0%	2 (2.9%)
0–15%	19 (27.1%)
15–25%	27 (38.6%)
25–40%	9 (12.9%)
over 40%	13 (18.6%)

3. As a result of boosting, have you had the unfortunate experience of becoming part of a liability situation?

   YES 3 (4.3%)   NO 67 (95.7%)

4. Do you presently have some mechanical means of protecting yourself against boosting a dead battery?

   YES 18 (25.7%)   NO 52 (74.3%)

5. Would you consider or do you own a vehicle specifically for boosting?

   YES 21 (30.0%)   NO 47 (61.1%)   BLANK 2 (2.9%)

6. Did you know that Goof Proof determines the condition of the battery to be boosted and can tell you when a vehicle should be towed as opposed to boosted?

   YES 60 (85.7%)   NO 9 (12.9%)   BLANK 1 (1.4%)

7. On what percentage of service calls do you experience a "dead" battery?

0%	7 (10.0%)	BLANK 5 (7.1%)
0–15%	34 (48.6%)	
15–25%	8 (11.4%)	
25–40%	8 (11.4%)	
over 40%	8 (11.4%)	

8. Is the Goof Proof protection feature of a built-in over-voltage (against power over 15 volts) a valuable feature?

   YES 62 (88.6%)   NO 4 (5.7%)   BLANK 4 (5.7%)

9. Would you agree that the features of Goof Proof offer a high degree of safety when boosting?

   YES 68 (97.1%)   NO 0   BLANK 2 (2.9%)

10. Will you buy a Goof Proof at $297.00 plus delivery and taxes?

   YES 47 (67.1%)   NO 12 (17.1%)   BLANK 3 (4.3%)

   MAYBE 4 (5.7%)   If less by $100.00 4 (5.7%)

had distributed over 2,800 of the 3,000 brochures (Exhibit 1) that were prepared the previous year. The brochures were sent to everyone who had called the 800 number, to all the CAA offices in Canada, and to anyone who had shown an interest in Goof Proof at the industry shows McLennan had attended.

Through fall 1993, sales grew to 20 to 30 units a month to various CAA offices, small towing firms, and individual tow truck operators. During this time Joannou had continued to assemble the units in his basement (all the components could be purchased from nearby

suppliers), but the level of sales required him to change this approach. By the end of 1993, he had outside contractors do most of the assembly and he did the final, now relatively simple, assembly in his basement.

During the fall, the partners also changed their financial arrangements. They agreed that Joannou, who owned the company, and had invested approximately $50,000 in the venture to this point in time (including the moulds for the cases which cost $15,000, promotional material, and trade show expenses), would keep the company and sell the units to McLennan for

EXHIBIT 3
Newspaper Article

Charleton Place men all charged up over new battery boosting system

LOOKING FOR THE RIGHT CONNECTION?

By Dianne Pinder-Moss
Staff Writer

If you want a real boost when you boost your vehicle, two Carleton Place men feel they have the right connection.

Frank McLennan and Dean Joannou are all charged up over their new invention — a "goof proof" boosting system.

The entrepreneurs claim this is the world's first error-free automatic boosting system.

"There's no wrong way to hook this thing up," McLennan explains.

"That's why the clamps are of the same color. They can be interchanged. It's a radically different technology."

With most boosting systems, if they are not operated correctly, there can be problems with sparking, shocks, etc., McLennan points out. He adds the dangers of boosting incorrectly are magnified in new vehicles which have many electronic parts.

"If you put a reverse polarity in a new car, it will blow up the battery, burn out the alternator, burn out the computer and burn out the digital readouts," he says.

According to McLennan, these risks disappear with the Goof Proof.

"This eliminates any sparking, any expensive errors and eliminates all fear," he says. "It eliminates your boosting liability."

So what gives the Goof Proof a boost over its counterparts? McLennan and Joannou will tell you the unit has several special features.

The eight-lb. box, approximately 175 cubic inches in size, consists of an electrical device used to determine the polarity of a dead battery. One of its unique components is a reversing relay which "effects" the correct transfer of power.

Likewise, the unit automatically disconnects the cables from the service battery when the clamps are removed. That means the cables are not "live" before or after the boosting operation.

Other features are a built-in over-voltage protection against power over 15 volts and a sounding device which lets the user know when the power is on.

"It's a very useful feature," McLennan says, "because you can't see power move."

If you're wondering what prompted McLennan and his partner to design such a product, it was McLennan's previous work in selling a similar "high quality" unit that was developed in Korea.

When his Korean associate stopped production, he decided to see if there was any way of re-inventing this technology in Canada.

In 1991, he met Joannou who brought the idea "to life."

Joannou, who has done several electro-mechanical designs over the years, says the project went rather quickly with a working model of the Goof Proof being completed in a few months.

Of course, like any first-time effort, there were some minor bugs that needed to be ironed out. For instance, the initial units were so sensitive that if the clamps touched wet concrete, they would show a charge. That was quickly corrected.

Currently, the Goof Proof, which was patented on April 7, 1992, is only available in the marketplace in an industrial version.

Units have been sold to several road sevice businesses. The Canadian Automobile Association (CAA) branches in Kitchener and Winnipeg and the Ministry of Transportation's road service operation in Toronto have been among the customers.

When contacted Thursday by *The EMC*, the fleet supervisor of CAA Midwestern (Ontario) only had positive things to say about the boosting system.

"So far, we love it," Henry Freriks said, citing the many safety benefits of the Goof Proof.

Along with eliminating a common problem for CAA drivers of being accused of hooking up the cables improperly, he pointed out that they also no longer have to worry about accidentally "spiking" the computer technology in new vehicles during a boost.

Likewise, Freriks said it was not unusual for CAA drivers in the past to forget to disconnect cables after a boost or the cables would inadvertently touch one another resulting in small fires or the cables shorting out.

"The Goof Proof is dead when it is (being) hooked up and dead when it is taken off," he said.

While CAA Midwestern currently has four of these systems in use, the fleet supervisor hopes to have all the branch's approximately 30 vehicles equipped by next year. In working towards this target, the CAA branch has been adding a new Goof Proof to its fleet each month.

Based on the success of the industrial unit, McLennan and Joannou are now intent on making their product available to all drivers.

The retail version is expected to be on store shelves by Christmas, 1994.

Already, they are working on designing the unit.

"We know how to make it more efficient and effective," McLennan said. "The whole design will be different but the technology will be the same."

Eventually, the entrepreneurs hope to have the Goof Proof boosting vehicles across Canada as well as in the U.S., Europe and Japan. "We want to become a world-scale supplier of this new technology here in Carleton Place," McLennan said.

Source: Story reproduced from *The Record News*. EMC article by staff writer Dianne Pinder-Moss.

$100 each. McLennan would then be responsible for marketing the product. At that time, future expenses for the venture were not discussed. Both men remained very interested in the product.

On many occasions, Joannou had discussed the product with his son-in-law, Alistair Macleod. Macleod, a school teacher, was taking his M.B.A. on a part-time basis at an Ontario university. Joannou asked him if he could help sort out how they might market the product. In September 1993, Macleod agreed to do a feasibility study and over the next few months collected information, prepared the report, and submitted it to the partners in December. What follows are selected aspects of that report, beginning with a list of benefits that Goof Proof would offer the market (Exhibit 4), followed by information on the competition, target buyers, financial aspects and marketing decisions.

EXHIBIT 4
Benefits of Goof Proof

Self-polarizing:	The unit senses the polarity of the connection and switches an internal relay to ensure a correct connection every time.
Safety:	The design prohibits the boosting of frozen batteries. It will not allow the mechanic to bypass an automatic feature which disconnects after boosting. The cables are not live before or after the boosting operation and no sparking can occur. A sounder is activated when power is delivered to the clamps.
Easy to Use:	Time is saved in setting the clamps on the battery and in storing the equipment after boosting. Both clamps included with the switch unit are coated in highly visible yellow plastic so that the service mechanic does not have to worry about making the right connections. The colour facilitates night use. No special user training is required.
Quality:	The switch unit to be introduced into the market is the third generation of the product. Design upgrades have resulted from test marketing: changes include the use of plastic casing to replace the metal cases of earlier models, and in assembly, which consists of precision injection-moulded parts that snap together.
Rugged:	The product is encased in a splash-proof box for mounting on all types of service vehicles.

Reliable:	The prototypes have never failed to make a correct polarity connection.
Options:	The basic product offered will be the switch unit with the same-colour clamps. The unit can also be provided with heavy gauge cables, battery, booster cart, and light upon request.
Brand Name:	The product will be known as Goof Proof, symbolizing the error-free connections made every time battery boosting is performed.
Warranties:	All test units returned for repair have been satisfactorily serviced and were promptly returned to the customer. On this basis, defective units can be returned for repair with labour and parts costs assumed by Goof Proof. It has been estimated that the return rate will be less than 1%. All users should be offered a money back guarantee.

COMPETITION

The Goof Proof system has four major competitors, including the standard booster cable. The strengths and weaknesses of each are summarized in Exhibit 5.

EXHIBIT 5
Competition Analysis

1. The FOX START System

The Product:	This system is a polarity protection device made in the United States and sold in Canada under the "Canadian" label. It includes two supply batteries, three 25-foot cables, a manual trigger switch, and a watertight metal control panel. The selling price is approximately $800.
Strengths:	FOX START checks the polarity of battery connections. After connection, the operator looks at an indicator light on a control panel to see if the polarity is correct. When the connections are correct, the operator activates a trigger to transfer the power. The American Automobile Association recommends this system.
Weaknesses:	This system is complicated, requiring two supply batteries which are mounted on back of the service truck. A lengthy connection is needed from the back of the truck to the alternator. FOX START won't operate if "dead" battery has less than 1.5 volts. The cables are awkward and are too long. The device requires manual intervention which will lead to liability claims. Price is high.

2. REVOLT

The Product: This polarity protection system is manufactured by Reid Electric in Montreal. Its selling price is $600, including cables and clamps.

Strengths: Polarity protection is given to the user.

Weaknesses: REVOLT will not boost batteries with less than 2.0 volts. Price is relatively high.

3. Solenoid-Based Polarity Protection Device

The Product: CAA makes this device for their service vehicles. The manufacturing cost to CAA is $200 per unit, not including servicing costs.

Strengths: The cost of the unit itself is the least expensive of all alternatives.

Weaknesses: Operators do not like them as they are awkward, slow to use, and only work 80% of the time. The solenoids eventually burn out and repair includes sending the truck to the site, therefore losing the use of the entire vehicle.

4. Consumer Booster Cables

Strengths: These cables are economical and easy to handle. They can be used by all markets, including the consumer market.

Weaknesses: They do not offer any safety features.

Aside from the standard booster cables, the competing products are costly, unreliable, and are frequently difficult to use. In comparison to these devices, the most significant advantage of the Goof Proof system is that, since no manual decision making is required, the insurance liability of roadside-assistance operators is reduced to virtually zero, resulting in a significant saving for the Goof Proof customer. In addition, testing of competitors' products shows that the polarity detection devices do not function when the battery voltage is below 2.0 volts (which occurs in 20% of all cases). This leads to operator dissatisfaction, since the reliability of the device is questioned each time it does not function properly.

The standard booster cables are obviously more economical, but such devices do not satisfactorily address the safety, reliability, and liability concerns of potential customers.

TARGET BUYERS

The primary target customers are those in the road service industry who offer automotive services to the public and those who transport people and/or goods via roads and highways.

Through their large coast-to-coast networks, automobile clubs such as the CAA and roadside assistance programs offered by the major car manufacturers present the most attractive segments since they are easily identified and since their needs are most completely met by the Goof Proof technology. It is estimated that, in total, the CAA has a fleet of approximately 2,000 vehicles. In addition, other road service companies have a total fleet of about 16,000 vehicles. It is estimated that the U.S. market would be 10 times the size of the Canadian market.

In conducting his research Macleod interviewed the road service manager of the CAA Kitchener office. The service manager had taken one unit on a trial basis in the late summer of 1992 and had purchased a number of units since that time. During the interview Macleod learned the following:

- The service manager was very positive about Goof Proof. He said that Goof Proof, when used properly, worked every time. To be used properly, first the Goof Proof unit had to be hooked up to the battery, then turned on. This required the driver to walk back to the truck to turn it on. In some instances, the tow truck operator had turned on the unit before hooking it up, and the unit "picked up" a small electrical charge from the operator. Then, when it was hooked up, a "dead" battery would register as a "live" battery, and charging would begin. At times, the consequence was a power "spike" that "fried" the computer components in the car.
- Each year, the problem of "spiking" dead batteries was increasing with the installation of more computer components within automobiles. The service manager felt that pre-1990 cars did not have this problem but from 1992 on, the cars were "loaded" with computer components.
- The service manager planned to install Goof Proof in all 35 of CAA-Kitchener's trucks on a phased basis. To date, he had purchased 14 units. In addition to owning and operating 35 trucks, CAA-Kitchener also contracted with 12 towing companies in the Kitchener region to handle road service. The service manag-

er had informed all 12 companies about the benefits of Goof Proof but only two had purchased units on a trial basis. He said the cost, $300, was a drawback but he also said that many of the independent operators were from the "old school" and didn't think that "spiking" was a problem. He said it was easier for these operators to keep the $300 "in their pockets."

- When asked about the Goof Proof company, the service manager said they could probably advertise a little more. When ordering a unit, he just called them up and the unit was there within a week.

Macleod also interviewed the Kitchener regional manager for CAA. The summary comments from the interview were:

- The regional manager was very impressed with Goof Proof and felt there was no equivalent competing product.
- He felt that the 17 CAA regional offices should all be interested in Goof Proof but that each office ran its own show and made their own purchasing decisions. As an example, he noted that one regional office might purchase Ford trucks while the adjacent regional office would purchase Chrysler trucks for their respective fleets. He said that the CAA was kind of a disjointed operation with each regional office doing "its own thing."
- Regarding tow truck operators who CAA contracted for service in smaller communities, he said the operators ranged from those who were on the "cutting edge of technology" with up-to-date equipment, to operators, often in very small communities, who had "ratty old trucks" and were not interested in spending any money to improve their service.
- He felt that "tow shows" were poorly organized and run and pointed out there was no overall association for the road service industry in Canada.
- He thought the marketing efforts for Goof Proof could be improved as he didn't see or hear much about the company or their product. He thought a "better" price for Goof Proof, somewhere below $300, would improve sales.

Macleod also talked to a manager at the Ottawa CAA office, which acted as a clearing house for the 17 member clubs. The manager provided the following information:

- The 17 member clubs were very independent with each having their own membership base; in total the CAA had 3.7 million members.
- The Ottawa CAA had 20 trucks and two towing firms on contract, each with between 30 and 50 trucks.
- He estimated that in total, across Canada, the CAA had contracts with 2,000 towing firms, who he thought had an average of 3 trucks each.
- He had not heard of Goof Proof.

MARKET MIX DECISIONS

In preparing the report, Macleod had given some thought to the various marketing mix decisions. With respect to pricing, he established an upper limit on the price by considering the value of the unit to potential customers; in particular to the segment offering roadside assistance. At a minimum, the product reduces the insurance liability of these companies to virtually zero. Using this fact as a basis for pricing, Exhibit 6 suggests an upper limit on the selling price of $500 for the boosting unit. The lower limit could be anything over variable costs which were $50 per unit.

EXHIBIT 6

Upper Limit on Selling Price

Average cost of an insurance claim for improper boosting	$ 1,500
Total cost per year in mid-west Ontario region (@ 1 claim/two weeks)	39,000
Total cost of insurance claims over a five-year period (expected useful life of a booster unit is five years)	195,000
Total cost of insurance claims per service vehicle (189 vehicles in mid-west Ontario region)	1,031
Present value of $1,031.00 over five years at 10% interest/yr.	702
Less 30% "incentive to purchase" discount	202
Upper limit on selling price:	500

Macleod saw two possible distribution channels. The first, which was very similar to current efforts, would be direct selling to larger groups such as the automobile associations who are likely to provide repeat purchases and gradually equip their trucks with Goof Proof. This would take advantage of centralized purchasing functions by the auto clubs (where they were present) and the existing 800 number for sales inquiries.

The second channel would require independent distributors, preferably existing companies within the automotive supply industry. A selective approach to the use of distributors would be taken with a view towards achieving adequate national distribution relatively quickly. One example of a possible distributor would be Snap-On Tools of Canada who have a fleet of trucks that visit their customers. Although Snap-On Tools' main products are wrenches and tools for mechanics of all types, one of their main markets is automobile mechanics. Typical margins on selling prices for distributors to the automotive trade were around 45%.

A number of other companies supplied equipment to garages and would be suitable for handling Goof Proof. There might be up to 10 distributors who regularly call on service stations, some on a regional and some on a national basis, who could handle the product. However, further investigation would be required to ascertain the suitability of the distributors and their willingness to carry Goof Proof.

Because of the changes in the partner's financial arrangements, Macleod did not prepare a budget for 1994. Instead he provided a list of estimated costs (Exhibit 7) and made the following comments.

- Advertising could be directed through trade magazines originating in the United States and would be expected to spill over into Canada as there were no equivalent Canadian magazines to reach those operating in the road service industry.
- A dedicated salesperson could handle incoming orders as well as introduce the product to potential customers. Personal selling would also take place through trade shows held regionally across Canada and the United States. Each year

EXHIBIT 7

Estimated Marketing and Other Costs

Advertising

One-half page ad in *Towing* or *American Tower* (monthly U.S. magazines)	$1,800	

Selling

1-800 number	1,050	per month
Person to answer "800" number	1,500	per month
Dedicated salesperson (salary and benefits)	5,800	per month
Travel expenses for salesperson		
— car	750	per month
— travel (meals, hotels)	1,000	per month
Trade shows		
— in Canada	3,000	per show
— in United States	5,000	per show

Office

Telephone	1,000	per month
Fax	500	per month
Postage	250	per month
Office supplies	350	per month

there were two trade shows in Canada and three in the U.S. that focused on the road service industry. As shown through experience at the trade shows, providing demonstrations greatly increased the likelihood of purchase.

- Offering units on a trial basis could be considered at a cost of $600 per trial to Goof Proof.
- If an office was established at CIMATEC, Joannou's company, to handle the Goof Proof product, total costs would be in the order of $2,100 per month.

Macleod ended the report with the following observations:

- The boosting system must be rugged to withstand frequent use as well as all types of weather. A high degree of product reliability is also crucial; it is unlikely that users will adopt the device unless it functions without error in repeated use.
- Goof Proof has a solution which meets all customer needs with its new "self-polarizing" technology, a switching unit with the potential to be the standard for the market segments identified. It is virtually error-free, easy to use, and is safe

for both the operator and all vehicles.

- The average age of registered automobiles on the road has increased to a level which is in excess of the average life expectancy of a battery, which is about five years. This trend enhances the likelihood of a continued active road service industry.
- A distribution channel has not been established to date; the ultimate success of this venture hinges on the development of an effective distribution network.
- Goof Proof represents a new product entering an existing market which is underdeveloped, judging by the small number of similar products available and their limited success. None of these competing products have greater than an 80% functioning rate. The "self-polarizing" concept and prototypes, in contrast, have *never failed* during the product introductory phase. New, improved designs have resulted from listening carefully to customer concerns and queries.
- In the long term, diversification of Goof Proof technology into portable industrial units and retail consumer models will be necessary to maintain a high rate of growth.
- Expansion into foreign markets will be necessary to continue the strong growth of Goof Proof due to the relatively small size of the Canadian market. Expansion will occur after the product is launched nationwide in Canada and after the first results of the distribution system and customer demand have been evaluated.
- A marketing program should be set up in 1994. The sales representative should initiate direct selling to service clubs and associations. The CAA is impressed with the device and has stated that it is willing to support the company by providing the mailing lists of all contracted road service operators across Canada. A concerted effort should be made to similarly access all service agencies.
- The sales representative should coordinate promotions at trade shows and road service educational seminars across Canada as well as advertising in towing magazines. As well, several automotive supply chains should be contracted to carry the product country-wide (e.g., Snap-on Tools).

THE DECISION

The next day the two partners met to discuss future plans for Goof Proof. Frank McLennan began the discussion, "I'm still in favour of going full-speed ahead. Let's start advertising, hire a full-time salesperson to cover Canada. I'll start on the U.S. market and you can get the units ready to be shipped out. We've got a winner."

Dean Joannou responded, "I agree this looks very promising but I still think we should be more cautious. Let's keep costs down to begin with by going slow and see how things go."

After considerable debate, McLennan said, "I'll put together a marketing plan for 1994 with some sales projections and costs. It will take about two days. Let's talk again when I've finished the plan."

The two agreed and McLennan began preparing the plan.

FORUM DES ARTS

"Denis, it has to be your call. This show matches our mission statement and exposes Forum des Arts to a young audience. I'm all for it," said Cassie Tichbourne, Director of Marketing. "In my heart, I'm for it too. But I have a responsibility to watch how we spend taxpayer dollars. This show could lose thirty or forty thousand dollars. At that level, we might be better off canceling the performance." These sentiments came from Henri Robillard, Director of Finance and Administration. Both viewpoints were being weighed by the Chief Executive Officer of Forum des Arts, Denis Fournier. The future of the Hozier concert had come up at the weekly Monday morning management meeting of March 14, 2016. The concert was scheduled for Friday, March 25 so he had to make a decision quickly.

The Deal

On Tuesday, February 23, 2016, a major Canadian promoter called with an offer to book Hozier for a concert at Forum des Arts on Friday, March 25, 2016 at 8:00 p.m. He believed he could get the show for Ottawa while booking a second show in Montreal at the Stage du Musique for Saturday, March 26. This promoter often booked stadium or arena acts like Eminem, Cher, Billy Joel, Elton John, and Madonna. As another division booked smaller acts, this call had come "out of the blue" and he required an answer within twenty-four hours.

Staff were quite pleased with the offer. Hozier was a name they recognized. Andrew Hozier-Byrne, known professionally as Hozier, was an Irish musician, singer and songwriter. He released a debut EP, featuring the hit single *"Take Me to Church"*, in 2013. It reached number one on iTunes on October 25, 2013. He followed this success with a second EP, *"From Eden,"* in early 2014. His debut studio album, *Hozier*, was released in Ireland in September 2014 and globally in October 2014. In the fall of 2014, he performed for the Victoria's Secret Fashion Show, *Saturday Night Live*, and *Late Night with Seth Meyers*.

To get further information, staff called a couple of record stores and radio stations. These sources confirmed that Hozier appealed to a younger audience (12 to 35) but that his music crossed many boundaries. Fans could view his work as Alternative, Rhythm & Blues, Adult Contemporary, Pop, or Rock. His latest album was selling well and one record store employee speculated on a response from students attending University of Ottawa, Carleton University, and Algonquin College. "End of term is a great time for a party."

While this data was gathered, staff from the Finance Department began to calculate a breakeven point for the event. (See Table 1) Forum des Arts could seat 2,191 patrons including ten positions for people in wheelchairs. Past experience suggested two ticket prices: one price for the

----

orchestra section, first balcony and the first rows of the second balcony (1,909 seats) and a second price for the rear part of the second balcony and wheelchair locations (282 seats). Ticket prices were quoted to the public with the Federal Goods and Services Tax (G.S.T.) and a capital improvement fund (C.I.F.) surcharge included. The latter was a $2.00 per ticket surcharge which was accumulated to pay for capital improvements to the Forum des Arts building. While the promoter had suggested a top ticket price of $60, staff felt more comfortable with prices of $55.50 and $51.50. SOCAN fees covered royalties to song-writers.

Table 1   **Hozier Concert - Breakeven Analysis**

Revenue:	1909 seats @ $55.50	$105,950
	282 seats @ $51.50	14,523
	Less: C.I.F.	4,382
	G.S.T.	8,433
Net Revenue:		$107,658
Fixed Expenses:	Main Act – Talent Fee	$60,000
	Advertising/Promotion	$ 8,150
	Production Cost (Ushers,	
	Cleaning, Stage Hands)	$10,000
Variable Expenses:	SOCAN	$2,013
	Credit Card Fees	$3,614
Total Variable Expenses		$5,627

Break-Even Point is ($78,150 + $5,627)/$107,658 = 78% of seats

Awards and Recognition

As a single, "*Take Me to Church*" reached number one on the Italian and Belgian music charts. It reached number two in Canada, the United States, United Kingdom, Australia, Germany, New Zealand, the Netherlands, and Ireland. On December 5, 2014, it was announced that " *Take Me to Church*" was nominated at the 57th Annual Grammy Awards for Song of the Year. Though he did not win a Grammy, he performed "*Take Me to Church*" with Annie Lennox at the award ceremony which happened in March, 2015.

Later in 2015, he performed the song at the *2015 Billboard Music Awards*. At that show, Hozier won Top Rock Artist and Top Rock Song for 2015. At the 2015 BBC Music Awards, he was nominated but did not win as International Artist of the Year but "*Take Me to Church*" did win Song of the Year. The song was nominated but did not win Best Rock Video at the 2015 MTV Music Awards. In mid-summer, "*Take Me to Church*" won Choice Rock Song at the American Teen Choice awards. On November12, 2015, he won the VH1 Artist of the Year, based on fan votes. He performed "*Take Me to Church*" and The Beatles' "*Blackbird*" with singer Tori Kelly at the awards show. In January, 2016, it was announced that the album "Hozier" was nominated as International Album of the Year at the Canadian Juno Awards which would happen in April, 2016.

In 2016, Hozier released the video for the song *"Cherry Wine"* to raise awareness of domestic violence. In January, 2016, he announced a new song *"Better Love"* would be included in *The Legend of Tarzan* soundtrack. An official video would be included with the movie when it was released on DVD.

The Booking Decision

All of this information was presented by Cassie Tichbourne to Denis Fournier on February 26, 2016. The two talked about the act, the potential for ticket sales, and the local market. The act fulfilled three mandates as specified in the corporate mission statement. (See Exhibit 1) Satisfied that the risk was worth taking and that Forum des Arts would likely break even on the concert, Cassie received direction to confirm the booking with the promoter.

Exhibit 1   Forum des Arts Corporate Mission Statement

1. *To maintain, operate, manage, and promote Forum des Arts on behalf of the City of Ottawa.*

2. *To have a positive impact on the economic health of the area through the increased use of hotels, restaurants, retail shops and services, by using the facility as the catalyst to retain local spending, and attract people from outside the region.*

3. *To maximize the use of the facility, while providing programming that reflects local interests, and contributes to the quality of life.*

4. *Via effective, efficient management to constantly work towards maintaining the 2003 subsidization by the corporation of the City of Ottawa at or below the current rate of inflation.*

5. *All of this is to be achieved while pursuing excellence of management and service, in a manner that fosters local pride and enhances the City's reputation and image.*

Cassie tried to contact the promoter that day but they did not connect. Confirmation of the performance was not made until February 29. A preliminary copy of the contract was forwarded. While each contract was different in some of its details, nothing in the twenty-five pages seemed out of the ordinary. The price was stipulated in the contract with half due when the contract was signed and the other half due on the night of the performance.

On Wednesday, March 2, an opening act was found. Wouter Andre De Backer, better known as *Gotye* (pronounced *GO-tee-ay*), was an Australian-Belgian multi-instrumentalist and singer-songwriter. He was best known for the single *"Somebody That I Used to Know."* In February, 2013, he won the Grammy Award for Record of the Year and Best Pop Duo/Group Performance for the song. He also won the Best Alternative Music Album for *"Making Mirrors"* on which that song was featured. The video for the song was originally released on

Vimeo and YouTube where it has been viewed 815 million times. In 2013, the single reached number one on the iTune charts in 46 countries.

The presence of a high profile, youth-oriented artist could only enhance the concert even though the artist's reasonable performance fee ($10,000) was an unbudgeted extra cost.

Also on March 2, the details of the advertising budget were confirmed. Three media were to be used. Ads would be placed in the Ottawa Citizen - the local daily newspaper. This paper published two special entertainment sections: "City Lights" on Thursdays and "Weekend" on Sundays. As can be seen in Table 2, these special sections would be used for maximum profile for the event.

Radio would also be used. MAJIC 100, an adult contemporary Ottawa-based station, had a package of promotional spots. For $1,200, the station would "present" the concert. In return, the station would provide extra unpaid advertising. Forum des Arts staff also identified a local dance radio station, KOOL-FM, and agreed to supply it with 24 tickets for "give-aways" in return for promoting the show.

Finally, Forum des Arts staff identified six local night clubs/discos: Topaz, The Pit, Ozzie's, Roxanne's, Woodsy's, and The Watering Hole. Forum des Arts agreed to supply each club with four tickets to "give-away" in return for promoting the show. In addition, 5,000 flyers were to be printed for $145. Some were to be placed in record stores. Some more would be sent to each of the six local dance clubs while the remainder would be placed under the windshield wipers of patron's cars parked in each club's parking lot.

Table 2   Newspaper Advertising for Hozier Concert in The Ottawa Citizen

Date	Columns X Lines	Cost per Column-Line	Cost	Section
Thurs, Mar. 10	3 x 100	$2.98	$ 894	City Lights
Fri, Mar. 11	3 x 100	$1.655	$ 497	Entertainment
Sun, Mar. 13	3 x 100	$3.61	$1,083	Weekend
Mon, Mar. 14	3 x 100	$1.655	$ 497	Entertainment
Sun, Mar. 20	2 x 65	$3.61	$ 469	Weekend
Mon, Mar. 21	2 x 65	$1.655	$ 215	Entertainment
			$3,655	

With these details confirmed, the contract was signed on Thursday, March 3. Tickets for both the Ottawa and Montreal shows were to go on sale on Monday, March 7.

The First Week of Sales

At both the Forum des Arts box office and at Ticketmaster outlets, sales the first day were disappointing. Forum des Arts staff contacted the promoter and were surprised to find Ottawa's sales figures to be slightly ahead of Montreal's. With the Easter season moving into full gear, information about the concert might not yet have reached the intended audience. Both groups decided to avoid passing judgement on ticket sales until after the first week of sales.

By Monday, March 14, the concert appeared to be in trouble. Over 1,700 seats had to be sold for the event to break even and sales had not yet reached half that number. (See Table 3) Forum des Arts staff decided to increase publicity for the event.

Lynn Saxberg, the pop music critic for the Ottawa Citizen, agreed to do a feature story about Hozier in the March 17 edition of City Lights. MAJIC 100 agreed to do telephone interviews with Hozier and Gotye during the week of March 21. MAJIC 100 had also agreed to "give-away" a pair of tickets during each of the last seven days before the concert. CJOH-TV was willing to do interviews with Hozier and Gotye. The latter would be interviewed on March 24 and the interview would include a video and a live performance. Management for Hozier was not certain about the live interview and felt it could be organized no earlier than the day of the concert. A press release was sent to all print, radio and television media in Eastern Ontario and the Outaouais region in Quebec in the hopes of generating news stories and free publicity.

Table 3   Day by Day Sales for Hozier Concert

Date	Number of Tickets Sold
Mar. 7	365
Mar. 8	580
Mar. 9	626
Mar. 10	663
Mar. 11	681
Mar. 12	714
Mar. 13	738

The Meeting

Every Monday morning, there was a Forum des Arts management meeting attended by the CEO (Denis Fournier), the Director of Finance and Administration (Henri Robillard), the Director of Marketing (Cassie Tichbourne) and the Director of Operations (Nikolai Litau). The first topic of the March 14 meeting was the Hozier concert.

"How are the ticket sales for the concert?", Denis asked.

"As of Sunday, March 13, we had sold 738 tickets not including any complimentary tickets given away as part of our promotional effort," Cassie responded.

"Wow. That's nowhere near our break-even point." Denis paused and thought for a second. "What are our options here?"

Henri Robillard was the first to speak. "We could cancel the show. The management group for Hozier already has half the money from us and I think we could negotiate with them on the remaining monies so that our loss could be kept to less than the performance fee. Think of the money they could earn from doing nothing! And I doubt they would want Hozier to play to a near-empty house a short time before the Juno Awards."

"I agree," Nik Litau said. "I thought this show was better suited to a bar. Forum des Arts has too many rules for the crowd he attracts. You know what I mean? They have to sit in their seats - no dancing in the aisles. There is no alcohol or smoking in the theatre itself. And thank goodness we have those restrictions as you can imagine the damage the audience could do to our upholstered chairs and carpets. This alternative music is just not appropriate to our venue. I don't know why he was booked in the first place."

"I disagree with Henri's scenario. Legally we haven't got a leg to stand on. The contract specifies a talent fee and they don't have to take anything less. Also we have committed advertising dollars and staff time to this project which would be lost. Canceling would also require more advertising to tell patrons about the canceled date and informing them about ticket refunds. As Marketing Director, I would prefer a different approach."

"Continue," Denis said.

"Ottawa has the reputation of being a 'walk-up' city. Translation - patrons just don't like to buy tickets in advance. You remember that NBA exhibition game last year. The Ottawa Civic Centre sold 7,000 of 13,000 tickets on the day of the game and I am sure you remember the hassles at the ticket windows. I believe our promotional strategies are working. We are in the Easter season and people may not be willing to commit to this show until they are sure they have the time. I bet we will have a big day-of-sale walk-up. All of our publicity work is supporting the last minute walk-up what with the newspaper, radio and television interviews, ticket giveaways and promotions at bars and clubs."

"Sure. And if the walk-up doesn't materialize we are stuck with little box office revenue, talent fees and the costs of mounting the show," added Henri. "Also imagine the newspaper reviews of the show. We have been stung before by poor attendance. And you know how the city councillors react to being called bush league. We are already receiving a subsidy from the City of Ottawa of over $800,000. If we blow a bundle here, we are guilty of fiscal mismanagement."

"Cassie does have a point, Henri. We're obligated for the talent fees. About 40% of the production costs are items over which we have some control. As we won't use the entire theatre, I can cut back on ushers and maybe there are a few other costs we can manage. The current box office revenue covers these expenses. Any additional revenue could go toward the talent fees. Even a poorly attended concert might be a better financial proposition than one which is canceled," Nik said.

"I hate to muddy the water but I just had another brainstorm," Cassie interrupted. "What if we paper the house?"

"You know my opposition to giving away blocks of free tickets," Henri retorted. "It can cause a lot of ill-will and complaints when paying customers find out they are sitting beside people who did not pay for their tickets. Some patrons demand a refund and when we don't give one, there are letters to city councillors and the local newspapers."

"Sure, that's one possibility," added Cassie. "But my records show that the average patron spends $10.00 at the concession areas in the lobby. They purchase liquor, wine, beer, soft drinks or the gourmet cookies and ice cream we stock. Our mark-up on cost is 100% so we stand to clear $5.00 per patron even if they haven't purchased a ticket. That could be several thousand dollars toward our bottom line. Unfortunately, we don't get any revenue from t-shirts or promotional programs sold by the act. But if we target an audience which rarely visits Forum des Arts, these free tickets could be an investment in audience development."

"Generally, I would agree," said Nik. "But remember the time of the year. If we have a sudden snow storm or freezing rain, all those people could really mess up the place. The additional cleaning costs and the lack of savings from having a full complement of ushers on hand could completely use up the additional revenues you just found!"

Denis had been quiet during the discussion. A good CEO lets his staff debate the merits of the options before him. Cassie turned to Denis. "There may be some other options we haven't considered but there you have the most likely scenarios. The concert is eleven days away and we should act today if any adjustment to our plans is to be made. How do you want to proceed?"

PORSCHE CARS CANADA LTD.

Dieter Heinlein, General Manager of Porsche Cars Canada, Ltd., was leafing through five proposals to establish new dealerships in Canada. As a preliminary screening move, Mr. Heinlein would need to make an assessment of the market potential and the qualifications of the person applying. He knew that any proposal that moved beyond the screening process would require several months of work both on the part of the applicant and the company. He was not committed to the idea of opening a new dealership but he needed to have his assessment finished for the June 1, 2016 quarterly meeting to be held at the Mississauga headquarters one week from now.

Company History

The Porsche firm came into existence in 1931 but the history of the German company could be traced to the turn of the century. In September 1900, a young Ferdinand Porsche, acting as both a designer and test driver, posted a record time on a race track near Vienna with a new automobile reaching a top speed of forty kilometres per hour.

From then until 1948, there were only automobiles designed by Porsche but none bearing his name. Porsche helped design and develop pumpers for the Vienna Fire Department, mortar tows for the Austrian artillery, tanks for the German army, Prince Henry touring cars, Sascha racing cars and the Mercedes SSK for the Daimler-Benz corporation. The most famous of all these vehicles was the Volkswagen. In 1931, Porsche designed the first Volkswagen "Beetle" and full production of the car began in 1938.

In 1948, the first sports car to carry Porsche's name was designed and built in Austria -- based on Volkswagen parts. This car, called the 356, was never intended to compete in races yet that same year it won a race in Innsbruck, Austria, reaching a speed of 140 kilometres per hour. In 1950, the company returned to Stuttgart-Zuffenhausen, West Germany after its exile in Austria and full-scale production began. By 1954, 5,000 Porsches had been built.

Professor Ferdinand Porsche died on January 30, 1951 at 75 years of age. His son, Professor Ferry Porsche took over as President of Germany's smallest automobile maker. In 1955, the first engine developed for and by Porsche went into production. When the American actor James Dean died in a Porsche during an automobile accident in Paso Robles, California on September 30, 1955, the car acquired a certain mystique. In 1963, with more than 60,000 Type 356 Porsches having been built, its successor, the Porsche 911, was introduced. In 1972, the Porsche firm became a joint-stock company and the Porsche family withdrew from active management.

In 2016, Porsche commercially manufactured five automobiles: the 911, the 718, the Panamera, the Cayenne and the Macan. North America was the major market for the cars though

----

Chinese and European purchases had been gaining steadily. (See Figure 1) Both latent demand (desire of people to one day own a Porsche) and true demand for Porsches was growing. With only a few exceptions in its history, demand for Porsches always outstripped supply. In 2015, Porsche produced approximately 225,000 cars up from 190,000 in 2014. (See Figure 2)

Figure 1 Porsche Main Worldwide Markets

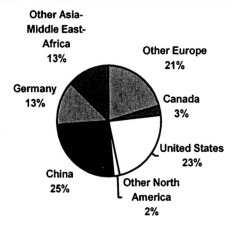

Figure 2 Porsche Annual Automobile Production

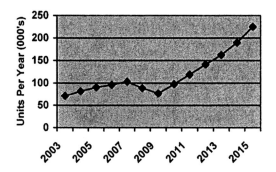

The History of Porsche in Canada

Canada and the United States were, from the beginning, the primary market for the expensive Porsches as Europe had been economically scarred by the Second World War. When the first Porsches were commercially produced in 1950, individual car dealers imported them to the United States. Canadian distribution evolved in a different direction. In 1952, Volkswagen established its first "daughter" company in Canada responsible for importing Volkswagen cars. As demand for Porsches in Canada at that time could be measured in single digits, it was convenient and less expensive for Porsche to "piggyback" efforts with Volkswagen Canada.

For the average person on the street, the relationships between Porsche, Volkswagen and Audi were confusing. Along with doing design work for Volkswagen, Porsche had done design work for Audi. Audi assembled 944's for Porsche under contract. Audi was purchased by Volkswagen in the mid 1970's and a grandson of Ferdinand Porsche sat on its Board of Directors as Chairman. Even in Germany, until 1990, all Porsche dealers also sold Volkswagen and Audi products. With increased sales in the 1970's, a dedicated Porsche presence emerged and in 1982 a separate Porsche division of Volkswagen Canada was created. In 1994, Porsche Cars Canada, Ltd. was created as a unique company for the management of Porsche in Canada. Importing was handled through Porsche Cars North America, Inc. headquartered since 1997 in Atlanta, Georgia.

In Canada, approximately 1,900,000 new automobiles were sold annually. Of that number, only 5% were luxury/sports cars and Porsche captured 10% of those purchases. In the early 1990's, Porsche Canada had reduced the number of cars it sold from 1,200 to 750 cars. But while volume declined, the average retail price of a Porsche sold in Canada had climbed from $50,000 in 1986 to $100,000 in 1990. A decade later volumes had grown to around 1,500 cars annually and average retail selling prices had declined to $95,000. The decrease in average retail price was related to the discontinuation of the more expensive 928 and 944 models and the introduction of the very popular, though cheaper priced, 718. When one new car and two new sport utility vehicles were introduced, sales volumes started to rise. In 2015, Porsche Cars Canada sold 6,413 vehicles at an average price of $92,000 each. The year 2016 business goals for Canada are shown in Table 1. Remarkably, this increase in units sold had occurred in the face of "hostile" changes to the tax act that made it more difficult to write-off the costs of a company car. As an "average" Porsche purchaser was a self-employed, "entrepreneurial" person between the ages of 30 and 55 earning at least $100,000 per year, tax implications were an important influence on the purchase decision.

The Product Line

It was difficult to describe the five basic models. Their shape and style were unique in the fine automobile world. Cars could be purchased as a coupe, cabriolet (convertible) or targa (centre section of roof was removable). Combining these designs with turbo-charged engines and other special features led to 25 models of 911's, four models of 718's, and nine models of Panameras. The sport utility vehicles differed in size and engine configuration. They did not come in cabriolet or targa versions. There were five models of Macans and eight models of Cayennes.

Table 1   Porsche Cars Canada: Key 2016 Business Goals

Ensure that:
* The Customer Comes First
  The most valuable capital Porsche has is its band of loyal customers with their sense of Porsche responsibility.
* Porsches Are Serviced Only By Porsche
  Porsche's commitment to every owner and to each Porsche extends for the life of the car.
* Porsche Controls the Used Porsche Business
  A Porsche is a Porsche is a Porsche.
* Each Potential Porsche Person is Introduced to the Marque With Care
  There are many people who would like to drive a Porsche if the idea was presented to them properly.

The Five Basic Porsche Models

The 911 – 31,300 sold worldwide

Since its debut in 1963, the Porsche 911 had been steadily refined by its designers, stylists and engineers into an undeniable classic. The rear-mounted, high performance engine, exceptionally solid body structure, high production quality, and elegant lines combined beautifully to characterize the timeless appeal of this universally desirable concept. Available in Coupe, Targa and Cabriolet form.

The Panamera – 17,200 sold worldwide

This was a four-door, four-seat luxury sedan with the engine in the front. The V8 normal-aspiration versions of the Panamera had rear-wheel drive as standard, while the Turbo version included standard all-wheel drive with PTM (Porsche Traction Management). The engine choices included the base model S, 4S, and Turbo. Canadian models included an engine start/stop system, and the Turbo version used active aerodynamics with a multi-stage, adjustable rear spoiler.

The 718 – 22,700 sold worldwide

This mid-engine car was launched in 2005 as a coupe version of its earlier "Boxster" model. It had become increasingly popular with customers as a more affordable and balanced proposition to the range-topping 911. The coupe came with either a 2.7-, 2.9-, or 3.4-liter, flat-four cylinder engine with as many as 340 horsepower and 273 pound-feet of torque. The Cayman model was a hardtop while the Boxster model was a "soft-top" which converted to a convertible.

The Cayenne – 73,100 sold worldwide

The Porsche Cayenne was a mid-size luxury crossover sport utility vehicle. It was launched in Canada in 2003. A second generation of the vehicle was launched in 2011. The car offered the first V8-engine built by Porsche since 1995, when the Porsche 928 was discontinued. It was also Porsche's first non-sports car and first vehicle with four doors. Since 2008, all engines featured direct injection technology. Although the Cayenne shared its platform, body frame, and doors with the similar Volkswagen Touareg, all other aspects of vehicle design, tuning and production were done in-house at Porsche. For 2014, Porsche introduced a plug-in E-Hybrid version.

The Macan – 80,200 sold worldwide

The Macan compact crossover sports utility vehicle offered a more compact body than the Cayenne. The Macan was sportier than the Cayenne; for instance the Macan had a standard 7-speed dual-clutch PDK gearbox which was more responsive while the Cayenne had an 8-speed Tiptronic transmission for smoother shifts. The Porsche Macan shared its platform with the Audi Q5. The wheelbase and suspension configuration were based on and heavily modified from the Audi, but the engine, transfer case, suspension tuning, interior and exterior are unique to Porsche. It was also 43 mm. longer and 36 mm. wider than a Q5. At launch, three different models and engines were available, all being V6 format: a 3.0-litre Macan S with 340 PS (250 kW; 335 bhp), a 3.6-litre Macan Turbo with 400 PS (294 kW; 395 bhp) and a 3.0-litre 258 PS (190 kW; 254 bhp) Diesel, with a CO_2 emissions of 159 g/km. The Macan GTS was launched in October 2015 to fit into the gap between the Macan S and Macan Turbo.

Distribution Decisions

Though in 1975, there were 72 authorized Porsche Dealers in Canada selling 226 cars annually, all of these dealers sold Audi and Volkswagen cars as well. The number of Volkswagen dealers carrying Porsche had grown quickly as Porsches provided an incremental source of profits. In the early days, with "Beetles" retailing at $2,000 each, an average Porsche might contribute $2,000 of gross profit to the dealership. With a slight downturn in the automotive market, the demise of the Porsche 914 (the low-priced, so-called "Volks-Porsche") and marketing research that showed Porsche purchasers wanted fewer barriers/ interfaces between them and the company, Porsche Cars Canada saw a chance to reduce some of the dealerships which sold only a few Porsches per year. By 1976, the number of Porsche dealers in Canada had been reduced to 33 and by 1979 that number was further reduced to 14. Over the next 35 years, the number of dealerships increased by three. (See Table 2 for a list of current dealer locations)

Table 2   List Of Dealer Locations

Vancouver (2)	Saskatoon	Ottawa
Victoria	Winnipeg	Quebec City
Edmonton	Toronto (2)	Montreal (3)
Calgary	Oakville	Halifax
	London (Ontario)	

The seventeen existing dealerships sold only Porsche vehicles. This requirement focused dealer resources totally on Porsche customer satisfaction. The best dealers were often "fanatic" Porsche lovers dedicated to the line and offering the best service. Dealers who carried Porsche as a side line were unable to properly sell and service the car and, over time, they were eliminated. A mechanic had to be properly trained to service a Porsche and if only a few Porsches were serviced each month, the mechanic would quickly lose his edge.

The financial structure of each dealership was quite different. A Porsche dealership with a large service business could sell only 200 to 250 new and used Porsches to earn acceptable profits. Another dealership with a smaller service business would have to sell 300 to 350 new and used Porsches. Mr. Heinlein felt that any new dealership should be capable of selling 250 to 300 new and used Porsches annually which would allow room to grow the business over time. To maintain a service support edge, at least 250 to 400 cars per year had to come into the shop.

Within the last three months, Mr. Heinlein had received proposals for five new dealerships. In evaluating a proposal, Mr. Heinlein looked both at the market potential and the person making the proposal. He felt that, at most, one dealership could be added while maintaining the 2016 Porsche business goals but that was not an absolute limit – if two locations made sense, he was prepared to consider them both. When looking at market potential, he looked at customer needs particularly in terms of servicing existing vehicles, geographic coverage of the dealership (helping to build a national network), the possibility of cannibalizing business from existing dealers, and a potential for selling an adequate volume of new and used cars. If this analysis was positive, he examined the person making the proposal by checking his or her general business references, his or her past experience in the car industry especially in the used car department, and the financial resources at the person's disposal. In particular, one would need $2 to $3 million equity to open a dealership exclusive of the land and the building.

Attitude was an important consideration in the examination of a dealership applicant. A Porsche purchaser, to acquire his or her car, would spend as much as many people would spend on a home. An average car salesperson, thinking that someone spending this much money on a car was quite foolish, would have a hard time communicating to a customer. Thus a good potential dealer had to be a lover of fine cars and of Porsches in particular.

Proposals for New Dealerships

1. Trois Rivieres, Quebec
   - nearest dealerships – Quebec City and Montreal - each about 110 kilometres away
   - population – 151,700
   - number of new and used cars sold – 45,000 to 55,000
   - number of Porsches in the area – 150
   - candidates felt they may need to use lower prices to entice customer purchases
   - proposal submitted by a father and son team aged 28 and 56 – father had owned the top Chrysler dealership in the region but sold out after a heart attack three years ago – son just finished a four year term in the Canadian army after completing a Business degree at the Royal Military College
   - father would supply the capital and son would run the dealership – father would also be involved in promotion
   - pair had $1,800,000 to invest and felt they could get by without any additional financing

2. St. John's, Newfoundland
   - nearest dealerships – Quebec City (about 2,300 kilometres) and Halifax (1,500 kilometres)
   - population – 196,970
   - number of new and used cars sold – 35,000 to 45,000
   - number of Porsches in the area – 120 to 160
   - proposal submitted by two former fishermen aged of 48 and 52 – each had twenty years work experience in fish processing plants attaining levels of Marketing Manager and Production Manager respectively – plant had recently closed and both took early retirement
   - one had worked for two years at a Ford dealership twenty-five years ago and the other had some experience as a mechanic on a fishing trawler nearly thirty years ago
   - pair had $1,300,000 to invest and felt that they could get government and bank financing for an additional $1,000,000

3. Kitchener-Waterloo, Ontario
   - nearest dealerships – London (109 kilometres), Toronto (107 kilometres), Oakville (85 kilometres)
   - population – 477,200
   - number of new and used cars sold – 75,000 to 85,000
   - hard to know buying habits as consumers were very mobile in the Golden Horseshoe area
   - number of Porsches in the area – 400 to 650
   - proposal submitted by three women between the ages of 35 and 43 – each had worked for ten years prior to leaving the work force to have children – one had worked as a bookkeeper at a car dealership, one was a lawyer and one was a pay equity consultant

- proposal would see each of the three women in the dealership but for less than thirty hours per week so that they could spend time with their young children
- group had $1,200,000 to invest and felt that they could get a bank loan for $800,000

4. Hamilton, Ontario

- nearest dealerships – Toronto (69 kilometres) and Oakville (33 kilometres)
- population – 721,000 (includes Burlington but does not include St. Catharines or Niagara Falls)
- number of new and used cars sold – 90,000 to 120,000
- number of Porsches in the area – 750 to 1,000
- some independent unauthorized service centres in Niagara region – this was a problem for Porsche Canada and it wanted them eliminated
- proposal submitted by a group of seven recent MBA grads between the ages of 25 and 27 – each had two to three years work experience in packaged goods firms like Procter and Gamble, Frito-Lay, or Cadbury-Schweppes
- four of the group would work at the dealership; the other three would be silent partners
- group had $280,000 to invest and felt that they could get a line of credit for $1,400,000

5. Regina, Saskatchewan

- nearest dealerships – Saskatoon (260 kilometres), Winnipeg (530 kilometres), Calgary (675 kilometres), and Edmonton (700 kilometres)
- population – 210,560
- number of new and used cars sold – 40,000 to 50,000
- number of Porsches in the area – 150 to 200
- proposal submitted by a former member of legislative assembly aged 45 – had been in politics for fifteen years attaining level of Assistant Minister of Industry and Trade – had owned a chain of hardware stores which had recently been sold
- had $10 million to invest; felt this would be one of a number of new ventures for him

The Decision

As Mr. Heinlein leafed through the proposals, he thought about Porsche Car Canada's goal of wanting to sell and service all new and used Porsches in Canada. He was aware that some of these proposals might only contribute marginally to sales, could take away sales from existing dealers, might eliminate some unauthorized Porsche service centres, and could lead to poor customer service in the smaller territories. Locating dealerships in high traffic areas or "automotive rows" was unnecessary as Porsche dealerships were a destination for a shopping trip. If only increased sales were needed, he could work with existing dealers to improve the situation.

The decision was not an easy one. He would have to think about the situation some more. There was no point making a hasty move.

FORTRON INTERNATIONAL INC.

When entering foreign markets, Fortron International Inc., a Hamilton, Ontario based producer of sport whistles, used a renewable sales agency agreement granting exclusive distribution rights to a country-specific distributor. Such an agreement with Allzweck-Sportartikel, a German wholesale catalogue store specializing in soccer equipment, was set to expire in October, 2015. Steve Foxcroft, General Manager of Fortron International Inc., felt the German market could be better exploited and was looking for alternative arrangements.

Product History

A conventional whistle produced its shrill "trill" through the movement of a small pea (a cork or plastic ball) in its interior. The pea alternately covered and uncovered a hole through which air was released producing a rapid cycle of sound and silence. Unfortunately, the pea would often stick especially if overblown or if water and debris got into the interior.

Ron Foxcroft and Joe Forte, professional basketball referees, perceived a need for a better, more dependable whistle. Along with dependability, they felt a new whistle had to have a louder, more penetrating sound, and an ability to be heard over the noise of a crowd. In short, the world needed a whistle that would not fail to perform under any conditions.

With the aid of an industrial designer, three and a half years of extensive development and testing, and $150,000 in start-up capital, the Fox 40 whistle was introduced as the only whistle without a pea. It had three air chambers that, when blown, created three different frequencies. As the frequencies were out of phase, they were alternately reinforced and cancelled resulting in a louder, piercing, intense vibrato. The Fox 40 whistle worked in all weather conditions and, also, floated on water. Patent protection for twenty years, from those firms that would try to copy the technology, was sought and received worldwide.

The whistle debuted at the Pan American Games. By 2015, the Fox 40 whistle was used in more than two dozen Olympic sports, the National and Canadian Football League (NFL, CFL), the National, American, and International Hockey Leagues (NHL, AHL, IHL), the World Basketball League (WBL), National Collegiate Athletic Association (NCAA) Basketball, the soccer World Cup, and the National Basketball Association (NBA). Since its introduction, many police departments and safety-oriented organizations adopted the whistle for standard use. The U.S. Cavalry and the Royal Life Saving Society endorsed the Fox 40 as their whistle of choice.

The Fox 40 whistle was available in thirteen models. For example, the "Classic" was sold in ten colours (red, orange, yellow, green, blue, pink, black, purple, white, and glow-in-the-dark), as was the "Mini-Fox." The "Referee" came in black and had six different finger grips.

Company History

Fortron International Inc. was created by Foxcroft and Forte to market the Fox 40 whistle. It was a lean organization with a staff of three executives, including Foxcroft's son, Steve, as General Manager, who shared responsibility for marketing and financial decisions and one secretarial assistant. For a dollar each, a nearby company, Promold Plastics, manufactured the whistle using injection moulding equipment and state of the art ultrasonic welding. In 2015, 10 million Fox 40 whistles would be sold worldwide and sales were expected to increase by ten percent in 2016. Revenue in 2015 exceeded $30 million and profits crossed the $3 million mark.

One of Fortron International's overseas sales agents was Allzweck-Sportartikel in Trechtingshausen, Germany. Exclusive distribution rights for Germany were granted in a three-year license agreement signed on October 8, 2012. Under the agreement, Fortron sold the whistles for $3.45 to Allzweck. Though Allzweck was free to negotiate discounts for volume purchases or promotional purposes, the suggested distributor selling price was $5.95. The suggested retail price was $9.95 per whistle.

Allzweck was a wholesale catalogue store specializing in soccer equipment. It distributed 5,000 catalogues annually within Germany and had four sales representatives. In addition, it operated a small booth at the most important sporting goods trade show (ISPO) held annually in Munich. Allzweck's sales of Fox 40 whistles are presented in Table 1. All of these sales were from Germany and most were from an area of thirty kilometres around Frankfurt including Trechtinghausen.

Table 1   Annual Sales of Fox 40 Whistles By Allzweck-Sportartikel

Year	Number of Whistles Sold
2013	18,680
2014	39,220
2015	59,700 (projected)

Competition

Conventional "pea" whistles retailed for half the price of the Fox 40. A number of small manufacturers were located in south-east Asia. These whistles were perceived to be a low quality, low price choice and were not used in sporting events. Instead, they were used recreationally and were common as children's gifts.

The major sporting whistle was made by ACME Whistles of Birmingham, England. This company had manufactured whistles for more than a century and held the original patents for the British bobby's whistle (registered in 1884) and the original pea whistle (1895). The sales director did not see Fox 40 as a threat to its major sports whistle -- the ACME Thunderer. "If you are implying that the Fox 40 is going to sweep ACME into liquidation, I think that's not the case." Nonetheless, it was rumoured that ACME was attempting to develop its own line of pea-less whistles.

There were no whistle manufacturers located in Germany.

The German Market

The breaching of the Berlin Wall in November, 1989, was the beginning of German reunification. On October 3, 1990, 45 years after being separated, West Germany (the Federal Republic of Germany) and East Germany (the German Democratic Republic) were reunited under the former's name. Germany covered 357,021 square kilometres and supported a population of 82 million in 2015.

On January 1, 2002, Germany abandoned its own currency, the Deutschmark, for the European Dollar or Euro. While the Euro would float on international currency exchanges, it was assumed that its value would be roughly equal to the American Dollar. By 2015, the Euro was worth about US$1.15 or about Cdn$1.40. The Gross Domestic Product (GDP) for Germany was US$3.7 trillion US which made it the fourth largest economy in the world. By comparison, Canada was the tenth largest economy in the world with a GDP of US$1.6 trillion. The German unemployment rate hit a twenty year low in June, 2015 at 4.6%. Germany had a trade surplus of US$245 billion in 2015 with forecast trade surpluses of US$260 billion in 2016 and US$265 billion in 2017.

In 2015, approximately 28% of the German population participated in sports. Of this number, only five percent were in training for national and international competition. Interestingly, nearly twice as many males participated than did females and the largest group of participants was 24 years and older (see Tables 2 and 3). Compared to the 1980's, many of the special sport schools for children and adolescents in East Germany were closed. A more decentralized sports movement was employed. As well, amateur sport budgets were dramatically cut from their peak in the 1980's and hundreds of full-time coaches and trainers had been dismissed.

Other German Markets

In addition to the sports market, Foxcroft wondered about the safety, fashion and education markets. Two blasts of a whistle were recognized internationally as an emergency signal. Since the Fox 40 whistle got louder as an individual blew harder and since it operated under any weather conditions, it was an ideal whistle in an emergency. In the 2000's, Germany had been faced with increased racist attacks on the poor and on new immigrants. Community groups were being formed to protect citizens and make neighbourhoods safer. Using a whistle as a signaling device would not require translation to be understood. While that unrest seemed to dissipate, a wave of Syrian refugees seeking resettlement in Germany had begun to see some racist graffiti and protest marches in German cities.

In the past decade, high fashion became prevalent in sportswear. The Fox 40 whistle had the potential of becoming a very fashionable, safety-oriented, accessory item. While limiting the extent to which it could spread in the sportswear industry, safety was particularly important in hunting, fishing, hiking, camping, skiing, cycling, and boating. Interestingly, the more expensive the apparel for a sport, the easier it could be to sell a whistle. After spending €2,000 on ski clothing and equipment, the price of a Fox 40 whistle would be almost unnoticeable.

In 2015, there were 7.0 million students enrolled in German schools and an additional 4.3 million enrolled in polytechnic schools. A safety education program coordinated through teachers and the schools could increase awareness of the Fox 40 whistle and lead to sales.

The German Consumer

In the "Guide for Canadian Exporters – The European Community" it was recommended that punctuality, politeness and a degree of formality were part of the keys to success in dealing with German consumers. Also, one needed to have a thorough knowledge of delivery periods, shipping costs, service requirements and performance characteristics. As holidays were very important to German workers, sales visits in July or August were avoided. A list of references was also useful.

By far the best sales vehicle for the German market was the appropriate trade fair. Germany had more world-class specialized industrial trade fairs than any other country. Because of this, many companies from beyond the German market attended, which extended selling opportunities.

Table 2   Participation in Sports By Age In Germany During 2015

Age Group	Number of Males	Number of Females
Under 15	2,531,602	1,975,214
15 to 19	1,378,683	865,851
20 to 23	1,022,576	586,453
24 and Over	9,688,417	5,162,853
Total	14,621,278	8,590,371

Table 3   Sports Participation in Germany During 2015

Sport	Number of Males	Number of Females
Football (soccer)	5,443,754	610,021
Gymnastics	1,545,399	3,363,648
Tennis	1,533,754	1,107,919
Hunting/Shooting	1,335,712	332,335
Table Tennis	673,333	226,644
Handball	649,548	324,858
Track and Field	570,071	459,837
Swimming	360,880	344,809
Volleyball	247,526	233,551
Judo	218,281	83,409
Other Sports	2,043,021	1,503,338
Total	14,621,278	8,590,371

International Options

Generally, there were six levels of involvement in international marketing. Casual exporting was the most passive and involved exporting only occasionally when surplus or obsolete inventory was available. This choice often led to losses and a fear of export markets.

Once a firm was making a continuous effort to sell its merchandise abroad, it moved to the level of active exporting. This was usually accomplished through sales agency agreements. A distributor in a foreign country was granted either exclusive or non-exclusive rights to sell a product in a geographic region. The manufacturing company only gained access to a market but no information about the business environment in that country. In return, the sales agency used its knowledge of distribution channels, consumer behaviour and local promotion to earn a healthy margin on each item sold. Foxcroft had such an agreement with Allzweck-Sportartikel. The spectrum of potential sales agents ranged from importers and wholesalers to department stores, mail order houses and buying cooperatives.

Licensing involved a formal agreement with a foreign company to produce Canadian merchandise. Like before, a company gained access to a market but no information about the business environment. The licensee was typically not responsible for sales of the product and so, often, a sales agency agreement was also required before a product could be distributed. Rather than make money through product production, the Canadian licensor would earn royalties either from a lump sum payment or on a per unit basis. Licensing was favoured for products with short life cycles, elementary technology, or technology nearing the end of patent protection. The potential was considerable for licensees to copy new or advanced technology or use the technology after the end of an agreement. Historically about 50% of all licensing agreements managed to satisfy both parties.

At a higher level, a Canadian company could maintain a separate sales/marketing operation in a foreign country. The product could be made at home or through foreign contract manufacturers but the Canadian company would control foreign sales either through its own sales force or through supervising a group of local sales agents. This path was often used when a company wanted to gather information about a country before it considered launching its own production facility. It was an especially attractive learning experience if the company could protect its technology with patents and thus have time to grow slowly.

Of course, the ultimate level of involvement occurred with a company both marketing and producing its product in a foreign country. A new plant could be built or an existing plant could be acquired. For Fortron, a foreign plant would cost $2.5 million and would require management time to establish and operate.

Another option at this level, however, would be a joint venture with a foreign firm. While this path offered the advantage of cutting in half the $2.5 million investment and reducing the commitment of managerial resources, there were some disadvantages. One was the sharing of profits. A second was the lack of control over the strategic and operational decisions which affected the joint venture. Perhaps the biggest drawback was the lack of a potential joint venture partner. One could, no doubt, be found but how long would the process take?

The European Community

If Fortron established a stronger presence in Germany, it could become a base for expanded operations in the European Union. The European Economic Community (EEC) came into being in Rome in 1957. A treaty was signed by Belgium, France, West Germany, Luxembourg, Italy and the Netherlands. In 1973, the EEC became a group of nine as Denmark, Ireland and the United Kingdom joined. It reached twelve member status when Greece joined in 1981 and Spain and Portugal joined in 1986. In 1993, the name was shortened to European Union (EU) to reflect new integration goals of the group rather than the original economic ones. In 1995, three more countries (Austria, Finland, and Sweden) joined the EU. A referendum in Norway that same year turned down admission to the EU. In 2004, the EU experienced its largest ever growth adding ten more countries including: Cyprus, the Czech Republic, Estonia, Hungary, Latvia, Lithuania, Malta, Poland, Slovenia, and the Slovak Republic. On January 1, 2007, Romania and Bulgaria joined followed by Croatia on July 1, 2013. The twenty-eight-member EU represented a large potential consumer market with its population of 510 million. More growth was being considered: Iceland, Turkey, Serbia, Albania, Montenegro, and Macedonia were being considered for membership.

On January 1, 1999, the Euro dollar (or Euro) was created. The currency existed only in electronic form until January 1, 2002 when coins and bank notes began to circulate. Not all members of the EU adopted the Euro as their currency. This created a separate "Eurozone." By 2015, 19 EU countries had joined the Eurozone.

The EU was striving to: 1) end intra-country customs checks; 2) create uniformity and mutual recognition of technical standards, university diplomas and apprenticeship courses; 3) create a common market in goods and services including a single broadcasting area; and 4) create an equal excise and national value added tax system. In 1993, the EU eliminated all barriers between member-countries so that people, capital and goods could move freely.

Since forming, the positive consequences of the EU included the overall improvement of economic conditions in member countries and easier and less costly access to member markets. Patents registered in one member-country would automatically be registered and recognized in all EU countries. For Canadian firms, the EU posed some risks including: 1) intensified competition in EU markets as European firms became more efficient and the interest of non-European firms in the EU increased; 2) more competition in North American markets and non-EU markets as the EU became more unified; and 3) another major bloc in the globalized world economy.

While the EU boasted much success in its integration of sovereign countries, there was a cloud on the horizon. The United Kingdom Independence Party (UKIP) was formed in 1993. At its core was strong opposition to and extreme criticism of the EU. In January, 2013, British Prime Minister David Cameron announced that a Conservative government would hold an in-out referendum on EU membership before the end of 2017, on a renegotiated membership package, if the party was elected in 2015. The Conservative Party won a majority and began a renegotiation with the EU centred on four key points: protection of the single market for non-eurozone countries; reduction of "red tape;" exempting Britain from "ever-closer union;" and restricting EU immigration. The government also announced a non-binding referendum would be held on June 23, 2016 based on any renegotiated deal. If the government lost the referendum,

Article 50 in its membership agreement would be triggered which would start a two-year negotiation to arrange for Britain's exit. While this would not cause the EU to collapse, such a move could undermine confidence in it.

The Decision

As Steve Foxcroft reviewed the information, he needed to make several preliminary decisions. Should Fortron be selling whistles in the German market? If so, what level of international marketing involvement was appropriate? Did existing management and financial resources preclude some forms of involvement? Not renewing the Allzweck license agreement would mean dissatisfaction with the number of whistles being sold. Steve felt the German market was capable of at least ten times the sales being generated by Allzweck. Could Fortron do better if it took control of all sales activities? Could a production centre, or other arrangement, be justified on the basis of entering the EU? With the patent expiring on the whistle in three years, he also had to consider the loss of any intellectual property rights.

Clearly any preliminary decision made would need follow-up research and information before being implemented. Still he could not afford to have his limited managerial staff pursuing a number of non-viable options.

CRAYOLA™ CANADA LTD.

As a member of the Business Development Team, Dinari Mrsic, Marketing Project Manager, had listened to presentations on three possible new products for the Crayola™ product line. These ideas had been selected as the most viable from more than twenty-five ideas generated at a brainstorming session held three weeks earlier. The other eleven people on the team included representatives from the Purchasing, Warehousing, Finance, Crayon, Marker, Clay & Paint, and Final Assembly teams. Any new product idea approved at this June meeting would attract significant company resources in support of its development. Dinari had to decide which, if any, of the ideas had the potential to become a successful new product.

Company History

In 1860, twenty-four year old Joseph W. Binney arrived in America from England. He settled in Shrub Oak, New York where, in 1864, he founded the Peekskill Chemical Works. This company manufactured iron oxide used to make red barn paint, and carbon black for printer's inks, carbon paper and automobile tires. When Joseph Binney retired in 1885, he left his business to a partnership of his son Edwin and a nephew, C. Harold Smith.

In 1902, the partners founded the Binney & Smith Company. Two years earlier they had purchased a second factory; this one near Easton, Pennsylvania. This stone mill was located near the region's slate quarries as its primary product was slate pencils. Among the first new products developed in Easton was Au-Du-Septic white dustless chalk, which earned a Gold Medal at the 1902 World Exposition in St. Louis. In talking with school teachers about the new chalk, company salespeople learned about the need for quality crayons in the classroom. Europe had been the birthplace of the "modern" crayon – a mixture of charcoal and oil. Over time, powdered pigments replaced the charcoal. It was subsequently discovered that substituting wax for the oil in the mixture made the resulting crayons sturdier and easier to handle. After months of laboratory research with pigments and paraffin wax, the company introduced its own crayons in 1903. The major hurdle researchers overcame was the toxicity of most available pigments. As crayons could be chewed or even digested, synthetic, non-toxic pigments were developed to replace organic colours.

The name "Crayola™", coined by school teacher Alice Binney, Edwin's wife, was derived from the French word "Craie" for stick of colour and "ola," from oleaginous, since paraffin wax was an oil derivative. The first box contained eight sticks (red, blue, yellow, green, violet, orange, black and brown) and sold for a nickel. Because of their colour depth and clarity, Crayola™ crayons won gold medals at Expositions in St. Louis (1903) and Paris (1904).

This case was written by Marvin Ryder. Case material is prepared as a basis for classroom discussion only. Copyright 2016 by Marvin Ryder, Michael G. DeGroote School of Business, McMaster University, Hamilton, Ontario. This case is not to be reproduced in whole or in part by any means without the express written consent of the author.

Canadian Operations

In 1926, James W. Gravestock of Toronto, founded the Canada Crayon Company. From his basement, Mr. Gravestock and his family moulded and hand wrapped the "Peacock" brand of wax crayons for the Canadian market. By 1927, Mr. Gravestock needed to expand his operations and increase his output, so he joined forces with the Binney & Smith Company of New York. In October, the partnership rented a three-storey factory in Peterborough, Ontario and transferred the manufacture of crayons from Toronto.

Within months, two new brands of children's crayons – "Radiants" and "Playtime" - were added to the line. Several brands of industrial crayons and chalks were also developed and manufactured in Peterborough. The Canada Crayon Company enjoyed tremendous success, and, in September 1933, moved to Lindsay, Ontario. In early 1934, the Canada Crayon Company introduced Canada's first "Crayola™" crayons.

In 1948, poster, finger and watercolour paints were added to the product line along with modelling clay, paste and glue. In October, 1958, Canada Crayon Company became a wholly owned subsidiary of Binney & Smith Inc. and two months later a national sales office was opened in Toronto. At the same time, Binney & Smith acquired Cosmic Crayon Co. Ltd. of Bedford, England. In 1964, Binney & Smith acquired Permanent Pigments Inc. of Cincinnati, Ohio. The company manufactured Liquitex™ acrylic colours, oil colours, watercolours, varnishes, media and other supplies for the fine artist. On November 1, 1965, on eight acres of land, a larger, combined factory and office building opened in Lindsay, Ontario and Canadian operations made its third and final move.

During 1976, Binney & Smith acquired the rights to Silly Putty™. Silly Putty™ was invented by James Gilbert Wright of New Haven, Connecticut, while working to produce a synthetic rubber at a General Electric lab. While no practical use of the material could be found in 1943, over the next few years it became a popular item at cocktail parties hosted by G.E. executives. In 1949, Peter Hodgson, a Montreal native, introduced the product commercially as an adult novelty by packing the material in plastic eggs and using surplus egg cartons for shipping purposes. Sales to children and adults rose quickly with each new wave of publicity and promotion surrounding the product – the biggest of which was a package of Silly Putty™ carried into space by the astronauts of Apollo 8. When Hodgson died in 1976, his estate was estimated to be worth $140 million. Other than adding colours (fluorescent green, yellow, orange and magenta) and four "glow-in-the-dark" shades, Binney & Smith had not altered Silly Putty™ in any way. Out of American facilities, Binney & Smith produced 12,000 eggs (150 kilograms) of Silly Putty™ daily or over 6 million eggs per year.

In 1984, Binney & Smith was acquired by Hallmark Cards, Inc., the world's largest greeting card manufacturer. Crayola™ products were sold in more than 60 countries from Iceland to Belize in Central America. They were packaged in eleven languages. The Crayola™ brand name was recognized by 99% of North Americans. In 1991, according to company promotional material, Crayola™ was ranked 51 of all world brands in terms of the brand's recognizability and consumers' esteem. The scent of Crayola™ crayons was among the twenty most recognizable to North American adults. Coffee and peanut butter were one and two. Crayola™ crayons were eighteen.

The years since the Hallmark acquisition had proven to be the most prosperous in the company's "colourful" history. Since 1985, sales from Binney & Smith's Canadian facility had almost tripled. Employing 150, Binney & Smith was the only crayon manufacturer in Canada. In 1992, the Canadian Toy Testing Council named the Crayola™ product line "Toy of the Year." In 1998, Crayola™ crayons were inducted into National Toy Hall of Fame. Silly Putty joined the Hall in 2001. In 2007, Binney & Smith was renamed Crayola™ Ltd. as part of a rebranding effort. In 2011, "My First Crayola™" was launched with triangular and egg-shaped crayons, and flat-tipped markers for children younger than four. In 2015, the company launched "Colour Escapes" to capitalize on the boom in adult colouring as a form of stress reduction.

Crayon Production

Outdoor heated tanks stored 82,000 kilograms of paraffin wax in a liquid state. This heated wax was pumped directly into a vat in which it was mixed with a predetermined amount of powdered pigment. Improvements and minor adjustments had taken place over the past 113 years, but Crayola™ crayons were made by essentially the same guarded formula as that of the original crayons made in 1903.

The wax was heated and poured from a double spouted bucket onto the moulding table. Each mould formed 2,500 crayons. As the wax-pigment blend settled into the cylindrical mould, it was cooled by water. The nature of each colour's pigments also determined how long the crayon would take to cool, anywhere from four to seven minutes. The typical crayon would begin to melt at forty degrees Celsius. After cooling, the crayons were hydraulically ejected from their mould into racks.

The mould operator then emptied the crayons from their racks onto a work table, where the first quality control check was made. Excess wax or any crayons with broken tips, chipped butt ends or inconsistent colour were returned to the mixing vat to be melted and remolded. Crayons were then placed in an automated labelling machine that wrapped and glued the labels. Labels were designed to encircle the crayon twice for sturdiness. This process was quite a bit faster than the hand labelling method that was used in the early and mid-1900's. From here, the crayons were fed into packing machines that collated the colours into different assortments for retail stores nationally.

Crayola™ crayons were available in package sizes of: two, three and four packs wrapped in cellophane; boxes of six, eight, sixteen, twenty-four, thirty-two, forty-eight, sixty-four, ninety-six, 120, and 150 which came in a portable plastic pyramid-shaped storage case. The box of twenty-four was the best selling of the package sizes. Red and black were the most popular crayon colours, mostly because children used them for outlining. The average child in North America wore down 730 crayons by their tenth birthday. Children, aged two through eight, spent an average of twenty-eight minutes each day colouring. Combined, children in North America spent 6.3 billion hours colouring annually -- almost 10,000 human lifetimes. Each year, the Lindsay plant produced 150 million crayons in 112 different shades and colours.

Marker Production

Eight brilliantly coloured Crayola™ Markers were introduced by Binney & Smith in 1978.

Since then, the company expanded the product line by developing new colours and adding decorative tips (nibs), often referred to as calligraphy tips for making double and triple lines. There were six basic components common to all Crayola™ Markers: a water-based colour ink blend, a porous (absorbent) nib, a plastic barrel, a polyester transorb (which, like an ink-pad, held the ink), a cap and a plastic plug to seal the barrel and prevent the inking from drying out.

The first step in marker production was making the non-toxic colour solution. The four ingredients (water, glycerine, preservative and colour/dye) were stored in the marker manufacturing area. Marker assembly machines produced approximately 50,000 markers per day. Bins, manually filled by marker machine operators, dispensed the five basic components into the marker assembly machines. Plastic barrels, held in place by grooves on a conveyor belt, began their journey down the assembly line. Pre-inked transorbs were inserted into the barrels and then the marker moved into position to receive its plug and nib to prevent leakage. Once sealed, the marker was fitted with a co-ordinating coloured cap. Each machine ran one colour at a time. Finished markers rolled into a final bin where they were inspected by machine operators for quality and packed into crates which proceeded to the marker packing machine. In 1988, markers containing "washable" inks were added to the product line. Annually, the Lindsay plant produced 30 million markers, 1,000,000 jars of paint and more than 300,000 pounds of clay.

The New Product Development Process

In 1990, Binney & Smith (Canada) Ltd. introduced high velocity manufacturing which was intended to stimulate profitable revenue growth through continuous improvement by the involvement of all employees. The latter was accomplished through a team approach to employment. Specialist functional teams for paint & modelling clay, marker, crayon and final assembly (for products that combined outputs, say, of markers and crayons) were established along with cross-functional teams for new product development, strategic planning, and operational monitoring. Another change was the concept of customer. For each team member, the customer became the person receiving the results of their work. By satisfying both internal and external customers, employees achieved continuous improvement, higher quality, faster delivery and lower costs.

In Easton, Pennsylvania, Binney & Smith maintained a research and development centre. It produced the new technologies that allowed the company to produce and sell washable markers and crayons, changeable markers (i.e., those that wrote in one colour and then could be changed to another colour with a special marker) and write-over markers (i.e., four markers which could be used to draw in the background with four markers that could overwrite them in the foreground with no colour bleeding). Canadian operations visited Easton in January and August to look at the new products being developed there and to pick and choose among them for launch in Canada. For new technologies, the rule of thumb was to wait a year to see how the product was accepted in the United States before launching in Canada. As a consequence, the United States operations had a larger product mix. In some cases, promotion surrounding the launch of a new product in Canada was completely different than in the United States.

Generally, the development of new products in Canada had been confined to the packaging of products into kits. Kits could combine crayons, markers, paint and modelling clay with outside inputs such as paper and fabric. On occasion, kit ideas developed in Canada were later adopted by the United States operations. The reverse was also true but it was not unusual for Canadian operations to make minor modifications in the kits including packaging, colours available, or brush types.

In keeping with the team approach, responsibility for new products along with continuous improvement rested with three Business Development teams. Each twelve person Business Development Team was cross-functional with representatives from Marketing, Purchasing, Warehousing, Finance, Crayon Production, Marker Production, Clay & Paint Production and Final Assembly.

For each team, the new product development process began with a "Team Talk." This was a brainstorming session with the goal of generating at least three viable new product ideas which could be developed further. The first half of the "Team Talk" was very non-judgemental – the purpose was simply to generate new ideas. The second half of the meeting allowed for criticism and discussion to focus efforts on those ideas most likely to succeed. To be viable, ideas had to: 1) have a likely retail price between $9.99 and $19.99 allowing for a company profit margin of 50% and retailer/wholesaler mark-ups; 2) be commercially viable (i.e., ready to sell to consumers) within six months; 3) have an expected product life span of from three to five years; 4) allow a parent and child to play or work together on a project; 5) be targeted to children three to ten years of age; 6) have no seasonal orientation (i.e., a Christmas theme); 7) be compatible with current production, technology and research & development capabilities; and 8) if a kit was being proposed, it would have additional play value after the objective of the kit had been constructed. The most recent "Team Talk" generated 25 potential new ideas and three were identified as the most viable.

Volunteers were solicited to act as "champions" for each idea and to develop it further. If no champion could be found, it was likely that the idea would not be developed further. The champions had three weeks to prepare a presentation which consisted of: 1) a set of components; 2) a rough cost estimate; 3) a rough retail selling price estimate; and 4) a mock-up of the finished product. To complete their task, champions were able to draw on the expertise of other team members as well as other company resources. An inability to convince other people in the company to support a product's development at this stage was seen as another sign of potential product failure. At the champion's presentation, the other nine members of the Business Development Team were able to ask questions and challenge assumptions. It was the goal of the team to find at least one viable idea from among the three by the end of this meeting.

Assuming that a viable idea could be found, the next three weeks would be spent getting very accurate measures of cost with the help of the purchasing department. Starting in week seven, the idea would be passed to production to have professional product mock-ups and artists renderings of any printed materials produced. In the third month, product testing would begin. Binney & Smith used several external testing approaches including telephone surveys, mall intercepts (where people would be exposed to the mock-up and asked questions) and focus group discussions (involving eight parents who considered themselves to be independent thinkers who had at least two children between the ages of four and twelve). The company also employed in-house testing whereby employees took home a sample product/kit and then evaluated it with their own children. Testing would take four to six months.

At the four and a half month point, the Business Development Team would have to make a go/no go decision on commercial launch of the product. A decision to commercially launch the product would mean that a launch date would be chosen and a schedule of activities leading to launch would be developed. The project would be handed over to the Final Assembly Team for execution of this "critical path." Leading to launch, the Business Development Team and Final Assembly Team would hold a joint meeting every Friday morning to track progress.

Once launched, the Sales and Operation Planning Team would review forecasts against actual sales. The team also monitored inventory levels and shipping reports for any problems. As Binney & Smith used a "just-in-time" approach to inventory management, only small inventory levels were kept on hand. Generally, the Final Assembly team produced to order. Any significant increase in inventory levels could signal a problem with the product launch. If problems arose, the Business Development Team would be brought back into the process for suggestions and the implementation of changes either to the product or launch strategies.

The Champions' Presentation

The Business Development Team had felt very positive about the three ideas developed during the "Team Talk" held three weeks earlier. In fact, some members of the team thought that all three new products could be winners. Each new product was a kit proposal combining Crayola™ products with other materials.

Project One

Leslie Henwood presented the idea of a papier maché mask-making kit. Each kit would contain an instruction sheet, six clear plastic mask forms, tissue paper strips, a package of dry paste, pipe cleaners, coloured sparkles, two paint brushes, two markers and three bottles of paint (in primary colours from which other colours could be derived). The kit would retail for $13.99 and had an in-house production cost of $4.00. The concept was that the parent and child would work together to make a mask which the child could later use in imaginary, playful games or on Hallowe'en night. Each day for two weeks, the parent and child would carefully mix some of the dry paste with water (to make sure the paste wasn't lumpy), soak about six paper strips in the paste and apply them to the mask form. Before the next layer could be applied, the mask would have to dry overnight. Instructions to make some sample masks (i.e., cat, dog, super-hero, monster) would be given but people would be free to be as creative as they wished. After two weeks, the mask would be complete and the parent and child would begin the process of decorating it. The kit also came with a re-order form should the parent and child need more mask forms, dry paste or paints.

Project Two

S. Jackson Zinger presented the idea of "Mold-a-saurus." Each kit would contain two packages of modelling clay, ten dinosaur moulds, two paint brushes, three bottles of paint, and an instruction booklet. The kit would retail for $17.49 and had an in-house production cost of $6.00. Using a recently developed modelling clay, children and parents could pick a mould, fill it with clay and overnight it would harden into a material resembling foam rubber. Unused modelling clay could be put back into the package, re-sealed and stored in the refrigerator without going hard for three weeks. After hardening, the palm-sized dinosaurs could be painted. The instruction booklet was in colour showing parents and children the scientifically derived colours for each dinosaur but children were free to use any combination of colours they wanted. The instruction booklet also came with some background historical information about each dinosaur so that parent and child could have an educational experience. It was intended that children would play creatively with the dinosaurs after they were painted. The kit also came with a re-order form should the parent and child need more modelling clay or paints.

Project Three

Mavis Leung presented the third new product idea – a sewing kit. Each kit would contain six pieces of coloured cloth, a package of six needles, four patterns, two spools of thread, a pair of scissors, a bottle of white glue, a package of eight markers, some coloured sparkles, pipe cleaners and a pair of funny "eyes." The kit would retail for $19.99 and had an in-house production cost of $11.00. With the kit, a parent and child could make fun things for the child to use or with which to play. Some potential projects were a hand puppet, doll clothes, bean bags, and wallets. Mavis had chosen the puppet project for her family and brought in a cow puppet with which she helped make her presentation. Her ten year old daughter had carefully cut the white material using the pattern enclosed. This had been difficult as the scissors used were a little dull. Fortunately, there had been enough material to cut an extra piece when her daughter had made a mistake. It took Mavis two hours to sew the puppet by hand and she had the needle pricks to prove it. Together they had coloured in the spots, added eyes and ears, and added a bell for effect.

The Decision

As one member of the committee, Dinari had to make a decision. Did any of these projects show the promise to justify further development into a new product? As a starting point, she thought she would use the eight defining criteria from the Team Talk to make sure each project passed. Beyond that, she wasn't sure what analyses were necessary to help pick a winner.

3 = Good
2 = Neutral
1 = Bad

	Paper	Mold	Sewing	
Child Safety	3	3	1	
Not Seasonal	2	3	3	
Good P/C Inter	3	3	2	
Gender Neutral	3	1	1	
Construction ≤ 5hrs	1	2	2	
Educational	1	3	3	
Total				

NATIONAL MUSIC STUDIO

Paul Robson, Manager of two Halifax-Dartmouth National Music Studio branches was studying the demographic data before him. He was also studying marketing surveys which included information on consumer attitudes and awareness. The owner of National Music Studio, Peter MacDonald, was considering adding another branch in the metro Halifax area and the two men were to meet in two weeks time to discuss the matter.

Before the meeting, Paul needed to evaluate the available information and present his conclusions regarding location, market potential and possible marketing strategies for the proposed branch. It was already March, 2012, and Paul knew that they had to proceed quickly if they were to open the new branch in time for the peak demand period which began in August.

The Company

National Music Studio (NMS), a chain of music schools, was started by Peter MacDonald in 1981 in Nova Scotia. The company had grown quickly, and by 2012, fifteen branches were spread throughout the Maritimes. Two were located in the Halifax-Dartmouth area and Paul Robson managed both. The Dartmouth branch opened in 1988 and the Halifax branch in 1994. Financially, the NMS outlets that Paul managed were sound.

The twin city area of Halifax-Dartmouth was the major urban centre in Nova Scotia. In Dartmouth, the NMS school was located on a main street (actually a small highway) in a business district with a major shopping centre. It was situated near two large upper middle class residential areas and one elementary and one junior high school. The NMS school was on the second floor of an old building that had been extensively renovated to improve the acoustics. Parking was a major problem and had been a frequent complaint of the clientele.

NMS had opened its Halifax school in a central residential area. It was near a junior high school and a major supermarket outlet. The building was relatively new and, again, the music school was located on the second floor.

The Service

In Paul's opinion, the personality of the instructors and their teaching methods had considerable impact on the students' perceptions of the quality of instruction. He was certain that these factors mattered more to students than did the technical skills and qualifications of their teachers. As these factors were intangible, it made the marketing of music instruction rather difficult. Over the years, NMS had gained a good reputation as a music school with high calibre instructors who provided individualized instruction. The teaching method used by the school was also considered unique and had led to good feedback from its students.

NMS provided instruction in voice training and a variety of instruments as well as in various styles of music. While most of its students were interested in learning to play an instrument for their own pleasure, some were interested in more formalized instruction. NMS did train students for the Royal Conservatory of Music exams and its students, who had taken these exams, had been very successful. In general, NMS had a reputation for having a good program in modern music.

Recently, Paul had started a music awareness program for pre-schoolers. Several pre-schools in the twin city area had agreed to have a music instructor from NMS come to its school to conduct a program for pre-school children. Mr. Robson hoped that many of these children would join NMS when they went to elementary school.

Location of a music school was not the deciding factor which led people to choose one music school over another for either their children or themselves. He frequently stated that "we are a second storey business. Certainly location is important. It does help to have ample parking and other facilities, like retail outlets, close by so that parents can drop off their children and do some shopping. If I were starting all over again, I would choose a different location for the store in Dartmouth - parking has always been a problem there. But I still feel that location is secondary to quality of instruction. If our instruction is good, they'll come - even to a difficult location."

The Competition

In addition to NMS, there were twelve other music schools in the metropolitan Halifax area. Of these, one was in Bedford and two were in Sackville. (Bedford and Sackville were widely regarded as "suburbs" of Halifax and Dartmouth.) Both music schools in Sackville were branches of larger local music schools operating in the Halifax-Dartmouth area. These two Sackville schools had very good reputations. There were also several music teachers in the Bedford-Sackville area who gave private lessons to students in their homes, and neighbourhood public schools offered music instruction to their students.

Paul did not think that the public school programs were real competition for his company. He had developed good relations with the music instructors in the public schools. In fact, many music instructors in the public schools recommended NMS to their students who were serious about music or had interests that the public school programs could not satisfy. This, combined with student exposure to NMS's successful pre-school program, minimized the threat to NMS from the public school music programs.

Promotion

Compared to some of the national music school chains, NMS was a relatively small operation. Before Paul began managing the Halifax and Dartmouth branches, the company had spent very little on promotions. Monthly advertisements in *The Mail Star* - a local newspaper - had been the only promotional tool used. The company had relied on personal referrals and the contacts that its instructors had established with music teachers in the public school system for stimulating demand for its services.

When Paul became manager, he had increased the company's promotional expenditures. In 2010, the company had conducted its first direct mail campaign. A small four-page brochure had been printed and distributed in certain parts of the city. Paul had limited the distribution of the brochures to high income, upper middle and higher social class neighbourhoods in Halifax and Dartmouth as he believed that this was the prime market for music schools. The brochure had stressed the variety of programs offered at NMS and the preparation for the Royal Conservatory exams. In Paul's opinion, the response to the campaign had been very positive - after the campaign, the Halifax-Dartmouth branches had experienced a 30% increase in inquiries and a 20% increase in registrations. The total cost of the campaign had been $10,000. Paul felt that Peter would not be willing to spend more than $20,000 this year on special promotional campaigns for the two existing and one new branch.

THE CUSTOMERS

Table 1 provides details of the age distribution and instruments preferred by the customers of NMS. Most students enrolled for an initial three-month program but many dropped out during this period. Those who stayed through the three-month period were likely to remain in the school for two to three years. Often, two children from the same family enrolled for music lessons at the same time.

Paul was not sure what the customers were looking for in a music school, or what made them choose one music school over another. Without this information, he felt that he could not formulate a marketing strategy for the NMS outlets he managed. Nor could he give advice to the owner on the market potential of the proposed new suburban branch, and on the best location for it. This led him to approach a local university to ask students from a marketing research course to collect data on customer preferences and attitudes toward music schools.

The students surveyed 180 residents drawn from Bedford, Sackville and outlying areas. The local telephone directory was used as the sampling frame. A random number between one and twenty was chosen, and beginning with that, every 40th residential listing in the telephone directory was contacted and the head of the household was interviewed. The first question was intended to measure the level of awareness of NMS (as indicated by aided and unaided recall). Only those families with at least one member currently taking (or planning to take) music lessons were asked to rate the attributes of a music school. (Information is provided in Tables 2 to 5)

PAUL'S DILEMMA

To prepare for his meeting with Peter, Paul had gathered some demographic information (Tables 6 to 9). Because he knew that parents often did shopping errands during their children's music lessons, Paul also gathered needed information on consumer shopping patterns in Halifax, Dartmouth, Bedford, Sackville and outlying areas (Table 10).

Paul was looking at the data that the students had gathered and was wondering how he could use it. He had to determine whether a market existed in these two suburbs for another music school. If there was, he knew that Peter would ask him to choose the best suburb for the new branch. He also knew that even if the operation was not profitable in the initial two or three years, Peter would be willing to open a new branch if there was sufficient long term potential. Paul also needed to formulate a marketing strategy for the new outlet.

The student survey seemed to indicate that awareness of NMS in the suburbs was rather low. Only five out of 180 respondents (or less than 3%) remembered its name in the unaided recall question. Even with prompting, only 68 of the respondents recognized the school. This worried Paul. Although he had complete control of the promotional budget, he would have too little money for a mass campaign.

Table 1   National Music Studio - Student Profile
Halifax - Dartmouth branches

	Dartmouth Age group						Halifax Age group				
Lesson Taken in	0-6	7-12	13-18	19-25	26+	**Total**	0-6	7-12	13-18	19-25	26+	**Total**
Electric Guitar	0	7	21	13	25	66	1	13	51	13	17	95
Drums	0	3	4	2	10	19	0	2	18	3	5	28
Piano	11	43	20	17	81	172	4	56	42	7	52	161
Organ	0	2	4	0	7	13	0	2	6	0	1	9
Saxophone	0	2	2	3	10	17	0	1	4	5	7	17
Violin	0	0	2	0	5	7	1	7	2	0	3	13
Other Instruments	0	2	8	2	15	27	0	8	26	3	26	63
Voice	0	0	2	4	8	14	0	0	7	2	12	21
Preschool Program	40	2	0	0	0	42	22	0	0	0	0	22
Total	**51**	**61**	**63**	**41**	**161**	**377**	**28**	**89**	**156**	**33**	**123**	**429**

Table 2   Awareness of National Music Studio and Competitors

Name of School	Unaided Recall*	Aided Recall**
NMS	5	68
B.J.'s	30	148
RCM	6	91
MCM+	23	145
McKenzie's+	21	147
Other	12	--
None	108	35

+ Branches of larger chains
* "Unaided recall" refers to the number of respondents who named a particular music school in response to the question "when you think of music schools, does any name come to your mind?"
** "Aided recall" refers to the number of respondents who, when asked if they had heard of a particular music school (by name) said "yes."
Totals do not add to 180 because some respondents named or had heard of more than one school.

Table 3   Interest in Music Lessons

Is any member of your household...	Bedford	Sackville	Outlying Areas	Total
Currently taking music lessons	12	13	4	29
Definitely planning to take music lessons	18	35	8	61
Likely take music lessons	7	23	6	36
Will not take music lessons	11	35	8	54
Total	**48**	**106**	**26**	**180**

Table 4   Important Attributes for a Music School

Attributes	Importance Rating*	Rating of NMS**
Quality of Instructors	87%	17%
Individualized Instruction	75%	65%
Location	71%	21%
Cost	50%	61%
Teaching Method Used	48%	73%
Flexible Timing	47%	49%
Number of Programs Offered	30%	65%

* Percentage of respondents giving a rating of 3 or 4 on a scale of 1 to 4 with 1 meaning "not at all important" and 4 meaning "very important." Only those families with someone currently enrolled in music lessons or planning to enroll were asked this question (n=126).

** Respondents' rating of NMS on the same items. Only 73 respondents who were aware of NMS were asked to answer this question. A five point scale with 1 = "very poor," 3 = "neither good nor bad" and 5 = "very good" was used. Only the percentage of respondents giving ratings of 4 or 5 are shown.

Table 5   Characteristics of People Interested in Music Lessons (n=180)

Interest in Music Lessons	Aware of NMS	Education High School	Some Univ	Income >$35K	<$35K	Household Size 1-3	4+	Total
Currently taking music lessons	22	11	18	20	9	10	19	**29**
Definitely planning to take lessons	42	27	34	33	28	30	31	**61**
May take music lessons	6	16	20	18	18	12	24	**36**
Will not take music lessons	3	27	27	11	43	17	37	**54**
TOTAL	**73**	**81**	**99**	**82**	**98**	**69**	**111**	**180**

Table 6   Population Distribution in the Metro Halifax Area

Halifax	280,321
Dartmouth	67,573
Bedford	18,533
Sackville-Windsor Junction	50,187*
Total	416,614

Source: Statistics Canada, 2011 Census.
* The 2011 population of Sackville alone was around 29,000

Table 7   Household Income - Metro Halifax Area

Income Ranges	Bedford	Sackville	Halifax	Dartmouth
Less than $15,000	2.5%	3.6%	6.3%	6.8%
$15,000 to $29,999	10.8%	11.1%	14.8%	14.9%
$30,000 to $44,999	11.5%	11.9%	16.3%	16.5%
$45,000 to $59,999	12.1%	12.3%	16.9%	17.1%
$60,000 to $74,999	13.2%	13.4%	14.1%	13.9%
$75,000 to $89,999	15.6%	16.1%	17.9%	17.6%
$90,000 and over	34.3%	31.6%	13.7%	13.2%
Median Household Income	$74,600	$64,100	$54,100	$52,300
Total Households	6,879	16,652*	104,045	28,174

* Total number of households in Sackville in 2011 was around 8,600.
Source: Statistics Canada, 2011 Census.

Table 8   Occupational Distribution - Metro Halifax Area

Occupational Category	Bedford	Sackville-Windsor Jn	Halifax	Dartmouth
Professional	34.5%	22.8%	32.3%	26.7%
White Collar	46.4%	49.4%	50.9%	52.6%
Blue Collar	19.1%	27.8%	15.8%	19.7%

Source: Statistics Canada, 2011 Census.

Table 9   School Population in Bedford and Sackville (2010/11 School Year)

Type of School	Number	Number of Students	% of total school population
Bedford			
Elementary Schools	4	1,683	10.2
Junior High Schools	1	765	4.9
High Schools	2	1,598	10.1
Total	**7**	**3,966**	**25.2**
Sackville			
Elementary Schools	13	6,111	38.8
Junior High Schools	4	3,016	19.2
High Schools	2	2,640	16.8
Total	**19**	**11,767**	**74.8**
Total School Population		**15,733**	**100.0**

Source: Statistics Canada, 2011 Census. Sackville figures include Windsor Junction.

Table 10   Retail Expenditures in Metro Halifax Area*

Customer Residence Location

Retail Area	Halifax	Dartmouth	Bedford	Sackville	Outlying Areas	Total
Halifax	82.0%	42.5%	33.9%	24.2%	38.3%	61.0%
Dartmouth	2.9	50.4	10.7	10.1	29.2	18.9
Bedford	7.3	3.2	32.2	26.4	3.4	8.5
Sackville	3.3	1.0	17.6	29.5	6.4	5.8
Outlying Areas	4.5	2.9	5.6	9.8	12.7	5.8
Total	**100.0%**	**100.0%**	**100.0%**	**100.0%**	**100.0%**	**100.0%**

* Indicates percentage of retail dollars spent in each location by residents of any one area. For example, people living in Halifax spent 82.0% of their retail dollars in Halifax itself, 2.9% in Dartmouth, 7.3% in Bedford, and so on. The last column indicates the percentage of retail expenditures spent in each of the specified areas. For example, the residents of all the areas combined spent 61% of their retail dollars in Halifax, 18.9% in Dartmouth, and so on.

DOMINION TANKING LIMITED

On March 1, 2012, Andrew Cheung, Red Deer, Alberta Branch Manager for Dominion Tanking Limited, was preparing the company's bid for a trucking contract. The bid, to deliver liquid fertilizer for Natural Fertilizers Limited, also of Red Deer, was due in two weeks and he expected intense competition. Dominion Tanking won the last bid, five years ago, and had operated under that contract, in Red Deer, to only serve Natural Fertilizers. Andrew knew that if this bid was unsuccessful, the Head Office would close his branch.

Company Background

Dominion Tanking Limited, a subsidiary of Canadian Hughes Trucking, was comprised of a series of Alberta branches administered through a Head Office in Calgary. The branch office in Red Deer consisted of eight truck drivers and the Branch Manager who operated out of a rented office inside the Natural Fertilizers Plant. The drivers were all members of the Teamsters Union, Local 141, and were paid on a combined basis of miles driven and time spent on delivery. Their average wage was approximately $26.50 per hour for a 35 hour regular work week. The drivers were paid time and a half for overtime (any hours worked over and above the 35 hour work week). Benefits such as Health Insurance, Canada Pension Plan, Employment Insurance, Vacation Pay, etc. were equal to 12% of regular wages and were paid over and above the weekly wages. No benefits were paid on overtime wages. The union agreement was coming up for renegotiation on January 1, 2013. Andrew was paid a straight annual salary plus benefits and was not a part of the union.

The company transported liquid fertilizer in eight stainless steel tank trucks ranging in capacity from 3,200 gallons to 5,800 gallons. The truck portion of each rig was leased from the RYDER Truck Company while Dominion owned the tanker trailers. The lease for the trucks was scheduled to expire on the anniversary of the trucking contract with Natural Fertilizers (i.e., January 1, 2013).

Dominion's tankers delivered an average of eight to nine loads of liquid fertilizer a day, five days a week. Though many deliveries were local, drivers were expected to deliver loads of fertilizer throughout Alberta and to near northern states. As could be expected, spring was a peak season for deliveries while the winter months experienced a decline in demand. In these months, drivers were allowed to take their holidays and the tanker trailers were serviced.

The Red Deer branch of the company existed solely to serve the delivery needs of Natural Fertilizers. Andrew knew the company would not allow him to solicit outside contracts to increase revenue. Further, should Natural Fertilizers go out of business, or should Dominion

----

Tanking lose its delivery contract, the branch would have no other source of business and the branch would be closed. Andrew knew closure was possible as a Wetaskiwin, Alberta branch had been closed, under similar circumstances, a year ago.

Competition

Dominion Tanking experienced competition from two other trucking companies: Ellsworth Transport of Innisfail, Alberta and Billings Equipment Leasing of Lacombe, Alberta. Both of these companies offered comparable service but with lower "per mile" rates than Dominion Tanking. One reason for the lower rate was the use of non-union labour by the two companies. Billings was the more aggressive company of the two. It had been formed little more than a year before and was operating with new equipment. Billings wanted the Natural Fertilizers trucking contract to give it more credibility. Management there could be expected to put in a low bid.

Natural Fertilizers also had the option of rejecting all submitted bids and purchasing its own trucks for delivery. Tanker prices varied from $100,000 for the 3,200 gallon size to $140,000 for the 5,800 gallon size. The truck or cab portion could either be leased or purchased. Prices for transport trucks varied, depending on options, from $100,000 to $120,000. The company would also have to hire and train drivers and a dispatcher. Andrew estimated that it would take at least one year to make a new fleet of trucks run efficiently.

The Bidding Process

Natural Fertilizers subcontracted delivery of its liquid fertilizer, to trucking firms, on a five-year basis. Over the period of the contract, the winner of the bidding process would be given first priority for all delivery assignments. If more fertilizer had to be shipped than the trucking company could handle, Natural Fertilizers was free to hire extra trucks as needed to make those deliveries. This situation often arose in the spring and summer months when drivers were working overtime to meet as many delivery schedules as possible yet they were still unable to meet them all.

While the sealed bids would be received on March 15, the actual contract would commence on January 1, 2013 and run for five years. In soliciting bids, Natural Fertilizers had made it clear to the three trucking firms that it wanted to lower its delivery costs from the $3.30 charge per mile that it currently paid. Each firm was attempting to come up with the lowest bid while maintaining adequate profit margins. Though timely delivery, friendly drivers and good service were important, the winning bid would be the lowest rate charged but only if that rate was acceptable to Natural Fertilizers.

The Problem

Dominion Tanking had been associated with Natural Fertilizers for twenty years, having won four consecutive contracts, yet Andrew knew that loyalty would only be a small factor in deciding the winning bid. Looking at a breakdown of the company's revenues and costs (Exhibit 1), he felt that the company's bid should be from 10 to 20% lower than the current rate to be competitive. The problem was further compounded by the uncertainty surrounding the bids of the other companies. His job depended on him coming up with a bid that attempted to maintain past margins and would win the five year contract.

Exhibit 1 Dominion Tanking Limited
Projected Revenue and Cost Analysis for Dominion Tanking
Red Deer Office -- Fiscal Year 2012

Revenues

Billings to Natural Fertilizers	$1,924,363	$3.30/mile
		= About 600,000 miles

Costs

Truck Drivers Wages & Benefits	$707,042
Fuel	$217,111
Leasing Costs	$242,612
Tanker Maintenance	$152,754
Depreciation on Tankers	$101,317
Administration & General Overhead	$110,915
Total Costs	$1,531,751
Gross Profit from Red Deer Operations	$ 392,612

	-10%	-15%	-20%
~~REVENUE~~	2.97/mile	2.80/mile	2.64/mile
REVENUE	1,780,000	1,680,000	1,580,000
FUEL↑	200,000	200,000	200,000
LEASING↓	240,000	240,000	240,000
↑ MAINTENANCE	150,000	150,000	150,000
↔ DEPRECIATION	100,000	100,000	100,000
ADMIN + OH	110,000	110,000	110,000
WAGES(Desired)	624,000 (-12%)	544,000 (-23%)	464,000 (-34%)
PROFIT = Desired Profit 20%	356,000	336,000	316,000

EAST HAMILTON MINIATURE GOLF

In January 2014, Jean-Guy Gauthier and Sonia Hamdani, two high school teachers, had just finished a proposal for a miniature golf course in Hamilton, Ontario. The idea developed after watching a miniature golf tournament on a cable sports network. They were discussing whether they should invest the time and money to make the proposal a reality. Jean-Guy felt the proposal would make money no matter where they located or how they promoted the venture.

"Sonia, there's not much primary competition and there are lots of people who would love to play miniature golf in Hamilton. I think we've got a potential gold mine on our hands. I've calculated that our maximum capacity for the course is 864 rounds per day, based on the assumption that there would be four people per hole and they would take one hour to play one round. Given that there are eighteen holes and the course will be open twelve hours per day, a total of (4 x 1 x 18 x 12) 864 rounds could be played every day."

Sonia was more cautious. "I think there are two important factors. First, if we don't get the Centre on Barton location, I wouldn't be too keen on the idea. Second, if we don't promote miniature golf properly, there's a chance that it won't succeed. I think we should have another look at our analysis and determine if this idea could work."

The Idea

Jean-Guy Gauthier and Sonia Hamdani often discussed ways of getting into business during their lunch hours at school. The months of July and August were relatively slow times for them at their work and they both liked the idea of earning a second income to supplement their base pay. The two teachers felt they could each invest $10,000 in a business venture if they could come up with a reasonable idea. After seeing the televised miniature golf tournament, they decided to do some research on miniature golf in Hamilton. The research included an analysis of competition, potential locations, consumers' needs, the Hamilton market, and the costs involved.

The Competition

YellowPages.ca revealed eight miniature golf courses in Burlington and Hamilton. **Wedgewood Golf Centre** was not analyzed as its target market was mostly Burlington. **Rock Chapel Golf Centre** was not analyzed as its target market was mostly Waterdown and Dundas. **Eagle Classic Golf Centre, Satellite Golf Centre,** and **Pros Golf Centre** were, at best, secondary competitors as they served people who lived on Hamilton Mountain or in Ancaster. That left three courses as primary competitors: **Adventure Village** (outdoor course connected to a water park)**, Putting Edge** (indoor course with glow-in-the-dark lighting) and **Glover Golf Driving Range** (outdoor course connected to a golf driving range).

The competitors were evaluated on a number of criteria (Exhibit 1), and the general conclusion reached by the partners was that the courses were either of poor quality or were too far away from the proposed location to pose much of a threat. It was felt that if a miniature golf course was constructed of high-quality materials and offered a fair degree of challenge, it would attract most of the competitions' customers. If they went ahead with the venture, the partners wanted to construct the best possible course in terms of challenge, materials, and craftsmanship.

Potential Locations

After looking at a number of areas, the partners concluded that any location should be readily accessible to the public. The basic idea was to "bring the game to the people" by having a convenient location in or near a shopping centre that had high traffic flows. The manager of Triovest Realty Advisors Inc., the company that operated the Centre on Barton, was contacted, and the idea of a miniature golf course located at the centre was discussed. The Centre on Barton was considered an ideal site as it was the most central of the "big box" shopping areas in the lower City of Hamilton with over 61 stores and services. Major tenants included Canadian Tire, Metro, Marshall's, The Brick, Wal-Mart, Michael's, Staples and Dollarama. Just 100 metres to the east was located East Hamilton Radio, a popular electronics store which drew customers from Niagara Falls to Toronto.

The number of visits to the Centre on Barton each month was estimated at around 340,000. The primary market of 136,685 patrons for the centre lived within a 15-minute commute. The secondary market of 159,250 patrons for the centre lived within a 30-minute commute. The centre had large areas of ground parking space (parking was available for 4,000 cars).

It was proposed that the miniature golf course be located in the parking lot near one of the anchor stores (Dollarama) for the period from May 1 to September 30. For the rest of the year, the wooden miniature golf course would be placed in storage. The manager, while interested in the proposal, did not commit himself to the venture. He suggested that the two partners return after they had finalized their plans. If they were allowed to locate at the Centre on Barton, the rental fee for the land would be 15% of gross sales.

Consumer Analysis

The next step in the project was to conduct a consumer analysis. The partners listed a number of consumer needs they felt miniature golf could satisfy and ranked them in terms of probable importance for three different consumer groups. The needs and rankings were:

Consumer Need	Pre-teen & Teen	Male Adults	Female Adults
Recreation/enjoyment	1	1	1
Challenge/competition	2	2	5
Socializing with friends	3	8	3
Family outing	4	4	2
Relaxation	5	5	4
Status	6	7	7
Convenience	7	3	8
Time available to play	8	6	6

This analysis indicated the primary needs satisfied would be enjoyment, challenge, and socializing with friends or family. Further information was collected through two consumer surveys. The first survey, shown in Exhibit 2, asked 100 adults if they would patronize a miniature golf course at the Centre on Barton. The results indicated that consumers might participate in miniature golf while shopping there.

The second questionnaire was designed and given to students at their high school. The results, shown in Exhibit 3, indicated that most students would play miniature golf at the Centre on Barton if they were already there. Approximately 50% would play miniature golf on a date, and 50% said they would come to the centre on Sunday and play. Approximately 77% said they felt that $8.00 was a reasonable price for mini-golf. Only 17% felt that $8.00 was too high a price.

The Hamilton Market

In 2012, Hamilton was Canada's ninth largest Census Metropolitan Area (which included Hamilton, Burlington, and Grimsby) with 761,346 people and 299,428 households. It was traditionally a heavy-industry community with large steel mills (US Steel and ArcelorMittal Dofasco) and manufacturing facilities using steel in their product lines. By 2014, seven of Hamilton's top ten employers were in the greater public sector including Hamilton Health Sciences, St. Joseph's Hospital, McMaster University, Hamilton-Wentworth Board of Education, Hamilton- Wentworth Separate Board of Education, Province of Ontario, and City of Hamilton. Mohawk College and the Government of Canada were also significant employers.

In 2012, the average annual pre-tax household income in the CMA was $90,500 compared to the Canadian average of $85,795. On a per capita basis, average annual pre-tax income in the CMA was $35,593 compared to the Canadian average of $34,352. (See Exhibit 4 for more age and income data).

In terms of weather, the average number of days with and without rain between May and September is presented in Exhibit 4. On average, there were 104 days without rain during the planned five operating months.

Cost Estimates

The partners calculated the costs of constructing the miniature golf course out of wood (Exhibit 5). The total estimated capital cost of $34,068.70 included the cost of building the eighteen holes plus a pro shop, fencing, and miscellaneous expenses. No budget was included for labour because the holes could be built by the industrial arts class at the high school where they taught. The only operating expenses would be advertising and hiring someone to operate the course. The cost of hiring student labour was estimated at $14,783, based on paying them $10.30 per hour (this was the new minimum wage for students being introduced on June 1, 2014), twelve hours per day for a season of 104 days. (If it rained, they planned that the students would not be asked to work and they would not be paid.) It also included a 15% premium to cover the required benefits (CPP, EI, vacation pay). The owners had planned to have the course operate from 10:00 a.m. to 10:00 p.m. each day.

While they had collected some data on advertising rates, they had not decided on any advertising campaign. The Hamilton Spectator, the local daily newspaper, had a city-wide circulation of 209,000 households. The cost of advertising for a full page, half-page, quarter-page, and one-eighth page was $23,750, $12,000, $6,000, and $3,000, respectively before any discounts for volume purchases of advertising. Hamilton was served by eight radio stations. CIOI and CFMU were based at Mohawk College and McMaster University respectively and were not available for standard commercial advertising. CHML, CHAM, and CKOC were AM stations while CHKX (New Country 94.7), CJXY (Y108 Classic Rock), CING (95.3 Fresh Radio) and CKLH (K-Lite) were FM stations. Radio advertising costs ranged from $25 for a thirty-second prime time spot on 95.3 Fresh (adult contemporary) to $250 for an equivalent spot on New Country 94.7 or K-Lite (continuous light hits). Discounts for volume purchasing of advertising could reduce these rates by up to 50%.

Decisions

The partners faced a number of decisions. They had not decided the final price to charge, either $8.00 or $10.00 per round; what advertising should be done, if any; or what they should do if the manager of the Centre on Barton did not agree to their proposal. They estimated the total capital cost would probably be around $34,069. A colleague in the Business Department recommended that they start the business with cash to cover two months of operating expenses (wages and advertising). They felt this would mean borrowing $15,000 to $25,000 from the bank. Finally, the major decision had to be made. Should they invest in this venture?

Exhibit 1   Primary Competitor Analysis

	Adventure Village	Putting Edge	Glover Golf Driving Range
Location – Accessibility	Excellent	Excellent	Good
– Built-in clientele	Excellent	Good	Fair
Cost – Per 18-hole round			
Adult	$11.00	$12.00	$6.00
Student	$11.00	N/A	$5.00
Children	$9.00	$9.00	$4.00
Course – Appearance	Excellent	Excellent	Fair
– Challenge Offered	Very Good	Excellent	Fair
– Material Quality	Very Good	Very Good	Fair
Promotion – Advertising	Fair	Good	Poor
– Tournaments	None	None	None
– Leagues	None	None	None
– Incentives	Poor	Fair	None
– Appeal to Market	Good	Excellent	Fair
Return on Investment	Good	Very Good	Poor

Exhibit 2   Adult Survey Results

- Sample Size of 100: 50 males and 50 females.
- Interviews were conducted at the Centre on Barton and with friends and colleagues.
- The respondents were informed of the miniature golf proposal and asked if they would patronize the service.
- Most frequent responses (i.e., those mentioned at least 10% of the time) were:
  - 24% Would serve as a family activity
  - 22% I would not use it as I don't have the time
  - 14% Children would be more likely to come shopping with us with a miniature golf course here
  - 10% I would play while waiting for my spouse to shop.

Exhibit 3   Student Survey Results

Sample size was 300 students aged eleven to twenty

Gender: Male – 144 (48%)   Female – 156 (52%)

1. Do you visit the Centre on Barton in the summer?
         Yes – 253 (84%)   No – 47 (16%)

2. a) If "Yes", would you play miniature golf?

	Yes	Maybe	No
Male	99 (84%)	7 (6%)	12 (10%)
Female	97 (72%)	14 (10%)	24 (18%)

   b) If "No", would you visit the centre for a recreational activity like miniature golf?

	Yes	Maybe	No
Male	4 (16%)	11 (42%)	11 (42%)
Female	4 (19%)	7 (33%)	10 (48%)

3. Do you think members of your family **older** than yourself would play miniature golf?
         Yes – 85 (28%)   Maybe – 154 (51%)   No – 61 (21%)

4. Do you think members of your family **younger** than yourself would play miniature golf?
         Yes – 126 (42%)   Maybe – 141 (47%)   No – 33 (11%)

5. Would you play miniature golf on a date?

	Yes	Maybe	No	No Answer
Male	80 (56%)	26 (18%)	14 (10%)	24 (16%)
Female	82 (53%)	32 (21%)	10 (6%)	32 (20%)

6. How do you view a price of $8.00 per round of miniature golf?

	High Price	Reasonable Price	Low Price
Male	34 (23%)	96 (67%)	14 (10%)
Female	18 (11%)	134 (86%)	4 (3%)

7. Would you come to the Centre on Barton on Sunday to play miniature golf?

	Yes	Maybe	No
Male	70 (49%)	32 (22%)	42 (29%)
Female	80 (51%)	45 (29%)	31 (20%)

Exhibit 4   Selected Statistics – Hamilton Census Metropolitan Area

Population by Age Group – 2012

	Male	Female
0 to 4	19,394	18,837
5 to 9	20,993	19,535
10 to 14	22,241	20,818
15 to 19	24,498	24,233
20 to 24	27,289	26,823
25 to 29	27,502	26,100
30 to 34	23,559	23,519
35 to 39	23,107	24,413
40 to 44	26,670	27,362
45 to 49	30,462	30,597
50 to 54	29,464	29,137
55 to 59	24,702	26,054
60 to 64	20,730	22,683
65 to 69	16,943	18,944
70 & Over	35,043	49,694
Total	**372,597**	**388,749**

Families: Number 216,145   Households: Number 299,428
Average Size 3.0   Average Size 2.5

Taxation Statistics – Income Class – Individuals – 2012

Under $5,000	38,220	$50,000 to $74,999	86,580
$5,000 to $9,999	36,530	$75,000 to $99,999	46,550
$10,000 to $14,999	48,650	$100,000 to $149,999	25,630
$15,000 to $19,999	47,190	$150,000 to $199,999	6,800
$20,000 to $24,999	43,170	$200,000 to $249,999	2,820
$25,000 to $34,999	67,330	$250,000 or more	4,220
$35,000 to $49,999	85,290	Total	**538,980**

Median Income   **$33,150**

Weather

	Avg. # of Days With Rain	Avg. # of Days Without Rain
May	11	20
June	10	20
July	9	22
August	9	22
September	10	20
Total	**49**	**104**

- Based on an accumulation of at least 0.25 millimetres. Averaged over the thirty year period 1981 to 2010. Most likely time of rainfall was 3:00 p.m. to 7:00 p.m. during these months.

Exhibit 5   Capital Cost Estimates for Miniature Golf Course

Material Costs

¾" Plywood	$32.50 per sheet
2" x 4" Lumber	$0.62 per linear foot
2" x 8" Lumber	$0.99 per linear foot
Paint	$47.00 per 3.78 litre pail
Carpeting	$55.40 per square metre

Average Construction Cost per Hole

    Material Cost

125 feet of 2" x 4" Lumber	$ 77.50
60 feet of 2" x 8" Lumber	$ 59.40
Four sheets of ¾" Plywood	$130.00
11.25 square metres of Carpeting Kentucky Blue Grass colour	$623.25
Miscellaneous (nails, sheet metal, batteries, motors, sand, shrubbery)	$250.00
Paint – one pail per hole	$ 47.00
Total Material Cost	$1,187.15

    Labour Cost

All construction to be done by the industrial
arts class at the high school under the super-
vision of a craftsman-certified teacher   FREE

Total Cost per Hole $1,187.15

Total Cost of Eighteen Holes = 18 x $1,187.15 $21,369

Other Expenses

Pro Shop	$5,000
Fencing	$4,450
Miscellaneous (putters, balls, cards, pencils)	$3,250
Total Other Expenses	$12,700

Total Capital Cost of Miniature Golf Course $34,069